Edward Henry Palmer

A history of the Jewish nation

From the earliest times to the present day

Edward Henry Palmer

A history of the Jewish nation
From the earliest times to the present day

ISBN/EAN: 9783337136376

Printed in Europe, USA, Canada, Australia, Japan

Cover: Foto ©ninafisch / pixelio.de

More available books at **www.hansebooks.com**

A

HISTORY

OF THE

JEWISH NATION;

from the Earliest Times to the Present Day.

By E. H. PALMER, M.A.,

*Of the Middle Temple, Barrister-at-Law, Fellow of St. John's College, and
Lord Almoner's Professor of Arabic in the University of Cambridge.*

AUTHOR OF "THE DESERT OF THE EXODUS," "A GRAMMAR OF THE ARABIC
LANGUAGE," ETC., AND JOINT AUTHOR OF "JERUSALEM THE
CITY OF HEROD AND SALADIN."

PUBLISHED UNDER THE DIRECTION OF THE
COMMITTEE OF GENERAL LITERATURE AND EDUCATION,
APPOINTED BY THE SOCIETY FOR PROMOTING
CHRISTIAN KNOWLEDGE.

LONDON:

SOCIETY FOR PROMOTING CHRISTIAN KNOWLEDGE.

NORTHUMBERLAND AVENUE, CHARING CROSS;

4, ROYAL EXCHANGE; AND 48, PICCADILLY.

NEW YORK: POTT, YOUNG & CO.

1883

PREFACE.

In this little work I have attempted to present a general view of the history of the Hebrew race, from their first appearance in the remote ages of antiquity to the present day. I have, to the best of my ability, grouped the broad facts of that history together in the form which appeared to me most likely to be easily retained in the student's memory; and while I have aimed at conciseness on the one hand, I have endeavoured to omit no important details on the other. Such illustrations as geography, ethnology, and archæology afford, I have occasionally introduced; and, following out the canon of criticism which I have laid down for myself in other works upon sacred subjects, I have preferred treating the history of the Jews entirely from a secular point of view, believing that physical and historical facts are themselves the best comment upon the inspired records or prophecies of God's dealings with His chosen people. I am sensible of the difficulties which beset one who ventures upon ground trodden by such masterly scholars as those who have treated the subject before me ; but my object has been, not presumptuously to rival their works, but humbly to supplement them, by bringing the main facts of the history to the notice of those who have neither time nor opportunity to study the larger books. I have had especially in my mind the requirements of Christian families and schools, and, hoping that I may number not a few children amongst my readers, I have told the story in as simple and unpretending a manner as I could.

It would be of little use to enumerate the works to which I have had recourse in compiling these pages; suffice it to say that I have derived much assistance from the publications of English and Continental scholars, some of them being brought to my notice for the first time by the kindness of Dr. Schiller Szinessy, Teacher of Talmudic and Rabbinic literature in the University of Cambridge, and that I am chiefly indebted to the immortal work of Milman, the best and completest yet written upon the history of the Jews.

TABLE OF CONTENTS.

THE OLD TESTAMENT HISTORY;

FROM

ABRAHAM TO THE CAPTIVITY OF BABYLON.

CHAPTER I.

THE PATRIARCHS.

CHAPTER II.

THE EXODUS AND WANDERINGS.

CHAPTER III.

THE SETTLEMENT IN PALESTINE.

CHAPTER IV.

THE JUDGES.

CHAPTER V.

THE MONARCHY.

CHAPTER VI.

THE KINGDOMS OF JUDAH AND ISRAEL.

PART THE SECOND.

POST-BIBLICAL HISTORY;

FROM THE CAPTIVITY OF BABYLON TO THE TAKING OF THE CITY BY TITUS.

CHAPTER VII.

THE RESTORATION.

CHAPTER VIII.

THE MACCABEES.

CHAPTER IX.

THE HERODIAN FAMILY.

CHAPTER X.

THE FALL OF JERUSALEM.

PART THE THIRD.

MODERN HISTORY;

FROM THE FALL OF THE ROMAN EMPIRE TO THE PRESENT TIME.

CHAPTER XI.

THE LAST DAYS OF THE ROMAN EMPIRE.

CHAPTER XII.

THE GOTHIC AND MOHAMMEDAN DOMINIONS.

CHAPTER XIII.

THE MIDDLE AGES.

CHAPTER XIV.

THE MIDDLE AGES—(continued).

CHAPTER XV.

THE JEWS IN RECENT TIMES.

ILLUSTRATIONS.

THE OLD TESTAMENT HISTORY,

FROM

ABRAHAM TO THE CAPTIVITY OF BABYLON.

◇

PART THE FIRST.

CHAPTER I.

THE PATRIARCHS.

Early history of the Semitic race—Abraham's migration into Canaan—His first military exploit—Birth of Ishmael and Isaac—Death of Sarah—Methods of interment amongst the ancients—Cave sepulture in Palestine—Uses of cave-tombs—Cave sepulture as illustrating the Bible—Noted tombs in Modern Jerusalem—Purity of descent in Abraham's offspring—Death of Abraham—Adventures of Jacob—Death of Isaac.

SHEM, Ham, and Japheth, the three sons of Noah, are the fathers of the human race, and we have it on the authority of Holy Writ that "by these were the nations of the earth divided after the flood." These three divisions correspond with the actual geographical distribution of races in the ancient world : Japheth representing the nations of the north, Ham the nations of the south, and Shem forming the great central group.

From this last family sprang the Hebrew or Jewish nation.

The history of the growth, development, and early migrations of the Semitic race, and its sub-division into the various families of Elam in Persia, Asshur in Assyria,

B

Arphaxad in Northern Assyria, Joktan in Arabia, Lud in
the Highlands of Armenia, and Aram in Mesopotamia and
Syria—this is all told in Gen. x., xi., in a concise form,
to the details of which ethnological investigations may
add some interesting facts, but to the accuracy and clearness of which they add little more than corroborating
evidence.

Our history commences with Terah, the ninth in descent from Noah, who "took Abram his son, and Lot the
son of Haran his son's son, and Sarai his daughter-in-law,
his son Abram's wife; and they went forth with them
from Ur of the Chaldees, to go unto the land of Canaan"
(Gen. xi. 31).

This migration is, as it were, the prologue to the great
drama which was to follow—the first shadowing forth of
the inscrutable purpose which was to make that "land
of Canaan" the scene of events the most important in
the history of humanity.

The family did not, however, reach their proposed desti-
nation, but stopped short at Haran in Mesopotamia, where
Terah died.

It was here that the Divine command came to Abram,
bidding him go out from his country and his father's
house unto the land of promise. This command he cheerfully obeyed; and, taking with him Sarai his wife, Lot his
nephew, and all the other members of his household, he
passed over into Canaan.

Egypt was the great centre of ancient civilisation.
supreme in arts, science, and commerce. To this favoured
land Canaan was but, as it were, the vestibule; and
Abram appears at first to have understood the promise as
tending ultimately to Egypt itself, and to have bent his
steps thither accordingly.

Later on, Isaac was only restrained by an express
Divine prohibition from attempting a settlement in the
same country (Gen. xxvi. 1—6).

It is not my intention in this work to dwell at length upon the details of the Bible narrative, which every Christian should read and learn from the sacred volume itself. But the history of the patriarchs demands an exceptional treatment, as, without it, the geographical and ethnical distributions of the tribes of Israel and of the surrounding nations cannot be properly understood.

This history is, indeed, the primeval history of the Hebrew race. The migration of the family of Terah from Ur of the Chaldees; the strong individuality of his son Abram; the history of Abram's first sojourn in Canaan, of his visit to Egypt, and of his later acquisition of territory in Canaan; the division of the land between Abram and Lot; the birth and fortunes of his two sons, Ishmael and Isaac, and of his grandsons Jacob and Esau; the rapid development of the families of Jacob's twelve sons into twelve tribes; and, lastly, the beautiful story of Joseph's adventures in Egypt, as they are told in the Book of Genesis,—these put us in possession of every fact necessary for the complete understanding of the political and geographical position of Israel at the time of the bondage in Egypt.

After a short sojourn in Egypt, Abraham returned to Canaan, where he and Lot parted, the latter choosing the fertile valley of the Jordan for his future possession. By this separation the purity of descent in Abraham's offspring was still further guaranteed.

Chedorlaomer, king of Elam, with three allies from the smaller chieftains of the country on the Euphrates and Tigris, invaded the rich valley of the Jordan, and compelled the kings of that district to pay him tribute. Thirteen years afterwards they rebelled; but Chedorlaomer returned, and subjugated the whole country to the south of Palestine as far as Kadesh, and, marching through the country of the Amorites towards the Dead Sea, took the important post of Hazezon-Tamar. The

PLAINS OF JERICHO.

princes of the Jordan gave them battle in the Plain of Siddim. The invaders were triumphant; the kings of Sodom and Gomorrah were routed amidst their own bitu· men pits and fissures ; their towns were pillaged; and the people carried away captive. Lot, who dwelt at Sodom, was among the captives.

Abram being apprised of this event by a fugitive, collected 318 of his own clansmen, and with the assistance of some neighbouring tribes, pursued Chedorlaomer and his army to Dan, at the head of the Jordan valley. Ey a night-surprise he was able to throw the enemy into confusion, and pursuing them with great slaughter as far as the neighbourhood of Damascus, rescued Lot and all his family.

This hardy exploit at once established the strength of Abram's position amongst the Canaanitish princes ; and it is a note-worthy fact that the Divine promise was on this occasion renewed, and the covenant ratified by a solemn sacrifice. On his way back to Mamre occurred the celebrated meeting between Abram and Melchisedec.

But, as time went on, Sarai, seeing that both she and her husband were well stricken in years, began to despair of the fulfilment of the promise in her own person, and attempted to compromise and hasten it by resorting to the not uncommon Oriental practice of giving her own Egyptian hand-maid, Hagar, to her husband as a concubine. The birth of Ishmael was the result. But Ishmael was not the child of the promise ; and fourteen years after his birth, when Abram was a hundred years old and Sarai ninety, a fresh revelation informed the patriarch that his aged wife should herself bear a son. At the same time they were commanded to change their names, and Abram became Abraham, "father of a great multitude ;" while Sarai was henceforth to be called Sarah, "a princess."

The events attending the birth and childhood of Isaac are of a remarkable character and full of deep import ;

the visit of the three mysterious strangers to Abraham
beneath the oak at Mamre; the destruction of Sodom
and Gomorrah; the incestuous birth of Lot's sons, Moab
and Ammon; the expulsion of Ishmael from his father's

WELL OF BEERSHEBA.

house; the trial of Abraham's faith when commanded to
sacrifice the child of all his hopes on Mount Moriah—
are incidents which, properly studied, throw a great light,

not only on the dealings of God with Israel, but on the rela-
tion of the chosen people with the neighbouring nations.

Sarah died at the old camping-ground in Mamre, and
was buried in the Cave of Machpelah. The whole question of cave-sepulture is so interesting, and so important
in its bearing upon the character of the Jewish people,
and upon the sacred narrative itself, that I must discuss
the subject at some length.

" Cain, the first murderer, in the frenzy of horror and
remorse, caught up the corpse of Abel in his arms and
fled he knew not whither. For days he wandered about
without being able to rid himself of his ghastly burden,
till at last, overcome by fatigue, he sank upon the ground.
Just then, two crows alighted near him and engaged in
mortal combat. When one of the two was stretched lifeless upon the ground, the victorious survivor scratched
a hole with its talons and covered the dead bird with
earth. Cain profited by the lesson, and, digging a grave
with his hands, buried his dead out of his sight."

So runs the quaint Mohammedan legend of the origin
of burial. Like most fables it contains a germ of truth,
for the problem how to dispose of the human body after
the life has left it must always have been an anxious and
difficult one in the earliest stages of society. Interment
was the most obvious solution of the problem ; but the
repugnance which we feel to parting altogether with a
beloved object must soon have exercised a modifying influence upon this practice ; and we find that various devices
for avoiding it were resorted to by different nations. The
most common of these were burning the dead and collecting the ashes as relics of the deceased, or the use of some
artificial means for the preservation of the body entire.
The last process was adopted by the Egyptians, to whom it
was naturally suggested by the presence in the soil of
their country of vast quantities of *natrin*, a bituminous
substance of great efficacy in arresting decay.

But to embalm a body is to set one's self up in direct
opposition to the laws of God and nature ; and the superstitious adjuncts of an Egyptian entombment show how
easily the practice led to idolatrous observances.   In this,
as in every other instance, the law of God, as enunciated
in His Word, indicates the right course to be pursued.
The sentence "Dust thou art, and unto dust shalt thou
return " is strictly conformable to nature, and points conclusively to interment as the proper method of disposing
of the dead.   To allow the gradual dissolution to proceed,
without either violently retarding or hastening the progress of decay, is manifestly more in accordance with the
sanctity of the human body as the temple of the Holy
Spirit than to subject it to the indignities of incremation
or embalming.

But the soil of Palestine offered facilities for a mode of
burial which combined the advantages of the natural and
artificial systems.   In the natural caves with which the
country abounded, the inhabitants of the Holy Land
found a last resting-place for their deceased friends, where
the bodies would be secure from the depredations of wild
beasts, and all danger of pollution to the living from contact with the dead would be avoided.

The Jews, therefore, invariably buried their dead, and
generally in a tomb hewn out of the rock, or already existing in it; the only recorded instances of a departure from
this rule being in the case of Jacob and Joseph, who were
embalmed, that they might be brought back to rest with
their forefathers, and that of Saul and his son, who were
burnt, to save their bodies from worse treatment at the
hands of their foes.   But even in the latter instance the
bones were only partially consumed, and were subsequently
interred with fitting honours.

In the unsettled nomad life of the patriarchs, the grave
was their only permanent home—their first as well as
last resting-place ; hence it is that the first record of the

purchase of land was that of a site for burial. The first piece of ground owned in Canaan by the father of the Jewish race was a tomb.

And a tomb is now the holiest spot in that Holy Land— the dearest to the Christian's heart.

The natural caves of Palestine, then, first served as sepulchres, and, when these were not easily obtainable, artificial ones were constructed for the same purpose.

When the cities became very populous, and all the available spaces were occupied, many persons, especially of the poorer classes, who could not afford to purchase a site or construct a tomb, would be obliged to resort to the more primitive and less ceremonious form of burial, namely, that of interment beneath the surface of the soil ; and in this way cemeteries came into existence outside the city walls.

Thus, in 2 Kings xxiii. 6, we read of the "graves of the children of the people," in the valley of Jehoshaphat. The "potter's field," which the chief priests purchased with the "price of blood" that Judas had restored, "to bury strangers in," is also an instance in point, the site having no doubt been selected from the fact that the holes from which the potter's clay had been dug could be easily utilised for graves. That such a consideration did influence the inhabitants of large cities we know from the example of Athens, where the principal cemetery was called the "Keramicon," or "Pottery," from this very cause.

With the Jews, contact with a dead body implied cere-monial defilement, which excluded the person so defiled from the performance of many of his religious and civil duties. Great care was therefore taken to prevent such accidental contact, and all sepulchres were required to be marked in such a manner as to be easily recognised. It was usual to surmount the grave with some pillar, pyra-mid, or other monument, or to ornament the face of the

rock with an inscription or *façade*. Where no other
means of distinguishing the spot were employed, the
sepulchre was conspicuously " whited " once a year. This
enables us to appreciate the point of our Lord's reproof,
" Woe unto you, scribes and Pharisees, hypocrites ! for
ye are like unto *whited sepulchres*, which indeed appear

TOMBS IN THE VALLEY OF JEHOSHAPHAT.

beautiful outward, but are within full of dead men's bones,
and of all uncleanness " (Matt. xxiii. 27).

" In the blessed hope of a resurrection," the Jews call
a cemetery, by a beautiful figure of speech, " the house of
the *living*."

The sanctity of a tomb, and the facilities for concealment afforded by its construction, rendered cave-sepul-
chres favourite places of refuge. The cave with two
columns in the front, represented in our engraving, is

called the tomb or cave of St. James, and receives its name from the tradition that St. James the apostle found a hiding-place in it during the anxious period intervening between the betrayal and resurrection of our Saviour. The catacombs at Rome are instances of a similar use of cave sepulchres for purposes of concealment in times of persecution. These caves did not always serve exclusively for tombs, but were frequently altered and enlarged so as to adapt them to purposes of residence for the living. The habits of the Horite or cave-dwelling aborigines of the country have not yet died out, and numerous instances are to be found in which caves, with a little rude addition of masonry in front, are still used as houses. The village of Silwan, or Siloam, in the Kedron valley, is entirely composed of such structures. The gloomy recesses of a cave-tomb also offer peculiar attractions for a gloomy and diseased mind, and we accordingly find that the demoniac (Mark v. 2) "had his dwelling among the tombs." The scarcely less gloomy and misguided hermits of early Christendom, when they fled from the duties of that state of life to which it had pleased God to call them, in like manner buried themselves in the fitting seclusion of the tombs.

The great masters who have transferred to canvas the most *spirituelles* conceptions of Divine grace, as exhibited in human form, have no doubt afforded important aid to devotion by their art; but yet, their disregard for correctness of detail in their pictures has done much to prevent our realising, as we might otherwise do, the great scenes of Scripture history.

Who is there, for example, whose conception of the resurrection is not influenced by Raphael's magnificent cartoon? And yet, the square box-shaped sepulchre from which the figure of the risen Saviour is seen to emerge is not only unlike any form of Jewish tomb, but is absolutely inconsistent with the Gospel account.

Let us see now how the facts connected with cave-sepulture in Palestine serve to illustrate that narrative. It was the usual custom for wealthy men to prepare tombs during their own lifetime for the reception of their bodies after death. These tombs were hewn out of the solid rock, and frequently in the proprietor's own garden or vineyard, or near his house. They were always outside the city, only kings and prophets being allowed the honour of burial within the walls. The following description, extracted from the Mishna, shows what constituted a perfect sepulchre according to Rabbinical ideas. A tomb consisted of a cavern about six cubits square, in three of the sides of which were cut niches, or *loculi*, each large enough to contain a corpse. In the fourth side was the entrance to the cave, approached by a small covered court or vestibule, sufficiently large to admit of the bier being brought in. The vestibule was usually open to the air, the small door which led from it into the inner cave or actual sepulchre being closed by a heavy stone (*golel*), capable of being rolled away upon emergency. Such in general is the construction of the numerous rock-tombs met with in Palestine. I need not point out how graphic the Gospel narrative becomes when read by the light of these details : " And when Joseph had taken the body, he wrapped it in a clean linen cloth, and laid it in his own new tomb which he had hewn out of the rock ; and he rolled a great stone to the door of the sepulchre, and departed" (Matt. xxvii. 59, 60).

The bodies were laid in the sepulchral niches uncovered, or if a coffin were used it was of stone and without a lid, and, as the tomb had to be opened from time to time, some precautions were necessary against corruption. Although the actual practice of embalming was not resorted to, spices were always made use of in a Jewish funeral. Some of these were burnt in the form of incense or pastilles during the performance of the rites of sepulture, and others were made into an unguent, with which the corpse was anointed previous to swathing it in the grave-cloths. It is this process which is alluded to in 2 Chron. xvi. 14: "And Asa slept with his fathers . . . and they buried him in his own sepulchres, which he had made for himself in the city of David, and laid him in the bed which was filled with sweet odours and divers kinds of spices prepared by the apothecaries' art; and they made a very great burning for him." We can understand, too, from this the full meaning of Christ's words respecting Mary the sister of Lazarus, who had anointed His feet with precious ointment, "Against the day of My burying hath she kept this" (John xii. 7). The hundred pounds weight of myrrh and aloes which were used at the interment of our Lord were destined to these purposes. Myrrh is a powerful antiseptic, and would enter largely into the composition of the preservative unguent, and Indian aloes wood (*ud*) is even to the present day the favourite fumigating substance employed in the East.

Amongst the common objects found in tombs are lamps, and lachrymatories, or small phials containing the tears of the bereaved survivors.

Jacob and Joseph were brought back from the land of Egypt to rest with their fathers, and, following their example, many Jews in later ages have sought to rest their weary bones in the sacred soil of Palestine. Thousands of aged Hebrews come up yearly to Jerusalem to die, and deem themselves happy indeed if they can be laid at last upon the hills on which their ancient glory stood. The thickly strewn stone slabs which cover the sides of the valley in our illustration (p. 10) are all the simple monuments of these pilgrims of the chosen race. The neighbourhood of Jerusalem contains many sepulchres of note, of the principal of which I will give a brief account.

The Holy Sepulchre itself stands in the centre of the rotunda of the church which bears its name. It consists of a small chapel containing two small apartments, the innermost one of which is said to be the actual sepulchre, "hewn out of a rock," in which the body of our Lord was laid. To outward appearance it is an erection of artificial masonry, but this is explained by saying that the architects of the Emperor Constantine, when they built the church, cut away the rock all round the tomb, leaving it an isolated block, which they then cased with masonry. There seems every probability that this statement is correct, and it is beyond all question that the tomb now shown as that of our Lord is the same which Constantine found. Whether he lit upon the actual spot cr not we cannot tell, but it is certain that the present sepulchre has been believed by Christians for all these centuries to be that of our Lord, and few will, I think, enter that shrine without emotion, or feel disposed to criticise too severely the authority for the identification of the spot.

Within the walls of the church, and near to the Holy Sepulchre itself, are two rock-hewn tombs, said to be those of Joseph of Arimathæa and Nicodemus. Whoever may have been their occupants, it is clear that they are *loculi* of Jewish sepulchres of the usual type, and this is interesting as giving additional probability to the authenticity of the site of the Holy Sepulchre.

Among other well-known tombs around Jerusalem is the Tomb or Pillar of Absalom. This is the monument with a conical roof on the left hand of the engraving on page 10. The tradition which connects it with Absalom dates at least as far back as the twelfth century. In 2 Sam. xviii. 18, we are told that "Absalom in his lifetime had taken and reared up for himself a pillar, which is in the King's Dale : for he said, I have no son to keep my name in remembrance ; and he called the pillar after his own name : and it is called unto this day, Absalom's Place." Josephus, in his "Antiquities," mentions the monument as still standing in his own day, and describes it as "a pillar of marble in the King's Dale, two furlongs distant from Jerusalem." It is interesting as an instance of the very same treatment as that to which the architects of Constantine are said to have subjected the Holy Sepulchre. A cavern was first excavated in the solid rock, and the rock then cut away round it, until the walls of the cavern stand out and form one isolated block. The only difference is that in this case the excavation of the chamber, and the isolation of the block containing it, were parts of one and the same design; while in the case of the Holy Sepulchre the cave had existed for centuries before the isolation of the block took place.

Of the cave or tomb of St. James I have already spoken. The square monument, with four columns and a pyramidal roof, to the right of this is known as the tomb of Zechariah, and immediately behind the tomb of Absalom is a fourth, which tradition points out as that of Jehoshaphat; of this nothing can now be seen but a handsome pediment above the surface of the ground. The so-called tomb of David is situated on Mount Zion, near the south-west corner of the city. This position agrees with the account given of it in Nehemiah iii. 16—19; and we know from Acts ii. 29 that the site was well known in our Lord's time, for the Apostle Peter, when speaking of David, declares that " he is both dead and buried, and his sepulchre is with us to this day." The tradition of the locality is not, however, to be traced down to the present time with such accuracy as that attaching to many other sites.

A very early tradition of the Christian Church connects the buildings which surround the tomb with the upper chamber in which the Last Supper was celebrated, and until a few centuries ago this place was occupied by a Franciscan convent founded in honour of that event. The local tradition in Jerusalem is that a Mohammedan beggar, having been refused alms by the friars, gave out. in revenge, that the convent stood on the site of the tomb of David, and that the populace immediately ejected the Christian occupants, and appropriated the block of buildings. This tale, however, instead of discrediting the identification, appears rather to strengthen its probability; for, unless there had been some popular tradition at the time connecting the site with the tomb of David, the revengeful beggar would hardly have been able to stir up the public mind to such decided action. Hyrcanus, the son and successor of Simon the Maccabee, and later still Herod the Great, are said to have respectively desecrated the tomb of David and despoiled it of treasure. Josephus adds that Herod was prevented from penetrating into the inner sanctuary, which contained the bodies of David and Solomon, by supernatural agency. This story of a person penetrating with sacrilegious intent into the cave-sepulchre of some great king or prophet, and being awed by the apparition of the supposed occupant of the tomb, and miraculously ejected, is common to all countries. It is told of the tombs of the patriarchs at Machpelah, of the cave of the seven sleepers at Ephesus, and of the cavern where our own King Arthur is fabled to await his recall to life.

Besides those already mentioned, there are several very remarkable mausoleums in the immediate vicinity of Jerusalem : such are the Tombs of the Prophets, the Tombs of the Judges, and the Tombs of the Kings. They differ from the other rock-hewn tombs chiefly in their extent and complex arrangement, consisting of an immense number of sepulchral chambers, connected by devious passages, and exhibiting wonderful ingenuity in their construction and in the devices employed for securing them against violation.

To describe these in detail would be foreign to my purpose, especially as the names by which they are known appear to have been given without any authority, either traditionally or otherwise, so that the interest attaching to them is merely archæological.

Of the celebrated tombs not situated in Jerusalem, the most important are that of Joseph, in the Vale of Sychem, near the modern city of Nablous; that of Rachel, on the road between Bethlehem and Hebron; and that of Mach-

TOMB OF RACHEL.

pelah, which, next to the Holy Sepulchre, possesses the greatest interest to the religious world, for it is the tomb of Abraham, the father of the faithful, and is venerated alike by Jew, Christian, and Mohammedan. The cave is jealously guarded by the Mohammedans, and no authentic accounts of its interior have ever been given. Of its existence there is, however, no doubt, and, were scientific explorers allowed to penetrate into its recesses, it is far

c

from improbable that the actual tombs of the patriarchs—nay, perhaps the very mummy of Jacob himself, embalmed after the fashion of the Egyptians—might be brought to light. The walls of the enclosure by which it is surrounded are built of massive masonry, dating, there is little doubt, as far back as the time of Solomon himself; they are deservedly reckoned amongst the most noble and interesting of the antiquities of Palestine. The tomb of Rachel and the cave of Machpelah are, perhaps, the best identified sites in the Holy Land, and authenticated by the most ancient and continuous traditions.

After the death of Sarah, Abraham took another wife, Keturah, by whom he had many sons. These were the founders of tribes and families and nations, and are often to be recognised in th. later history as coming in contact from time to time with the Jews; but only Isaac, the child of the promise, and Abraham's son by his Mesopotamian wife, was permitted to remain in and inherit the Promised Land.

In order to maintain the purity of descent from the old Mesopotamian stock, Abraham would not allow Isaac to intermarry with his Canaanitish neighbours, but sent a trusty messenger to his native country to fetch him a wife from thence. The patriarch died at the age of 175 years, and was buried by his two sons, Isaac and Ishmael, in the cave of Machpelah.

The life of Isaac, though full of interest, is not so important to our history. The birth of his twin sons; their early struggles for supremacy, and the ultimate triumph of the younger but more crafty Jacob over his fierce and reckless, but more frank and simple, brother, Esau; and the loss of his birthright by the latter,—present a very typical picture of the early growth and development of a nation, and of the necessary ultimate triumph of the intellectual element over mere physical qualities.

The young Jacob is sent by his mother into Mesopotamia, not only to withdraw him from his brother's vengeance, but to procure for him a wife from his ancestral home, and so preserve the unmixed purity of the race.

The confirmation of Jacob's newly acquired right to be the head of the family and the recipient of the promise, by the express renewal at Bethel (where he received his name Israel) of the covenant with Abraham ; and the story of his previous adventures in Mesopotamia, of his reconciliation with his offended brother and return to his father in Canaan, are incidents which not only bear the stamp of truth, but strikingly illustrate the unswerving purpose of the Almighty, both in the literal fulfilment of His promise to Abraham, and in working out the regeneration of the world by means of the specially favoured nation which should be born unto him.

Isaac had, in the meantime, made the first step towards taking actual possession of the land, for he had commenced to dig wells and cultivate the soil in that portion of the south country of Canaan where he dwelt.

When Jacob rejoined his father Isaac at Hebron, he brought with him twelve sons, the last, indeed, a new-born infant, whose mother, Rachel, Jacob's favourite wife, had died on the way, and been buried near Bethlehem. The dying woman called her son Benoni, " the son of my grief"; but the father called him Benjamin, " son of the right hand," or " of happiness."

Of the meeting between Isaac and his son we are told nothing, but we learn from the Bible that the old patriarch died at the age of 180 years, and was buried by his two sons, Esau and Jacob, who, like Isaac himself and Ishmael, appeared to have finally reconciled their differences at their father's grave.

CHAPTER II.

THE EXODUS AND WANDERINGS.

The migration to Egypt—Settlement in the land of Goshen—The bondage in Egypt—Egyptian records—Moses the deliverer of Israel—The Exodus from Egypt—Topography of the Exodus—Sinai; the lawgiving—The forty years' wanderings—Topography and vestiges of the wanderings—Kadesh—Condition of the Israelites in the wilderness—Death of Moses—Joshua the leader of Israel—The entry into Canaan—Topographical proofs of the truth of the narrative—The conquest of Canaan.

An event now occurred which seemed to put an end to all hopes of the fulfilment of the promise made to Abraham; and it is a remarkable instance of the mysterious, though certain, working of the Divine Providence, that this very circumstance, which seemed fatal to the possession of Canaan by Abraham's descendants, in reality ultimately led to their entire conquest and undisputed possession of the country. These events are so familiar to every reader of the Bible that I need only glance at them here.

The jealousy of his brethren towards Joseph, Jacob's favourite son, causes them to sell him as a slave to a caravan of Midianite merchants; after various adventures at the court of Pharaoh, he is promoted to the highest rank in the kingdom, and becomes the Prime Minister of the Egyptian sovereign. A subsequent famine in the land of Canaan leads to the reunion of Joseph with his aged father and his brethren, for whom, through his influence with Pharaoh, he procures a settlement on Egyptian territory, in the land of Goshen. Here the patriarch Jacob dies, pronouncing on his death-bed a grand poetic blessing, in which the future fortunes and relative positions of his sons, and of the twelve tribes who should be descended from them, are graphically and distinctly sketched. Jacob's body is removed to Canaan, and buried with great pomp in the sepulchre of his fathers at Hebron. After this, the Land of Promise appears almost forgotten by his descendants, who in their Egyptian home increased and multiplied until they grew in time to be a great nation. For 430 years the history of the chosen people is almost a blank ; but at the expiration of that period we find them no longer the honoured and welcomed guests of a friendly sovereign, but oppressed and tyrannised over by a strange people in the midst of whom they dwelt, and who would fain have crushed them out altogether, but for that distinct and persistent nationality, the vitality of which the persecution of ages has never yet been able to repress.

The Bible dismisses the subject in a few words, and the only notice of the political changes which led to this alteration in the position of the Hebrews is contained in the statement that "there arose up a new king over Egypt which knew not Joseph" (Exod. i. 8).

The Egyptian accounts do not supply the deficiency, and, beyond a confirmation of the main facts of the history, we learn but little from the Egyptian documents which have been either preserved in the writings of the ancients, or recovered from monuments by modern research.

For many generations before the seventeenth dynasty of the kings of Egypt, a prolonged struggle had been carried on between the stationary inhabitants of that country and a certain nomad people called by the ancient writers "shepherds ;" and the contest ended in the peaceable establishment of a dynasty of these people upon the throne of Egypt, under the name of Hyksos, or "shepherd kings."

They were, no doubt, of Semitic origin, and probably came from the land of Canaan, since Manetho and Eusebius, from whom our information is chiefly derived, speak of them as Phœnicians. It was during the reign of one of these shepherd kings that the patriarch Joseph came to Egypt, and this fact throws much light upon the subject of the relations existing between the Egyptian prince and the Hebrew captive boy. It was by no sovereign of a strange race that Joseph was raised to be the first man in Egypt, but by a son of Shem, like himself—by one whose ancestral home was in the fair land of Canaan.

The national characteristics of the Egyptians and the Hebrews present a marked contrast. The Egyptians were an intellectual people, delighting in subtle studies and refined arts, while their religion, though degraded by the introduction of the worship of animals and of the dead, with other gross and sensual notions, yet contained many true and noble ideas, such as the doctrine of a final judgment, and of a future state of reward and punishment.

The Hebrews, on the other hand, were a simple, pastoral people, of nomad habits and great physical power and energy, but with little sympathy for many intellectual pursuits. Their primitive Semitic notions of religion had been elevated far above the most advanced ideas of their age, for the one true God had vouchsafed to their father Abraham knowledge of Himself.

Still, it was but natural that so long a sojourn in Egypt should exercise a lasting impression on the Israelites, and the Bible speaks with no uncertain sound of the intimate nature of the relations which existed between the two peoples. Joseph's assumption of an Egyptian title, Zaphnath-paaneah (Gen. xli. 45) and his marriage with Asenath, daughter of Potipherah, priest of On ; the adoption of Moses by a daughter of Pharaoh, and his education in all the learning and wisdom of the Egyptians, are facts which point to a more close connection between the two races than we are at first inclined to suspect. So, too, the constant rebellious longings of the people in the wilderness after the fleshpots of Egypt and its rich vegetable produce, and, still more, their deplorable lapse into Egypt's besetting sin, the worship of the bull-god Apis, prove incontestably that the refined but corrupt civilisation of Egypt had exercised an influence upon the national character which time and altered circumstances could not efface.

The Egyptians had always cherished a violent animosity against the stranger "shepherd" kings, and, although they submitted to their authority for a long period, yet as soon as an opportunity offered they rose up and shook off the foreign yoke.

The expulsion of the Hyksos was probably the beginning of Israel's troubles, for the native sovereign who now occupied the throne would not be likely to regard with favour a race connected with their defeated enemies by such close family ties as those which we have just seen bound the Hebrews to the shepherd rulers. The restoration of the native Egyptian dynasty is doubtless, therefore, the meaning of the words, "There rose up a new king which knew not Joseph."

The Hebrew race had in the meantime increased prodigiously in numbers, and (as the incidental notices in the Old Testament teach us) were still vastly superior in physical development to the people amongst whom they dwelt. Under a friendly dynasty they lived prosperously; and although, as I have just said, they were affected by Egyptian institutions, they had preserved their nationality intact. But having once become objects of fear and aversion to their rulers, it would seem that there was nothing left for them but to become absorbed into the mass of the population, and consequently lose their nationality, or else to maintain an unequal struggle, which must ultimately be decided against them.

But the Hebrews were no ordinary nation; they were God's own people, chosen to work out His own divine purposes, and their destinies were therefore made His own peculiar care. No greater proof of this can be given than the fact, admitted on all hands, and proved by contemporary history, that, after more than 400 years of sojourning in a strange land they were neither expelled, exterminated, nor absorbed, but marched out from the land in battle array—the same people, serving the same God, actuated by the same lofty aims and confiding in the same divine promise which had encouraged their father Abraham to separate himself from his kindred and leave his old Mesopotamian home.

And now a wondrous figure appears upon the scene. When the people are groaning under their heaviest burden of oppression and wrong, when their hopes seem almost lost, and when their very existence is threatened by Pharaoh's arbitrary and inhuman decree that every male Hebrew child should be murdered at its birth, then God vindicated the promises which He had made to their forefathers, and raised up for them a mighty deliverer.

Around this central figure the events of the next period of Hebrew history cluster.

I need not here enter into the details of the birth and early life of Moses, with which every reader of the Bible is, of course, acquainted; but I will just point out how he came to assume the character of the deliverer of his people, which God had assigned to him. Bred up in the luxurious court of Pharaoh, and cut off from all communication with, or share in, the sufferings of his people, he might well have been expected to appear devoid of sympathy with them. But the inspired mission for which he was destined influenced his character from the very first, and we find him early evincing sympathy with the sufferings of his compatriots, and even betrayed by his zeal into the crime of homicide. "And it came to pass in those days when Moses was grown, that he went out unto his brethren, and looked on their burdens; and he spied an Egyptian smiting an Hebrew, one of his brethren. And he looked this way and that way, and when he saw that there was no man, he slew the Egyptian, and hid him in the sand '' (Exod. ij. 11, 12). By this rash act he was driven into exile, and sought refuge amidst the nomad tribes dwelling on the borders of Palestine and Arabia.

But the Divine purpose was not to be thwarted by the imprudence of its human instrument. After years of exile,

SUMMIT OF JEBEL MÚSA (SINAI).

during which Moses was so completely alienated from his people, and had so forgotten their laws and customs, that he had neglected the national rite of circumcision in his family—and during which he had shown no extraordinary talents or enterprise,—he suddenly receives the call.

He, the humble shepherd, stricken in years, and labouring

under the physical defect of an impediment in his speech—
he, the lonely exile, in whose aged bosom the fire of youth
and of ambition has long been quenched,—is suddenly
brought face to face with God on Sinai, and is sent with all
the authority of præternatural powers to deliver the nation
of Israel from their Egyptian bondage.

Backed by such credentials, all difficulties give way before him; the abject spirit of his enslaved countrymen is
aroused; the obstinacy of Pharaoh and the craft of Pharaoh's magicians are overcome; and amidst dreadful visitations, which cow the proud Egyptians and force even the
impious Pharaoh to acknowledge the power of Israel's God.
Moses leads the people out of the house of bondage to the
Promised Land. The history of the chosen people as a
nation begins with the Exodus, their departure from
Egyptian soil being signalised by the miraculous deliverance at the passage of the Red Sea.

In order to make the account of this migration intelligible
to the reader, it will be necessary to treat the question from
a geographical point of view.

The children of Israel might have been expected to take
the ordinary route from Egypt to the Promised Land, but
this lay through Philistine territory, and we are expressly
told that " God led them not through the way of the land
of the Philistines, although that was near, for God said,
Lest peradventure the people repent when they see war,
and they return to Egypt; but God led the people about,
through the way of the wilderness of the Red Sea " (Exod.
xiii. 17, 18). This " way of the wilderness " passes round
the head of the Gulf of Suez, the western arm of the Red
Sea. Now in Exod. xiv. we are told that the Egyptians
came upon them before they had rounded the head of the
gulf, so that nothing was left for the fugitives but to take
to the water or fall into their enemies' hands, either of
which alternatives appeared to involve certain destruction.

But the Lord was ever present to help them : " And the Lord caused the sea to go back by a strong east wind all that night, and made the sea dry land, and the waters were divided. And the children of Israel went into the midst of the sea upon the dry ground. And the waters were a wall unto them on their right hand and on their left."

The exact site of this miracle it is of course impossible to fix ; but it is certain that the Israelites must have crossed somewhere in the neighbourhood of the present head of the gulf. The spot now called 'Ayún Músa, or " Moses' wells," is evidently connected traditionally with the Exodus, and might have been their first camping-ground. From this point their road is plain for the first three days ; for it is nothing more than the straightest path one can choose across a flat strip of desert. The Bible tells us that " they went out into the wilderness of Shur ; and they went three days in the wilderness and found no water " (Exod. xv. 22). Now there are two remarkable things which the modern traveller must notice here ; first, that the desert is bounded on his left by a lofty *wall* (Hebrew, *shur*) of mountain; and, secondly, that for the first three days he traverses a perfectly waterless track. " And when they came to Marah, they could not drink of the waters of Marah, for they were bitter " (Exod. xv. 23). Again the traveller finds the Bible corroborated, for the first spring which he finds is too bitter to drink. This spring, now called 'Ain Hawwárah, may or may not be the identical Marah at which Moses and the Israelites drank, but the well of Marah was doubtless in this neighbourhood, and bitter from the same cause as that which affects the existing spring, viz. : the presence of a substance called *natrún* in the soil. At any rate the spring must, from the geological conformation of the country, have been somewhere in the neighbourhood ; and the reason for its extreme bitterness—namely, the presence of a substance called *natrún* in the soil—must have been the same then as now. Elim, their next station, " where were twelve wells of water, and threescore and ten palm trees," may be placed in the vicinity of the present springs and palm grove of Wády Gharandel, a pleasant valley to which we next come a few miles farther on.

From Num. xxxiii. 10, we learn that "they removed from Elim, and encamped by the Red Sea." To reach the sea-coast, they must have turned down a broad valley called Wády Taiyebeh, at the mouth of which is a convenient open space which might well have served for the camping-ground of such a host. There are two roads by which the modern traveller can reach the central group of mountains in which Mount Sinai is situated. One of these, the upper road, passes by Sarábít-el-Khádim, an Egyptian mining station, which the children of Israel would have good reason to avoid; the other road is that by the Wády Taiyebeh, just referred to; so that there is little doubt but that we are now upon their track.

Besides the camp in the "Wilderness of Sin," which is probably on the coast near the mouth of a broad valley called Seih Sidreh, two other stations are now mentioned in the Bible, Dophkah and Alush; it is unimportant to identify these, but it is worthy of note that, proceeding on our way, we halt for two successive nights without finding anything worthy of record, but another day's journey will bring us to the mouth of the most fertile valley in the peninsula, Wády Feirán. This, too, is the first valley turning inland which is sufficiently broad and open to admit of the passage of a large body of men and cattle. And now comes a most wonderful confirmation of the truth of the Mosaic narrative. The next station after Alush was Rephidim. Here the Amalekites assembled to defend their fertile valley and their streams of fresh water from the invading host; and here, when the tribes, thirsty and disappointed, murmured against the Lord and against Moses, the lawgiver of Israel smote the rock, and the waters gushed forth at the command of the Most High. And

what do we find at the present day? We find that some
way up Wády Feirán, *a few miles before the fertile part
begins*, there is a rock, of which the simple Bedawín (who
never so much as heard of the Bible) still tell that " our
lord Moses smote it, and water miraculously flowed from
the stone." The old travellers all identify Feirán with
Rephidim, and Antoninus Martyr, writing in the seventh
century, mentions his having seen a chapel or oratorium
built in honour of Moses on the very hill upon which
he stood when Aaron and Hur held up his hands at the
battle with the Amalekites : " And it came to pass, when
Moses held up his hand, that Israel prevailed, and when
he let down his hand, Amalek prevailed " (Exod. xvii. 11).
The ruins of this chapel still remain upon the summit of
a small conical mountain called Jebel et Tahúneh, and
the view which it commands of the valley beneath, in which
the fight must have taken place, is at once impressive and
grand.

The children of Israel " departed from Rephidim, and
pitched in the wilderness of Sinai, and there Israel encamped before the mount " (Exod. xix. 2). This verse
evidently implies a break in the march between Rephidim
and Sinai, and the account exactly accords with the route
now followed. The traveller sends his baggage round by
Wády-es-Sheikh, and he himself, mounted on his drome-
dary and attended by lightly laden camels, may reach
Jebel Músa (the mount of Moses) in a single day's march.
Tradition and probability alike single out this mountain as
the Mount of the Law, and a spot more fitted by nature
for the awful scenes transacted there can scarcely be
imagined.

Mount Sinai is an immense block, isolated from the surrounding mountains by deep valleys, so that it would be
an easy task to set bounds round it, and prevent persons
from making the ascent. The " nether end of the mountain " is a magnificent bluff rising precipitously from the

plain—truly a "mount which might be touched." In front of this stretches a broad plain, which has been ascertained by Captain H. S. Palmer, R.E., from the actual measurements of the Ordnance Survey, to be capable of containing *over a million of spectators.* The highest summit of the mountain is completely hidden from this plain; and on this secluded peak Moses might well have remained for forty days until the people "wot not what had become of him." The Arabs here show the traditional spot in which the law was delivered to Moses; from the lower peak, overlooking the plain, the law-giver of Israel must have proclaimed the commandments of God to the expectant hosts assembled beneath.

The distance from Egypt to Jebel Músa, exactly accords with the number of stations or days' journey mentioned in the Bible; the physical aspect of the mountain and its surroundings exactly answer the description given in the Bible of the mountain of the law; traditions of the events recorded in the Bible still linger in the tales which the untutored Arabs tell to their children over their camp fires.

The events of the Exodus lie within a small compass, and the scenes of the law-giving took place in a country not altogether unknown to geographers; it is, therefore, comparatively easy to arrive at a decision upon the whole question. But with the forty years' wanderings of Israel the case is far different, and the great and terrible wilderness had until lately scarcely ever been visited and never carefully examined. Accordingly, in treating of this part of my subject, I am compelled to fall back upon my own experiences in that barren region, which my companion, Mr. Tyrwhitt-Drake, and I were the first to thoroughly explore.

The ordinary road from the convent of Mount Sinai to the little seaport of 'Akabah, at the head of the eastern arm of the Red Sea, crosses a sandy plain in the north-

SINAI.

east of the Sinaitic peninsula. This plain is apparently one of the dreariest spots in the whole desert, but the neighbourhood is a most deeply-interesting one, for a few hours short of the plain, the remains of an Israelitish camp may still Le seen ; and a little further on is Hazeroth, the second permanent encampment of the children of Israel after their departure from the mountain of the law. When making a previous excursion to Hazeroth we had come across some curious stone-heaps and circles, and on asking the Arabs what these might be, we were told that they were the remains of a large Hajj caravan which had lost its way at this point and wandered off into the desert of Et Tíh. Now the word *Hajj* is applied by the Mohammedans to the great caravan of pilgrims which yearly crosses the desert to Mecca; and it may seem at first sight that no possible connection could exist between this caravan and the Exodus of Israel. And yet that such connection does exist I do not hesitate to assert. In the first place, the Mohammedan pilgrims would not, under any circumstances, have passed by this road, and the story must, therefore, apply to some other caravan. Secondly, the word *Hajj*, although now appropriated by the Mohammedans, has been borrowed by them from the Hebrew; and the first use of the word in the Bible occurs in the passage in Exodus where Moses begs of Pharaoh to let the people go " to sacrifice" (literally, " to a Hajj") " in the wilderness." Again, the word used in the legend by the Arabs, signifying " they lost their way," is identical with that used in the Bible to express the *wanderings* of the Israelites. All these considerations and the additional fact that the remains are evidently of high antiquity and different from any others which I have ever seen in the desert, leave little doubt upon my mind but that in them we discovered the real vestiges of an Israelite camp. They are situated rather more than half-way between Sinai and Hazeroth, and this is just the position which the Bible assigns to the station of Kibroth-hattaavah, where Israel was fed with the miraculous flight of quails ; and where, "while the flesh was yet between their teeth, ere it was chewed, the wrath of the Lord was kindled against the people, and the Lord smote the people with a very great plague." As if to place the identity beyond question, we found outside the camp an immense number of tombs, doubtless the very *Kibroth-hattaavah* (graves of gluttony) of which the Bible speaks.

About a day's journey past 'Ain Hudherah, which is the present Arabic form of the Hebrew word Hazeroth, we come to Jebel 'Arádeh, a name which, allowing in the same way for the difference between the two languages, is identical with Haradah,—another station of the Israelites, which has hitherto remained unrecognised. Shortly after this point we entered the wilderness called *Bádiet et Tíh*, "the Desert of the Wandering," as the name implies. This is a broad plateau of limestone, the southern end of which projects wedgewise into the Sinaitic peninsula. It is bounded on the north by the Mediterranean Sea and the mountains of Judah, on the west by the Isthmus of Suez, and on the east by the Wády el 'Arabeh, that large depression or valley which runs between the Gulf of 'Akabah and the Dead Sea.

Across this tract of desert lay the road down into Egypt, along which Jacob travelled to visit his long-lost son Joseph ; and across the same unpromising waste the Virgin mother fled with her Holy Child ; and the hilly plateau in its north-east corner was once the home and pasture-ground of the patriarchs, the "south country" of Scripture.

The key to the movements of the Israelites after their departure from Hazeroth is the position of Kadesh-barnea, as we see from Deut. i. 19, "And when we departed from Horeb, we went through all that great and terrible wilderness which ye saw by the way of the mountain of the

D

Amorites, as the Lord our God commanded us : and we
came to Kadesh-barnea." This is found on the western
edge of the plateau last mentioned, and consists of a
large tract of open wilderness, stretching out from the
foot of a long line of cliffs, in which may yet be seen
a fountain, bearing the name of Gadís, or Kadesh. In
the immediate neighbourhood are the mountains of the

KADESH-BARNEA.

Amorites (Deut. ii. 19, 20), still called by their scriptural
name, in its Arabic form, 'Amarin. An ancient fort
guards a mountain pass in these hills, by which we reach
a fertile plain, having the ruins of a fine town in its midst.
The city is named Sebaitah (the Hebrew Zephath, or
" watch-tower "), and the fort is called by an Arabic
word, meaning also watch-tower. The importance of

these two places, which Mr. Tyrwhitt-Drake and I had
the good fortune to discover, will be best seen from two
passages of Scripture. In Num. xiv. 43, 45, we read
that " the Amalekites and Canaanites which dwelt in that
hill" came down and smote the people, even unto Hormah. And in Judges i. 17 we are told that " Judah went
with Simeon his brother, and they slew the Canaanites that
inhabited Zephath, and utterly destroyed it; and the
name of the city was called Hormah." Thus we find
that Hormah and Zephath are the same, or rather that
Hormah was called the city of the Zephath or watch-
tower, because of the tower or fort which guarded the
approach to it.

Now, this city and tower we find in the mountains of
the Amorites, within a short distance of Kadesh, thus
conclusively proving the accuracy of that part of the
narrative of the wanderings of the Israelites which relates
to their sojourn at Kadesh and defeat at Hormah. But
the battle took place after the return of the spies; these
had brought with them specimens of the monstrous grapes
which Palestine then produced, and as the nearest place at
which grapes are now found is at least four or five days'
journey distant, and as grapes will not keep good so long in
a hot climate, it may, at first sight, appear impossible that
Kadesh could be where I place it. We must remember,
however, that this country was not always as barren and
dry as it is now; when the children of Israel sought to
enter the land, this outpost was defended by its inhabitants,
as Rephidim had been by the Amalekites, because it was
the commencement of the fertile district: it must always
have been remarkable for its extensive vineyards, for even
to the present day miles and miles of the valleys and hill-
sides are covered with regular swathes of small stones,
along which the grapes were trained, and which are still
called by the Arabs, *Telailât el 'Anab*, or "grape mounds,"
and we may certainly place Eshkol in this neighbourhood.

Hitherto, the children of Israel had been led towards the Promised Land, and but for their constant murmurings and disobedience would, no doubt, have been permitted to enter in at this point. But their neglect of God's express command, in " having presumed to go up into the hill-top " to attack the enemy, resulted, as might have been expected, in defeat and disappointment. And then came the dreadful punishment, forty years of wandering in that cheerless wilderness. It must not be supposed that during all this time the hosts of Israel were continually on the move, or that they wandered about in the strict sense of being unable to find their way. What is, no doubt, intended by the expression is that, instead of marching onward and conquering—a triumphant nation, strong in the invisible presence of Jehovah—they were beaten back at every point by the peoples who held the Promised Land, and were compelled to linger on, as do the Bedawin Arabs of the present day, in a half-savage, homeless state, moving about from place to place, and pitching their tents wherever they could find pasture for their flocks and herds. During all this time the Bible is almost silent as to their doings, or what it does tell us is little more than a sad record of murmurings, rebellions, sorrows and forebodings. As God's people and the chosen instruments of His vengeance, their least act and smallest journey had been chronicled in the inspired Word; but now that His presence was withdrawn, they sank down to the mere level of a Bedawin tribe, and their history during the whole dismal period of their wandering is almost a blank. But in the fortieth year they again assembled at Kadesh; the Lord was once more with them, and the kings of Moab and Edom were powerless to prevent their onward march to Canaan. Along the self-same track my companion and I journeyed, not without encountering many dangers and difficulties which I have not space to record here. I shall not easily forget the feelings which overpowered

me when our wanderings in the wilderness were at an
end. We stood upon the heights of Mount Nebo, where
Moses, the aged lawgiver of Israel, gazed for the first time
on the Promised Land, and looked his last upon the world.
The hills of Palestine rose up before us ; at our feet the
Jordan meandered along its noble valley to the calm blue
waters of the Dead Sea ; and, as we meditated on the
scene, the solemn words of Deut. xxiv. 4, came to our
minds with a reality they had never before assumed—
" This is the land which I sware unto Abraham, unto
Isaac, and unto Jacob, saying, I will give it unto thy
seed ; I have caused thee to see it with thine eyes."

During the Exodus of the Israelites, and their subsequent
wanderings in the wilderness, they were led by the visible
presence of Jehovah, and this was the cause of their great
and wonderful success. The periods of reverse and
failure which they from time to time encountered were
consequent upon their own sin and murmuring, to punish
which that presence was withdrawn. The government of
the people was thus a theocracy in the purest and fullest
acceptation of the term ; it was God Who ruled their coun-
cils, and Moses their earthly leader was the prophet, that
is, the mouth-piece and oracle, of their God. It is very
important to bear this fact in mind, for the fortunes of the
Hebrew nation depended entirely upon this Divine constitution, and in the subsequent periods of their history we
see them rising or falling, victorious or conquered, united
or dispersed, according as they accepted or rejected this
direct government of God.

The grand earthly aim which Moses and the hosts of
Israel had in view was the conquest of Canaan, and to
this purpose they were constantly commanded to adhere.
When the weary wanderings came to an end with the fulfilment of the term for which that heavy curse was laid
upon them, the young generation which had in the meantime grown up to man's estate must have looked forward

with joyous anticipation to the moment when the promise should at last be fulfilled, and the Land of Canaan become their own. The death of Moses must have cast a heavy cloud over their prospects, for they could never hope again to see at their head one so favoured by Divine grace, or so able to cope with every unforeseen difficulty or political crisis.

But, when God has a purpose to fulfil, the history of the whole world teaches us that an instrument is never wanting, and while men are wondering who next shall take up the cause and fulfil the mission, the man is found, and the people recognise with wonder and with awe that from the very first God has prepared him for the work. Thus, after the death of Moses, the leadership of the people fell upon Joshua the son of Nun. All previous mention of him points to his fitness for the post, and to his gradual preparation for the lofty destiny to which he had been ordained.

We early meet with him as the confidential servant and companion of Moses, and at the first great crisis in their affairs—the rebellion of the people at Kadesh on the southern border of Canaan—we find him, together with Caleb, the brave prince of the tribe of Judah, leading to a successful issue the difficult expedition to spy out the resources and defences of the Promised Land. At that time he was called Hoshea, " help," but on his being selected for the accomplishment of this mission his name was changed by Moses to Joshua, " Jehovah's help," a title significant and earnest of the part he was afterwards to perform.

But both Moses and Joshua were not only God's instruments in the accomplishment of His purpose, not merely the leaders of a young nation struggling up to power and greatness, but they were types of a much higher and more spiritual progress ; hence it is, no doubt, that we see in the lives and actions of both of them certain curious parallels.

Joshua was to complete the work begun by Moses, but, as though to prove that his success was no mere result of human energy or foresight, but part of one and the same Divine scheme, the very incident in the completion of that scheme was a reflection of the one which marked its commencement. As, before leaving Egypt, they were commanded to prepare themselves for the wondrous events that were to follow by eating the Passover as a sacrament and token of their covenant with God, so, before entering the Promised Land, they received the command, "Sanctify yourselves, for to-morrow the Lord will do wonders among you." As the waters of the Red Sea divided to let the people pass from the bondage of Egypt to the freedom of the wilderness, and to allow them to enter into the glorious heritage of the law proclaimed by God's own lips from the rugged peaks of Sinai, so, after their probationary wanderings, the swollen flood of Jordan was parted asunder, and the people marched over on dry land to take possession of their earthly heritage.

And now Joshua, at the command of God, bade one man from each tribe set a stone in the midst of Jordan, and as the memorial act was completed, the waters rushed back again into their channel. This miraculous act, so strictly parallel to the incident which accompanied the deliverance of Israel under Moses, was recognised by the people as an authoritative proof that Joshua was the divinely appointed successor of the deceased lawgiver, and as if in gracious token of his acceptance, the God of Israel appeared to Joshua nigh unto the spot where he had led the children of Israel across the Jordan, and, revealing to him, as He had done to Moses, the splendour of His Divine Majesty, spake to him in the self-same words, "Loose the shoes from off thy feet, for the place whereon thou standest is holy."

Joshua pitched his camp at Gilgal, a place on the western bank of the Jordan a little to the south-east of

Jericho, and from this as his head-quarters he speedily accomplished the subjugation of the land. Jericho was the first town which fell, and, as though to teach them that it was not in the strength of man that they should prevail, the city fell, not to the clash of arms and the shout of battle, but to the sound of the trumpets of the priests, and the utterance of the ineffable name of God.

Some writers have expressed wonder that no collateral accounts have reached us from ancient times of so important an event as the conquest and occupation of Canaan by the Israelites. We have, however, a testimony to the truth and accuracy of the Bible history even more startling and convincing than written or traditional records; this testimony we owe to modern science, and, although some people would fain have us believe science to be antagonistic to Scripture truth, yet, in the case of Palestine, scientific research has proved itself in every instance the handmaid of that truth.

After the fall of Ai, Joshua led the conquering army northwards to Mount Ebal, where the covenant between God and His people was solemnly renewed by the setting up of an altar to the Lord; by the engraving of the law on stone, and reading it in the presence of the whole congregation; and, finally, by the recital of the blessings and curses from Mounts Ebal and Gerizim. After this solemn ceremony, Joshua "wrote these words in the book of the Law of God, and took a great stone, and set it up there by the oak, that was in the sanctuary of the Lord." (Josh. xxiv. 26.) Judges xi. 6, again mentions both the sanctuary and the "pillar that was in Shechem."

Here, again, a wonderful confirmation of Scripture is afforded us by modern discovery. The Rev. George Williams was the first to notice the important fact, that in this valley of Shechem there is a natural amphitheatre, formed by a recess in Mount Ebal, exactly facing a similar recess in Mount Gerizim; this amphitheatre the subsequent investi-

FORD OF THE JORDAN.

gations of Captains Wilson and Anderson, of the Palestine
Exploration Fund, proved to be admirably adapted, both
in size and acoustic properties, for the assemblage of a
large concourse of persons to hear the reading of the Law.
But, stranger still, close by this very spot is a sanctuary
still called El 'Amúd, " the pillar," containing the very
stone set up by Joshua, and venerated alike by Mohammedans and Samaritans.

We must not omit to notice the parallel between the
circumstances attending this first decisive battle of Joshua
with the Canaanites, and those of Moses' first decisive
battle with Amalek. At the battle of Rephidim, Moses held
up his hands and Israel prevailed, while at the battle of
Ai, the brandishing of Joshua's spear over the doomed city
was the signal of success to the hosts of the Lord.

The country to the east of Jordan was now in the hands
of the Israelites; while by the destruction of Jericho and
Ai, the peaceable submission of the city of Gibeon, and
the establishment of the camp at Gilgal, a firm footing had
been established in Palestine itself.

The principal tribes of the country, led by the chief of
the Jebusites, now formed an alliance against the invaders,
and turned the first fury of their desperate indignation
upon the Gibeonites, whom they regarded as having betrayed the common cause. Joshua received news of the
attack at his camp at Gilgal, and, marching through the
night with amazing rapidity to the relief of his allies, appeared in the morning before the walls of Gibeon.

The battle that followed was the death-blow to heathen-
dom in Canaan, the crowning victory to the banner of the
Lord. Discomfited before Israel, fleeing in blind confusion
through the intricacies of their own mountain passes, the
Amorites fell before the avenging sword of Joshua and the
terrible hailstones from on high, while the very " sun stood
still and the moon stayed, until the people had avenged
themselves upon their enemies."

One last and unsuccessful struggle was made by the Canaanites; Jabin, the king of Hazor, capital of the northern kingdom, assembled together all the neighbouring chiefs with their followers, and made a stand against Joshua at the Lake Merom. The Canaanite army was most formidable in numbers and equipment, " they were like the sand that is upon the sea-shore in multitude, with chariots and horses very many." Joshua lost no time in giving them battle, " and the Lord delivered them into the hand of Israel, who smote them and chased them as far as great Zidon and Misrephoth-maim, and to the valley of Mizpah eastward, and they smote them until they left them none remaining" (Josh. xi. 4, 8).

After this event, the subjugation of Palestine was slowly but surely accomplished, and although the Canaanites now and then rallied sufficiently to give considerable trouble to Joshua and his generals, they were never able again to endanger the stability of the Israelite occupation of the land.

CHAPTER III.

THE SETTLEMENT IN PALESTINE.

Final subjugation of the country and partition amongst the tribes—Harmony between the physical and historical aspects—Detailed description—The netherlands—The "hill country" of Judah—The Dead Sea and its neighbourhood—The "hill country" of Benjamin—Territory of Manasseh—Mount Carmel; the scene of Elijah's sacrifice—The Plain of Esdraelon—Upper and Lower Galilee—Lake of Galilee—Gergesa, Chorazin, and Capernaum—Kedesh-Naphthali; traces of Canaanite occupation—Maritime territory of Asher—The Trans-Jordanic tribes; district of Bashan, Gilead, and Moab—Ethnography of Palestine—Persistence of racial characteristics—Modern Anakim—Manners and customs—Illustrations of Biblical incidents.

AFTER a war which lasted about seven years, the complete subjugation had, as we have seen, been effected, and the various tribes, tired of hostilities, desired to settle down into the peaceful occupation of their conquered territory. Thus they disobeyed the command of God, Who had bidden them utterly exterminate the Canaanites. In after years the nation proved how disobedience to the least of God's commands entails a dreadful punishment, however late that punishment may come. The remnant thus left of the heathen nations in Palestine not only constantly harassed the Israelites, but, by seducing the people from time to time into following their own idolatrous customs, was the immediate cause of all the visitations and chastisements which subsequently befel the Hebrew race.

Joshua's first act when peace was fairly established was the survey of the country, and its partition amongst the various tribes.

To make this division intelligible to my readers, I must give a brief sketch of the geographical aspect of the Promised Land.

Nothing, perhaps, more strikingly exemplifies the unity of purpose in God's government of the world than the universal harmony which exists between the moral and the physical in nature, and between revelation itself and the scenes in the midst of which it was vouchsafed, or to which it immediately refers.

For instance, the geologist tells us that the rugged rocks of Sinai belong to the earliest formation ; that they are, in fact, the primeval rocks of which the body of this ancient world is formed ; that some volcanic convulsion has upheaved them and caused them to burst through the crust of the globe ; and that it was these rocks which witnessed the promulgation of *the* primeval law, when, amidst a terrible convulsion of nature, thunder and lightning and earthquake, those commandments which form the body and essence of all law and morality were made known—when, in a word, the Divine Will burst through the thick crust of man's fallen nature, and stood revealed. So, too, the Promised Land was destined to be the scene of events, not only of paramount importance in their influence upon the world at large, but types of what should come hereafter— events which should contain lessons applicable to all people, ages, or lands.

Accordingly, we find this country to be as unique in its physical and geographical aspects as it is in its historical points of view. Small in extent, it yet embraces within its narrow limits some type or specimen of almost every possible feature of which physical geography treats. Within that narrow compass you have land and sea, mountain and plain, fertile fields and well-watered gardens, with parched and arid desert tracks, and the climate and fauna of the arctic zone* almost side by side with the hot, heavy atmosphere and the luxurious vegetation of the tropics.†

Of the southern portion of the Holy Land, the Negeb,

* In the Hermon and Lebanon districts.
† In the Ghor, or deep depression in which the Dead Sea lies.

or, as it is called in the Authorised Version, "the south country," I have already spoken in the account of the Exodus and forty years' wanderings.

Between the long mountainous ridge, which forms, as it were, the backbone of the country, and the sea, there extends a broad low-lying plain, partly desert and partly cultivated. This is called in the Bible "the Shephelah," or netherlands, rendered in our version sometimes "valley" and sometimes "plain." The lower portion of this maritime plain was called Philistia, and was chiefly assigned to the tribe of Judah, while the northern portion, which is terminated by the promontory of Mount Carmel jutting out into the sea, was known as the Plain of Sharon, and assigned to the tribe of Dan. The southern portion of the maritime plain was assigned to Simeon.

Philistia was not subjugated at the time of the conquest by Joshua, but maintained its independence until the time of the first monarchy. Perhaps no part of the country has preserved its ethnological characteristics so long, for the Fellahín, or peasantry, are a race distinct from the rest of the inhabitants of Palestine; and the principal towns of the region, Gaza, Ascalon, Joppa, Ashdod, Lachish, and Gath, have never once disappeared from history, but exist at the present day under the names of Gazzeh, Askalún, Yáfá, Esdad, Umm-Lakis, and Beit Jibrín, that is, Beth Gubrin, "the house of the giants."

Many other of the modern names also preserve the memory of the old Philistine history and worship. A small village, about nine miles inland from Joppa, for instance, being still called Beit Dijan, "the house of Dagon."

Still proceeding northward, the next division of the country which claims our attention is the "hill country" east of the maritime plain just mentioned, and which formed the chief portion of the tribe of Judah.

In the Book of Joshua, thirty-eight cities are enumerated as belonging to this part of the country, and their number was, as we know, greatly increased during its subsequent occupation by the large and powerful tribe of Judah.

South of Hebron, the "hill country" is scarcely less barren than the Negeb itself; but the ruins of the ancient towns are scattered in immense numbers over the whole district. Here, too, the names are scarcely altered from the Hebrew appellations given them in the Bible, and in Attir, Semú'ah, Tell Zíf, Ma'in, Kirmil, and the like, we can easily recognise the ancient Jattir, Eshtemoah, Ziph, Maon, Carmel, &c. The culminating point of the "hill country" is at Hebron, the chief city of the region, and, as the Bible itself tells us, almost the oldest city in the world.

The neighbourhood of Hebron is identical with the plains, or, more correctly, the "oaks" of Mamre, the scene of so many important events in Abraham's career; and within the present town is a structure, venerated alike by Christians, Jews, and Mohammedans, namely, the enclosure built by Solomon around the burial-place of the patriarch and his family, the Cave of Machpelah.

Within this region are comprised many remarkable spots. Bethlehem, the birth-place of our Lord, and near it the burial-place of Rachel, "in the way to Ephrath which is Bethlehem" (Gen. xxxv. 19), whose tomb is still to be seen, an object of veneration to all the three conflicting sects of Palestine.

Within this district also lie the caves of Khuretun, the traditional site of the Cave of Adullam. Caves are found in greater numbers in this part of the country than in any other, and many of the villages, such as Dhahariyeh and Siloam, are still little more than a collection of cave-dwellings, reminding us that the ancient Horites, or "cave-dwellers," who were dispossessed by the Israelites, have left abundant traces of their existence and mode of life.

Leaving Hebron and Bethlehem, and proceeding eastwards towards the Dead Sea, we find a large and barren tract which has evidently been uncultivated and uninhabited from the remotest times, for here only in all Palestine do we find no traces of the ruins of former cities. This is the wilderness of Judea. It slopes eastward gradually to the Dead Sea, close to which it suddenly terminates in precipitous cliffs. At the foot of the cliffs lies the Buheirat Lút, " Lot's Lake," or, as we are accustomed to call it, the Dead Sea. It lies no less than 1,300 feet below the level of the

CAVE OF ADULLAM.

Mediterranean, and the climate in this deep and sheltered spot is almost tropical.

The Dead Sea is always spoken of in Scripture as the Salt Sea, its waters being so intensely salt and bitter that no form of life whatever exists within them. This condition they owe to the presence, at the southern end, of an immense mass of rock-salt, no less than 300 feet high, and known by the name of Jebel Usdum. At the northern end of the lake, in all probability, were situated the cities of the plain, upon which fell so signal and terrible a punishment.

The tradition of this event, which has never ceased to cling to the spot, and the sulphurous and bituminous nature of the soil, indicating some great volcanic convulsion, have invested the Dead Sea with so weird an interest that few persons form a really clear conception of what it is like. I will venture to give my own impressions of the scene, written upon the spot.

"The sky was overcast with clouds, and a dense haze obscuring the mountains made the landscape as dreary and monotonous as it could be. In an aspect such as this, the Dead Sea seemed more than ever to deserve its name; not a sign of life was there, not even any motion, save a dull, mechanical surging of the waters. The barren shore was covered with a white incrustation of salt, relieved only by occasional patches of black rotting mud, or by stagnant pools of brine. All along the dismal beach, large quantities of drift-wood were thickly strewn, and amongst this might be detected the blackened trunks of palms. The palm-tree has disappeared from Palestine for centuries, but here its body is embalmed, the only record of that grove which, in olden times, gave to Jericho the title of the City of Palm-trees (Deut. xxxiv. 3).

"But on a sunny day the Dead Sea presents a very different appearance. The waters, which are remarkably transparent, sparkle with a bright azure hue, and the mountains on either side assume the most gorgeous tints. Nor does it then wear the same aspect of utter sterility; for, although the immediate vicinity of the lake is barren enough, the Ghor, or deep depression at the northern and southern extremities, teems with life and vegetation; and, even where the cliffs rise sheer up from the water's edge, streams of fresh water dash down the ravines and bring the verdure with them almost to the Salt Sea's brink. Even on the barest parts of the beach, immense numbers

E

of storks may be observed, and these also help to give life and animation to the scene."*

It is impossible to fix precisely the site of Sodom and Gomorrah and the other cities of the plain; but there is no doubt that they were situated in the neighbourhood of the various streams which run down from the ravines and produce large patches of luxurious vegetation.

On the western side of the lake is 'Ain Jídy, the ancient Engedi. We learn also from Chronicles (2 Chron. xx. 2) that it was identical with Hazezon-Tamar, the fortress

THE DEAD SEA.

taken by Chedorlaomer, who invaded Palestine in the time of Abraham.

Not far from 'Ain Jídy, and lying between the latter place and the southern end of the Dead Sea, are the ruins of the ancient fortress of Masada, which, though not mentioned in the Bible, played a most important part in later Jewish history, and formed the last refuge of the Jews during the war of independence. Between 'Ain Jídy and the northern end of the lake are several oases, where the little mountain streams leap forth upon the plain. The

* " The Desert of the Exodus," pp. 464, 465.

last of these is called 'Ain Feskhah, and here the Ghor, or Plain of Jordan, commences. From the junction of Jordan with the Dead Sea, at this point, " the bay of the sea at the uttermost part of Jordan," a line drawn westward over the hills marks the boundary between Judah and Benjamin. This frontier line passed by Beth-hogla, Beth-arabah, the stone of Bohan, the valley of Achor, and the " going up to Adummim."

The course of this boundary line may be easily traced at the present day. Beth-hogla is the present 'Ain Hajleh ; a little to the south-east of Jericho, the " going up of Adummim " is the pass on the south side of the great Wády Kelt, the ordinary road between Jericho and Jerusalem. The stone of Bohan has been recently identified in an ingenious and convincing manner by Monsieur Ganneau (the discoverer of the Moabite Stone) with a rock now known by the name of Hajar el Asbah.* Proceeding up the Jordan valley, the first important place to which we come is Jericho, which, although now but a mere collection of hovels, was a wealthy and strongly fortified town at the time of the conquest of Canaan by Joshua, and continued to play an important part in history even as late as the crusading times. Its present name, Er Riha, is absolutely identical, letter for letter, with the ancient name Jericho, little as our spelling of the latter word would seem to indicate the fact.

Immediately opposite to Jericho, on the eastern side of the Jordan, is a large barren plain, " the Plain of Shittim," upon which the Israelitish hosts encamped before their invasion of the Promised Land.

The southern boundary of Benjamin, as we have just seen, ran up the steep ascent from the northern end of

* *Bohan* signifies "the thumb," and the name *Hajar el Asbah*, by a simple change in the last letter, becomes Hajar el Asbâ, the "finger stone." This interchange of letters is very common in the Bedawín dialects, and M. Ganneau and myself have collected a great number of instances in proof of it.

the Dead Sea to Jerusalem. Taking in the latter town, it ran north-west to a point on the western slopes of the "hill country," where the latter sinks into the Plain of Sharon. From this point its northern boundary starts, and, passing north of Bethel, crosses the hills, and descends into the Jordan valley. It is thus, although very small as compared with the allotments of the other tribes, one of the most important of all the divisions of the country, including the two great passes into the centre of the country, Michmash on the east, and Beth-horan on the west, Jerusalem, the capital, being also situated in its border. Within these narrow limits, too, are comprised the sites of Bethel, Ai, Gibeon, Mizpah, and many other names familiar in our mouths as household words.

The central "hill country" of Palestine, a much more fertile and more diversified tract of land than that of Judah, was nearly equally divided between the tribe of Ephraim and the half tribe of Manasseh; the portion of the former comprising the region of Shechem. I have already alluded (p. 42) to the identification of the spot, El 'Amúd, in the valley between Mounts Ebal and Gerizim, where Joshua assembled the tribes at the conclusion of the war of conquest, and solemnly ratified the covenant with the Almighty. The other chief points of interest in the same neighbourhood—the well of Jacob, where our Lord discoursed with the woman of Samaria, the tomb of Joseph hard by in the same valley of Shechem, and the ruins of the Temple of Samaria on Mount Gerizim—are too well known to need further mention here.

Just within the southern limits of Ephraim, a little north of Bethel, is Seilún, the ancient Shiloh, where Eli and Samuel dwelt, and where the Ark of the Lord rested for so many years. The portion of the tribe of Manasseh on the western side of Jordan stretches right across Palestine; its southern border is difficult to define, being somewhat confused with the possessions of Ephraim. The northern border begins at Beth-shean on the east, and then takes a bold sweep round to the north as far as the promontory of Mount Carmel. The territory of Manasseh thus includes the passes of Esdraelon and the Plain of Jezreel, the scene of Gideon's exploits against the Midianite invaders. On the mountain ridge which terminates at Carmel, and overlooking the great Plain of Esdraelon, lie the ruins of the ancient Megiddo, in front of which two of the greatest battles of the Bible history were fought: the first was that in which the Canaanites were routed by Barak when Sisera, their leader, fell; the second that in which Josiah, king of Judah, lost his life in endeavouring to oppose the hosts of Pharaoh-Necho, king of Egypt, who was advancing against the king of Syria. Along the foot of the self-same hills runs the Nahr el Makatta, " that ancient river, the river Kishon."

About six miles from Megiddo, in the same chain, there suddenly rises a bold bluff, the east end of Mount Carmel, which, stretching to the north-west for about eighteen miles, as suddenly terminates in a similar bluff running down to the Mediterranean. The east end of Carmel was the scene of the great contest between Elijah and the priests of Baal. The very spot at which this event took place has been identified, and is still known as El Mahrakah, " the place of burning or sacrifice," and, as Dr. Tristram, its discoverer, aptly remarks, " from the El Mahrakah, or place of burning, a slippery path leads down to the Kishon, which now bears, in memory of that awful day, the name of Nahr el Makatta, " the river of slaughter."

At the foot of the mountains which mark the territory of Manasseh, a fine undulating plain, some twelve miles in width at its narrowest part, stretches right across the country, sinking imperceptibly into the Jordan valley on the east. The western portion is cut off from the rest of the maritime plain by the promontory of Carmel on the south, and on the north by another fine headland called Râs en-Nakûra, which is really a spur of the Galilean hills. This part of the plain is known as the Plain of Acre, and is divided from the Plain of Esdraelon by a sparsely-wooded ridge. In the centre of the Plain of Esdraelon, at the foot of a low spur of Mount Gilboa, stands the little hamlet of Zer'ín, the site of the ancient Jezreel. The modern Arabic name is identical with the Hebrew word which in our version of the Bible is spelt Jezreel, and the name Esdraelon given to it in the Septuagint is merely the Greek rendering of the same word. Nothing but a few ruined columns and broken sarcophagi remain of the city which was once the capital and pride of Israel.

The Plain of Esdraelon is diversified by the hills of Tabor and Gilboa, and the hill of Moreh, generally known as the Little Hermon. Amongst the numerous ruined sites in the district we may notice those of Sulem, 'Ain Dûr, and Nain, which are identical with the Shunem, Endor, and Nain of the Bible. The whole of this district belonged to the tribe of Issachar, and is identical with the Lower Galilee of the New Testament.

The hilly district which lies to the north of the Plain of Esdraelon was apportioned to the tribes of Zebulon and Naphthali; it was known later on by the name of Upper Galilee.

It is chiefly as the scene of our Lord's ministry that Galilee is so full of interest for us. The frontier of Zebulon stretched from the Sea of Galilee to Mount Carmel and the sea. The territory of Zebulon thus included the Plain of Acre, and it is to the immediate connection with the trade of Phœnicia which this situation gave it that the prophetic blessing of Jacob alludes: " Zebulon shall dwell at the haven of the sea, and he shall be an haven of ships, and his border shall be unto Zidon " (Gen. xlix. 13). The actual sea-coast district, as

far as the frontier of Sidon, was assigned to the tribe of
Asher. The portion of Naphthali included the north-
western side of the Lake of Galilee, and ran up into the
fertile valleys of the Anti - Libanus, including Mount
Hermon, with its well-watered and vine-clad slopes. The
Lake of Galilee is about 12¼ miles long by 6¾ miles broad ;
it lies about 650 feet below the level of the Mediterranean,
and the climate, when contrasted with the fresh, cool air
of the highlands above it, is almost tropical.

At the time of the New Testament history, its neighbourhood was, as Josephus tells us, the most densely
populated part of the country, and no less than nine
cities existed on its shores, of which the miserable town of
Tiberias alone remains. On the east side of the lake the
cliffs are very steep, and at one or two places come down
nearly to the water's edge. A few miles from the northern
end of the lake, a deep valley, called Wády Semahk, runs
down from the mountains, and a little to the south of this
are some ruins now called Khersa ; this is the site of the
ancient Gergesa, the scene of the healing of the demoniac
and of the destruction of the herd of swine.

Captain Wilson, in his account of the spot, says, " The
hills, which everywhere else on the eastern side are recessed
from a half to three-quarters of a mile from the water's
edge, approach within forty feet of it. They do not terminate abruptly, but there is a steep, even slope, which
we identify with the ' steep place ' down which the herd
of swine ran violently into the sea, and so were choked."

Of the ruins which still exist on the western side of the
lake, the most important are Kerazeh and Tell Húm, the
Chorazin and Capernaum of the New Testament. At the
latter, the ruins of a synagogue have been found, and on
the lintel the sculptured representation of a pot of manna
may still be seen. In all human probability, this synagogue was the very one in which our Lord discoursed, and
that figured pot of manna may have suggested the speech

of the unbelieving Jews who listened to Him, " What sign showest Thou then, that we may see, and believe Thee ? what dost Thou work ? Our fathers did eat manna in the desert ; as it is written, He gave them bread from heaven to eat " (St. John vi. 30, 31).

Following the course of the Jordan northwards, we come to a little lake, about ten miles from the Lake of Galilee ; this is the "Waters of Merom," the site of the great battle in which Joshua crushed the Canaanitish power by the conquest of King Jabin of Hazor and his allies. It is a curious fact that in this district, which was the last strong- hold of the Canaanites, traces of that people may still be found in the peculiar ethnological characteristics of the inhabitants, and of some of their customs and legends, which mark them as a race distinct from the other inha- bitants of Palestine.

One of the old Canaanitish towns, Kedesh-Naphthali, may still be identified in the modern village of Cadis, and it is a noteworthy fact that both the ancient and modern names are identical with that of the Canaanitish outpost on the southern frontier, which played so important a part in the history of the forty years' wandering. It was near Kedesh-Naphthali that Sisera, the Canaanite leader, died, pierced to the brain by the nail,* or rather tent-pin, of Jael.

A few miles north of Merom, we come to Tell el Cádhí, the " Judge's Mound," from which gushes forth one of the principal sources of the River Jordan ; this is identical with the ancient Laish or Dan. The name of Dan signi- fies in Hebrew " a judge," and still exists in the Arabic name of the place.

Here was a small colony of the tribe of Dan, whose narrow strip of land between Philistia and Ephraim was found too small to contain them.

---

* The nail was undoubtedly a sharp pin of hard wood, such as is used by the Bedawín at the present day to fasten together the various portions of the haircloth, which form walls, roof, &c., of their tents.

The territory of Asher, as I have just said, lay by the sea-coast: it embraced the Plain of Acre, and extended some way into the hills of Galilee eastward, being there conterminous with Zebulun and Naphthali. The whole of the coast-line never fell into the possession of the tribe of Asher, and Phœnicia Proper maintained its position as an independent kingdom, and held the maritime plain as far south as Tyre.

Half the tribe of Manasseh never entered into their possession of the Promised Land, but, together with Gad and Reuben, were content in the fertile region to the east of Jordan. Of this country, the northern portion, extending southward from the slopes of Hermon to the River Hieromax (a stream which enters the Jordan a little below the Sea of Galilee), is identical with the kingdom of "Og the king of Bashan," who was defeated by the Israelites at Edrei, before the conquest of Canaan. This was the inheritance of the half-tribe of Manasseh. The next division of the country extends from the River Hieromax to the River Arnon, the immense ravine which opens out in the centre of the mountains on the eastern side of the Dead Sea. This large mountainous district is divided into two nearly equal parts by the River Jabbok, and is identical with the Gilead of Scripture. The northern half was allotted to the tribe of Gad; the southern moiety to Reuben. A little south of the Jabbok is one of the highest points of the range; it is called Jebel Jilád, thus perpetuating the ancient name of Gilead.

Such were the geographical and tribal divisions of the Promised Land. To complete the sketch, I will say a few words about the ethnography of the country before proceeding to relate the further details of its history.

The people of Palestine—the chosen people—have paid the penalty of their sins, and are dispersed over the face of the world; those Hebrews who now sojourn there are strangers in the land of their fathers.

It may at first sight appear, then, that with them would have been lost the distinctive characteristics of the inhabitants, and that the manners and customs of the Bible could no longer exist in the country. Such, however, is not the case, for, although the Jews—that is, the distinctive race who conquered the country and held it for so many ages—are gone, yet the inhabitants of Palestine are no more supplanted by the new-comers and invaders than are the inhabitants of England extinguished by the Danish and Norman invasion. Invasions and political changes of course alter the character of a people, who become more of a mixed race, but their nationality is never entirely lost; the primitive habits, the local customs, and the native traditions will ever linger on. The present inhabitants of Palestine—Fellahs or peasants—are called Arabs, because they have adopted the language and religion of their Desert conquerors, the Bedawín, who are the lineal descendants of the fierce border tribes whom we know under the names of Hivites, Midianites, &c., &c., as the troublesome border-foes of Israel.

This peasant population exhibits some remarkable peculiarities, and a study of their ethnography will tend more than almost anything else to illustrate the reality and truth of the Bible. I have already alluded in a previous chapter to the men of Gath, or, as it is now called, Beit Jibrin, or " the House of the Giants." We still find the neighbourhood of this town producing an exceptionally tall and fine race of peasants, greater and more stalwart men than those found in any other part of the country. Yet men hesitate to believe the Bible when it speaks of a race of "giants." as existing there, and discredit the mention of the Anakim and Rephaim who so terrified the Israelite spies when they visited this and the surrounding districts. It is a commonly known fact that the Patagonians are an exceptionally tall race of men. Now, if there existed ancient heathen records containing allusions to Patagonian giants in former ages, scientific men (anthropologists, as they are called) would sing triumphant pæans over the consonance between the old account and the existing facts, nor would they ever dream of throwing discredit upon the former, or of explaining away the latter. But, alas! this is not the spirit in which modern science always approaches the Bible. Some men in the present day spare no pains to bring into disrepute the Holy Book by which their forefathers lived, and for which they died. The manners and customs of the modern inhabitants of Palestine present but little variation from those described in the Bible, and the modern traveller in the Holy Land is continually coming across scenes which form the very counterpart of scenes and incidents described in Holy Writ. To treat of this subject in an exhaustive manner, and to point out the numerous and minute details in which the modern habits of the people conform to the ancient usage, would require a large volume of itself ; I will, therefore, content myself in this place with a few instances in which the more characteristic features of the life described in the Bible are exemplified.

As in the ancient times, so in the present day, the population of Palestine and the countries immediately bordering upon it, is partly nomad and partly stationary. The habits of the nomad tribes are absolutely unchanged, and the constitution of society amongst them is strictly patriarchal.

The reception of Sisera by Jael, the wife of Heber the Kenite (as narrated in Judges iv. 18, 19), might serve as a general description of our own visits to the tents of the Moabite Arabs : " And when he had turned in unto her into the tent, she covered him with a mantle. And he said unto her, Give me, I pray thee, a little water to drink, for I am thirsty : and she opened a bottle of milk and gave him drink, and covered him." If by " bottle " we understand a small skin, in which the *Leben*, or sour milk, is kept, the picture is complete.

Again, to take an example from my own experience. On the occasion of my first visit to Sinai, and just as the Mountain of the Law burst for the first time upon our gaze, we found ourselves in the neighbourhood of the tents of our Sheikh 'Eid, whose wife and two children, accompanied by an aged male relative, came out to meet him.

GROUP OF BEDAWÍN ARABS AT SINAI.

'Eid saluted the old man, embraced him, and kissed him on either cheek, and the pair then, with right hands clasped, repeated over and over again the words, *Taiyibin?* ("Are you well?") with the answer, *Al hamdu lillah taiyibin!* ("Thank God, well!") Does not such a scene as this vividly call to mind the words of Exodus (xviii.

5—7) : " And Jethro, Moses' father-in-law, came with his sons and his wife unto Moses in the wilderness, where he encamped at the mount of God : and he said unto Moses, I thy father-in-law Jethro am come unto thee, and thy wife and her two sons with her. And Moses went out to meet his father-in-law, and did obeisance, and kissed him ; and they asked each other of their welfare ; and they came into the tent."

In the heart of those same Sinai mountains, too, I have seen a woman of the desert weaving, with a primitive loom of her own construction, a cloth of goats' hair for her tent, just as, 3,000 years before, the Bible tells us that on that self-same spot " all the women, whose hearts stirred them up in wisdom, spun goats' hair " (Exod. xxxv. 26) for the adornment of the tabernacle.

The Bedawin tribes who now wander in the wilderness of the south country, where the patriarchs aforetime made their home, still lead their flocks and herds to pasture in the self-same valleys, and even to drink at the self-same wells.

The description which I have elsewhere given of El Biyár, "the Wells," situated at the northern edge of the Sinai peninsula, would apply to almost every well in Palestine : " Several large stone troughs are provided for the purpose of watering the flocks and herds, and the mouth of the well itself is stopped up with a large stone, to be rolled away when occasion requires, precisely in the manner described in Genesis (xxix. 10) : ' And it came to pass, when Jacob saw Rachel the daughter of Laban his mother's brother, and the sheep of Laban his mother's brother, that Jacob went near, and rolled the stone from the well's mouth, and watered the flock.' "

In their wars and predatory excursions, too, the Bedawín enact over and over again the scenes of Scripture history. Here is a description of the raids made by the Arabs of the Teyáheh tribe, amongst whom I sojourned for many months :—

"Once at least every year they collect in force, often mustering as many as 1,000 guns, and set off on camels for the country of the 'Anazeh, a distance of more than twenty days' journey. Having chosen for their expedition the season of the year when the camels are sent out to graze, they seldom fail to come across some large herd feeding at a distance from the camp, and watched by a few attendants only. These they drive off, the Bawárideh, that is, "those who possess guns," forming a guard on either side and in the rear, and the rest leading the beasts. It sometimes, though rarely, happens that they get off clear with their booty before the owners are aware of the invasion; but in many cases they are hotly pursued, and compelled to relinquish their prey and take to their heels."

. . . .

"Indeed the state of desert society has but little changed since the messenger came in to the tent of Job and said : ' The Chaldeans made out bands, and fell upon the camels, and have carried them away, yea, and slain the servants with the edge of the sword ' (Job. i. 17)."

"Robbery is not regarded by the Bedawín as in the least a disgraceful thing, but ' a man taketh his sword, and goeth his way to rob and steal ' (Esdras iv. 23), with a profound feeling of conscious rectitude and respectability." *

To commemorate the spot upon which a battle was fought, or on which a warrior fell, and, indeed, to perpetuate the memory of any important event, the Bedawí Arab of the present day sets up a cairn, or pillar of stones, just as Jacob, when he had spoken with God, "set up a pillar in the place where he talked with Him, *even* a pillar of stone : and he poured a drink offering thereon, and he poured oil thereon " (Genesis xxxv. 14).

At any spot to which a remote traditionary interest attaches, and notably at the tombs of their sheikhs and

* The Desert of the Exodus." pp. 295 and 296.

saints, the Arabs are wont to offer up sacrifices. These
sacrifices are attended with great rejoicings. Arabs from
all the neighbouring tribes flock in and pitch their tents;
a kind of fair is held, camel-races and other sports take
place, and the whole concludes with a *mesámereh*, or
" Arabian Night's Entertainment," something between a
concert and a rustic ball, in which the women take part.

The animals slaughtered for the sacrifices are eaten by
the assembled guests, who make the occasion one of unusual indulgence. Does not this afford a clue to the
motives which led the children of Israel astray; and
enable us to understand how it was that idol-worship
possessed such attractions for them that they could turn
from the worship of the true God, Who had wrought such
signal deliverance for them, to bow down before Baal-peor,
and " eat the offerings of the dead " ?

No less striking is the parallel afforded between the life
of the settled inhabitants of Palestine in the present day
and that described in the Bible. In Europe, we are so
accustomed to the supremacy of the state that the individual existence of separate towns is hardly recognised
and appreciated among us; in the East it is quite different.
The government never interferes in the affairs of the
smaller towns and municipalities, except it be to compel
the payment of taxes, or to levy a fine upon some particular district for a flagrant act of violence or insubordi-
nation. Each town thus virtually governs itself by its
own laws, and stands in the position of an independent
state, though under the protectorate of, and paying tribute
to, the Imperial Government.

The affairs of these little commonwealths are administered by a council of elders, with a sheikh, or chief man, at
their head, and we find them from time to time combining
against their Bedawín neighbours, or against the government, much in the same way as alliances are made between
nations in other parts of the world. It is very important

to bear this state of things in mind, for otherwise such histories as those which we continually read of in the Bible, where the kings of such cities as Sodom, and Gomorrah, and Admah, and Zeboiim, and Zoar, engage in war, would seem inconsistent with the undoubted geographical fact that they are all comprised within a district scarcely larger than one of the English counties.

In the cities, and still more in the villages, of Palestine, the mode of life is now just what it was centuries upon centuries ago. The houses, the food, even the dresses, are the same; the potter with his rude potter's wheel turns out vessels of the same shape as those ancient ones which excavations from time to time bring to light, and he even marks them with the ancient trade-mark, of which he knows not the import, but which has been handed down to him from generation to generation; the peasant's dark hovel is lighted by lamps of the same pattern as those found in the oldest tombs; the earth is still turned up by the primitive ploughs which we see figured in the older sculptures; the wheat is trodden out by bullocks, as the Bible so often describes, and on the self-same threshing-floors as of old— flat terraces on a hill-side, from which the inequalities have been cut away by Jebusite and Canaanitish hands; the same old stories and traditions linger amongst the people, and beneath the external disguise of Mohammedan worship the older forms of religion are kept up; the common par- lance of the people is still that of the Bible, so that the most ordinary phrases of their common life, when literally translated, have a solemn and stately ring to an European ear.

In a word, the people of the Holy Land are a living memorial of the accuracy and reality of the Bible; a standing and incontrovertible proof that the Word of God is no vague, unreal rhapsody, but an intensely true, vivid, and life-like reality.

CHAPTER IV.

THE JUDGES.

Characteristics of the period—Wars with the Canaanites—Emigration of part of the tribe of Dan to Laish—Corruption of the national faith–Invasion by the King of Mesopotamia—The first judge, Othniel—Ehud—Shamgar–Deborah : defeat of Sisera—Incursions of the Midianites; Oreb and Zeb; Gideon—Abimelech ; attempt to found a monarchy at Shechem—Provision of the Mosaic law for the conduct of a king—Tolar and Shamgar—Further invasions by the Ammonites; Jephthah—Civil war between Ephraim and Gilead—Ibzan—Elon—Abdon—Samson—War with the Philistines—Eli ; High Priest and Judge—The call of Samuel—Battle of Aphek and capture of the Ark—Restoration of the Ark—Samuel a judge—School of the prophets—Evacuation of the country by the Philistines—Union of the tribes under Samuel—Election of a king—Saul anointed ; his first military success—Renunciation of the judicial authority by Samuel.

The early annals of the Hebrew Republic present a series of pictures of wild adventure and romantic incident rather than the continuous history of a nation. In fact, immediately after the establishment in Canaan there appears to have been no settled government representing a confederation of all the tribes, and the Judges* of Israel were little more than leaders, called into prominent action by some danger which threatened the particular tribe to which they belonged, and supported only by such other sections of the community as had an immediate interest in repelling the attacks of a foreign enemy or repressing some internecine quarrel.

After the death of Joshua, the Israelites soon began to pay the penalty of their disobedience, and the heathen nations whom they had allowed to continue in their midst caused them constant annoyance. Judah and Simeon

* The Hebrew word for judges is Shophetim, which, as Milman points out, is probably identical with the name " Suffetes," given by the Carthaginians to their chief magistrates.

P

banded together, and defeated the combined armies of the Canaanites and Perizzites at Bezek, and took their chief prisoner, and cut off his thumbs and great toes. Such mutilation of prisoners of war was common in ancient times, and Adoni-Bezek, being notorious for the practice, was justly punished.

GAZA.

After taking and burning Jerusalem, they then marched southward, expelling the inhabitants of Hebron, and conquering the country as far as Zephath or Hormah. This place is identical with the city mentioned (Numbers xxi.

3) as one of those places which ineffectually opposed the progress of the Israelites on their first approach to the Promised Land.*

The more powerful cities of the Philistine Plain—Gaza, Ascalon, and Ekron—were attacked, but not thoroughly reduced. Ephraim gained possession of the town of Bethel. The tribe of Dan, being worsted by the Amorites, were driven into the mountains, and a part of the tribe pressed northwards and took the town of Laish at the head of the Jordan valley, which they colonised and called by their own name. The history of this expedition is very curious. Five men had been sent forward as spies to reconnoitre their intended point of attack in the north, and on the way these scouts passed by the house of one Micah; this man, according to the prevailing custom, had associated the idolatrous ceremonies of the Canaanites with the national faith of Israel, and had constructed for himself a silver idol and an ephod and teraphim. To this private shrine he had appointed a poor and unscrupulous Levite as priest, for he really appears to have believed that it was the God of Israel Whom he was serving under these strange heathen forms. The Danite spies were anxious to inquire of this local oracle as to the success of their expedition, and received an encouraging reply, which was confirmed by their own subsequent experience. Six hundred men of the tribe marched out to take possession of Laish, and, having heard from their scouts of the success of Micah's divining apparatus, they seized the graven image, carried it with them to Laish, and set it up as an object of worship in that city : " And Jonathan the son of Gershom, the son of Manasseh, he and his sons were priests to the tribe of Dan until the day of the captivity of the land. And they set them up Micah's graven image, which he made, all the time that the house of God was in Shiloh " (Judges xviii. 30, 31).

* See page 34.

F 2

The corruption of national manners consequent upon this forsaking of the national faith led to the most disastrous consequences, and a crime committed by the inhabitants of Gibeah, a city of Benjamin, gave rise to a fearful civil war, which nearly resulted in the extermination of the offending tribe.*

These events, although recorded later on in the Book of Judges, are, it is generally agreed, anterior to the time of the Judges.† The first symptoms of the re-organisation of the federal league was the revolt of the tribes under the leadership of Othniel of Judah against Chushan-Rishathaim, king of Mesopotamia, who had invaded Palestine and compelled the people to pay him tribute. At the end of another forty years, the tribes of the east of Jordan were assailed by the Ammonites, Amalekites, and Moabites, under Eglon, king of Moab. The capture of Jericho by the confederate forces of the enemy seems to have alarmed the hill-tribes for their own safety; and Ehud, from the tribe of Benjamin, appeared as the deliverer of the people at this important crisis. Eglon, who seems to have been by his generalship the main instrument of the enemy's success, was assassinated by Ehud, a Benjamite, and the latter, escaping into the territory of Ephraim, obtained the assistance of that powerful tribe, and effectually delivered the country from the Moabites.

Eighty years now passed away, during which the land had rest, but it would appear that the peace and prosperity were only comparative, and those tribes at least who bordered on Philistia experienced molestation at the hands of that people, for after Ehud came " Shamgar the son of Anath, which slew of the Philistines six hundred men with an ox-goad : and he also delivered Israel " (Judges iii. 81).

Troubles next began to arise in the north, and a similar confederation to that which Joshua had defeated at Merom again threatened the Hebrews. As on the previous occa-

* Judges xix., xx., xxi.   † Milman, vol. i., p. 242, Note.

sion, the Canaanites were under the leadership of a king of Hazor, who bore the same name as his predecessor, Jabin. His forces, under the command of Sisera, a fierce and able general, held the northern tribes in subjection for twenty years, but were at last signally defeated, thanks to the enthusiasm and patriotic ardour kindled by the fervent appeal of the inspired prophetess Deborah.

The details of this victory, and of the flight and death of Sisera, are familiar to all readers of the Bible; Deborah's triumphant song uttered on the occasion, which has been preserved amongst the sacred records, forms one of the most magnificent specimens extant of ancient Hebrew poetry.

Another forty years of peace were passed after these events, with the usual result, "the children of Israel did evil in the sight of the Lord : and the Lord delivered them into the hand of Midian seven years" (Judges vi. 1).

The Midianites and the Amalekites were the prototypes of the modern Bedawín, and those who have seen, as I have, the effect upon a peaceful and flourishing district of an incursion from these nomadic tribes, will appreciate the graphic description of this pest given at the beginning of the sixth chapter of the Book of Judges, and will not wonder that famine and misery were the result, and that the children of Israel fled to dens and caverns in the mountains when " the Midianites came up, and the Amalekites, and the children of the East, even they came up against them." *

* As a practical comment on the Biblical description here alluded to, I may, perhaps, be permitted to quote my own impressions of the Bedawín, written while actually sojourning amongst them.

"The Bedawí regards the Fellah with unutterable scorn. He has a constitutional dislike to work, and is entirely unscrupulous as to the means he employs to live without it. These qualities (which also adorn and make the thief and burglar of civilisation) he mistakes for evidences of thorough breeding, and prides himself accordingly upon being one of nature's gentlemen.

"Camels and sheep are, as I have before said, the Bedawí's only

In the midst of all this distress God raised up a deliverer in the person of Gideon, of the tribe of Manasseh, who, encouraged by visible signs of Divine favour and support, rallied a large army from Manasseh, Zebulun, Naphtali, and Asher, and declared war against the oppressors. With a picked band of his bravest followers, he surprised them in a night attack, put them to utter rout, and expelled them from the land with a loss of 120,000 men, their head sheikhs, or princes, Oreb and Zeb, Zebah and

BEDAWÍN HORSEMEN.

Zalmunna, being among the slain.   The names of the first

means of subsistence; so long, then, as he lives his present unsettled life, and can support himself with the milk which they produce, he is independent of all occupation save plundering. The effect of this is that the soil he owns deteriorates, and his neighbours are either driven away or reduced to beggary by his raids and depredations."—"The Desert of the Exodus," p. 299.

two Midianite princes, Oreb and Zeb, mean respectively
" the raven " and " the wolf " ; and it is a curious coinci-
dence that the latter name is still the appellation of one of
the chief families of the large and powerful trans-Jordanic
tribe of the Adwán Arabs, while the Beni Sakar, " sons of
the *kite*," are perhaps amongst the most formidable of the
neighbouring Bedawín tribes. As a reward for these
signal services, Gideon was offered the name and title of a
king, which dignity he, however, refused. But even he,
the direct recipient of a Divine revelation, he who had
risked his life and incurred the displeasure of his compatriots by overthrowing the altar of Baal at Ophrah, was
no sooner possessed of the spoils of the Midianites than he
made of them an ephod and other religious symbols, and
set up an idolatrous and fictitious worship of Jehovah in
the self-same city.

Forty years more, and idolatry was again rife in Israel;
Gideon died, and Abimelech, an illegitimate son of the
great leader, aspired to grasp the crown which his father
had refused. Gathering round him a desperate band at
Shechem, where his mother's kindred dwelt, he fell on the
city of Ophrah, and murdered all his seventy brethren,
with the sole exception of Jotham, the youngest, who
escaped. After this treacherous act, he was proclaimed
king by the inhabitants of Shechem and the neighbouring
towns, in spite of the remonstrances of Jotham, who denounced the usurper with bitter satire in the well-known
parable of the trees who would fain elect a king, but could
find none to reign over them except the worthless bramble.
Three years sufficed to convince the Shechemites of the folly
of their choice ; the people rose against Abimelech, and,
just as he seemed on the point of suppressing the insurrection, he fell, wounded by a woman's hand, and only escaped
that ignominious end by falling on his armour-bearer's sword.
This unsuccessful attempt to found a monarchy over part,
at least, of the tribes of Israel was but a prelude to that

movement which was shortly to follow, when the whole
nation, tired of the simplicity and restraint which the
government of the Law imposed upon them, sighed after
the luxuries and vain dignities of heathen nations, and clamoured for a king. The Mosaic Law, though strictly en-
joining an adherence to the divinely-prescribed form of
government, yet wisely contemplated the possibility of
this undesirable change, and appointed rules for the conduct of the king with a view to moderating the effects of
the change (Deut. xvii. 14—20). Joshua, by his fair
partition of the country, and by enforcing the law as
to the inalienability of property in land, set a strong
barrier against the encroachments of individual ambition,
and so put off the evil day; for, so long as it was
impossible for large estates and districts to fall into the
possession of a few, the growth of an oppressive oligarchical
aristocracy was nipped in the bud as often as it appeared.
As the people fell away from their allegiance to God, and
their observance of His laws, the bond of national union
became more and more relaxed, and there was no great
power left which might be brought to bear in repressing
any unfair assumption of the authority of one person over
his fellows.

The next two Judges were Tola, of the tribe of Isaachar,
who exercised his authority at Shamar, in Mount Ephraim,
for twenty-three years, and Jair of Gilead, who ruled for
twenty-two years, and of whom nothing further is told us
than that " he had thirty sons that rode on thirty ass colts,
and they had thirty cities " (Judges x. 4). During these
forty-five years, the Israelites had, as usual, relapsed into
the grossest idolatry, and the usual punishment followed.
The Philistines invaded the southern border of Palestine,
and the Ammonites, overcoming the trans-Jordanic tribes,
had even marched across the river, and attacked the allied
armies of Judah, Ephraim, and Benjamin.

The inhabitants of Gilead had, from their position, suffered most severely from the incursions of the Ammonites, and at Mizpah, a town in that country (built upon the site of the stone set up by Jacob and Laban in token of their covenant), the Israelites had mustered their forces, and were concerting measures to repel the invaders. At Mizpah, too, there dwelt a famous outlaw and freebooter, Jephthah, an illegitimate son of Gilead, who had been expelled from his father's house. In their extremity, the elders of Gilead entreated Jephthah to return and lead their armies against the Ammonites. This he consented to do, and, after vainly attempting to come to terms, he set out for battle, vowing that, should success attend his arms, he would sacrifice to Jehovah the first thing that met him on his return. The sequel of the story is familiar to the reader. Jephthah, returning to Mizpah after a glorious and decisive victory, was met by his only daughter, and the misguided, but devout, soldier sacrificed her in fulfilment of his vow.

The country was scarcely delivered from the Ammonites when Ephraim declared war against Gilead, jealous of the laurels which the latter had won, and at the slight they themselves had received in not being asked to participate in the war. Jephthah at once marched against them, defeated them, and occupied the passages of the Jordan before the Ephraimites could retreat into their own territory: "And it was so, that when those Ephraimites which were escaped said, Let me go over, that the men of Gilead said unto him, Art thou an Ephraimite? If he said, Nay; then said they unto him, Say now Shibboleth; and he said Sibboleth : for he could not frame to pronounce it right. Then they took him, and slew him at the passages of Jordan : and there fell at that time of the Ephraimites forty and two thousand " (Judges xii. 5, 6).

Jephthah ruled for seven years, and after him came three other Judges, of whom we know nothing more than the names ; they are Ibzan of Bethlehem, Elon of Zebulun, and Abdon of Ephraim, the period of their authority extending over twenty-five years. The next Judge who appears upon the scene is Samson. The Philistines had by this time overrun the south country, and caused great and continued annoyance to the Israelites, and the record of Samson's strange adventures and personal prowess against them seems to indicate little more than that the free spirit of the Hebrew nation was chafing under a foreign yoke, but that as yet no organised federation had taken up arms, although gigantic, but useless, efforts were made by individual chieftains or families. The memories of such attempts would naturally group themselves around so imposing a figure as the Herculean Nazarite hero, Samson. In the meanwhile, Divine Providence was gradually, but wisely, shaping the course of events. Hitherto, heroes and deliverers had started into prominence from the various tribes, but no rallying point for the whole nation had as yet appeared. This was obviously to be looked for at Shiloh, where the only authorised symbols of the national worship were placed, and, if a personal leader were to be found in the theocracy, it was evident that his appointment must proceed from the seat of the Divine government. So loose had the bonds become which held together the different communities of the Hebrew Republic, that, unless some such a leader should soon arise to knit them once more together, the very existence of the Republic would be threatened. God, at this critical juncture, interfered to save His chosen people.

The offices of Judge, or civil leader, and of high priest, were for the first time combined in the person of Eli; but his great age and physical infirmities rendered him unfit for the assumption of so great a responsibility, while his criminal weakness in sanctioning, or at least overlooking, the excesses of his sons Phinehas and Hophni, had introduced fresh complications into the situation. But it was not to Eli or his house that Israel was to look

for a deliverer. Attached to the service of the tabernacle was a youth, dedicated to God even before his birth,
and from his earliest years educated to the ministry.
To him the Divine commission came, and the youthful
Samuel was commanded to bear to the aged high priest
the message of vengeance against the house of Eli. A
desperate struggle was now made by the Israelites to
throw off the Philistine yoke ; but they were totally
defeated in a battle which occurred at Aphek in Judah.
In their despair, they bethought them of the Ark, which
had been a sure pledge of victory to Joshua's armies.
The proud Judah was forced to humble itself before its
powerful rival Ephraim, and to demand permission for the
Ark to be removed from its resting-place in Shiloh. This
request was granted. The Ark, under the safe-conduct of
the two priests Phinchas and Hophni, was carried out to
the camp, and around that sacred emblem the tribes of
Israel rallied, for the first time united in one common cause.

The Philistines advanced to battle with sore misgivings
when they saw the symbol of that mighty God Who had
wrought such wonders in Egypt and Canaan. But, though
the Israelites fought with unwonted ardour, the iron
chariots and the numbers of Philistia prevailed, 30,000 of
the chosen people fell, and the Ark of God was taken.
Terrible, indeed, was the consternation with which the
news was received at Shiloh ; and when the messenger
told Eli, "Israel is fled before the Philistines, and there
has been a great slaughter among the people, and thy two
sons also, Hophni and Phinchas, are dead, and the Ark of
God is taken," the aged high priest fell from his seat,
breaking his neck, and died ; while the wife of Phinchas,
giving premature birth to a son, expressed the general
feeling of Israel when, unmindful of her own pains, and
heedless of the loss of husband and friends, she wailed
Ichabod, " the glory is departed from Israel," and gave
that mournful name to the son of her tribulation.

But the acquisition of the Ark proved an unfortunate one for the Philistines. Wherever the holy shrine was brought, plagues and troubles fell upon its possessors, and Dagon, their idol, fell prostrate and broken before it. After seven months, they determined to restore it, together with a propitiatory offering, consisting of golden emerods and mice, representing the plagues by which they had been smitten.*

Two milch kine were yoked to the car which bore the Ark, and, without the guidance of mortal hands, the kine set off upon the direct road to Beth-shemesh, within the Israelite frontier. The returning Ark was welcomed with great rejoicings by the Israelites, and a sacrifice was at once offered up, the kine which drew the Ark being slaughtered for the occasion, and the car which bore it being broken up for fuel.

The profane inhabitants of Beth-shemesh were rash enough to look into the holy chest, and their profane curiosity was punished by the death of a large number. The Ark was then solemnly removed to Kirjath-jearim, a neighbouring hill-city, and Shiloh ceased to be regarded as a holy place. For twenty years after this the Philistines continued to oppress Israel ; but Samuel, who had now grown to man's estate, and succeeded Eli in the exercise of the double functions of leader and judge, found means to kindle an enthusiasm amongst the people and induce them to struggle to throw off the yoke. His first care was to eradicate the love of idolatry from their hearts: and, in order to excite a spirit of devotion and religious fervour, he gathered round him a number of men like himself,

* It is curious to note the persistence of this heathen custom of offering at a shrine a representation of any limb or member affected, in hopes of, or in gratitude for, a cure. The recent excavations in the Venus Temples at Cyprus have brought to light thousands of such objects, and even at the present day there is scarcely an image of the Virgin in Roman Catholic Europe that has not some such tribute hung up at her shrine.

earnest for the cause of God, who devoted themselves entirely to promoting a religious revival.

This was the origin of the School of the Prophets, which continued till the fall of the kingdom to exercise such an astonishing influence upon the Jewish nation. From the description given of them in the Bible, we learn that the constitution of their society and the ceremonies practised at their meetings were almost identical with those of the Eastern dervishes of the present day; and that it was when wrought up to a pitch of ecstatic excitement by music and dancing that they uttered those inspired strains with which we are all so familiar.

Samuel's movement so far succeeded that he was able to summon the people to a general convention at Mizpah, and there to receive from them a solemn promise to repent, and to put away the images of Baal and Astarte, and to serve the Lord alone. The Philistines, taking this assembly as an expression of revolt, hastily collected their forces and marched upon the assembly ; but Samuel's prayers prevailed, and the people—nerved to valour by the promise of help from God, and convinced of His visible presence by a terrible storm which helped to discomfit the enemy—obtained a signal victory and drove the Philistines out of the land.

The influence and authority of Samuel enabled him to unite the greater part of the scattered tribes, especially those of the south, and once more to give life to the nation. So long as he could personally direct them, the affairs of the commonwealth prospered ; but when, in his old age, the duties of government devolved upon his two sons, these latter proved venal and corrupt, and the people began to murmur for a more settled form of government, and bade Samuel make them a king, to judge them like the nations. They doubtless felt, too, that their guerilla warfare was of little avail against the powerful monarchies with which they had to contend, and

desired a more complete military organisation, and therefore they cried that their king might go before them and
fight their battles.

Samuel pointed out all the disadvantages of a despotic
rule, but the people were importunate, and the Lord at
last commanded the aged Judge to hearken unto their
request, and to anoint a king.

The choice, directed by Divine inspiration, fell upon
one Saul, a young man of good presence and commanding
stature, and descended from one of the chief families of
the tribe of Benjamin. He was at first privately anointed
by Samuel, by whom he was sent to the School of the
Prophets, that he might receive that training and feel
those influences of religion and patriotism that should fit
him for his high station. Later on, a solemn assembly of
all the tribes was held at Mizpah. The tribe of Benjamin
was designated by lot from all the rest, and Saul was
received as king.

The monarch-elect did not enter at once upon his
functions, and the whole authority of the state was really
still exercised by Samuel; but an occasion shortly presented itself in which Saul was able to prove his fitness
to wield the sovereign power. Nahash, king of the Ammonites, had invaded Gilead, and demanded that the inhabitants of the city of Jabesh, which he was now besieging,
should submit to have their right eyes put out, in token
of subjection. In their despair, they appealed to Saul,
who " took a yoke of oxen, and hewed them in pieces,
and sent them throughout all the coasts of Israel by the
hands of messengers, saying, Whosoever cometh not forth
after Saul and after Samuel, so shall it be done unto his
oxen " (1 Sam. xi. 7). The signal was at once responded
to ; the tribes of Israel mustered to the number of 330,000
men, and a complete victory was the result. This act of
promptitude and vigour completely established the young
king in his position, and Samuel thereupon called the

people together at Gilgal, and, having given an account of his own stewardship, resigned the administration into the hands of Saul ; not, however, before he had rebuked the people for their violation of the constitution divinely framed for them, by a sign from heaven, confirming and approving his words.

CHAPTER V.

THE MONARCHY.

AFTER the events narrated in the last chapter, an hiatus occurs in the sacred narrative; and Saul next appears, no longer an ardent youth, but mature in years, and the father of a brave young warrior, Jonathan.

The Philistines were now meditating a formidable invasion of the Hebrew territory, against which Saul, on his part, was also making active preparations. Jonathan, his son, rashly precipitated matters by risking an attack before the preparations were complete, and the result was a temporary success, shortly followed by a disastrous rout of the Israelite forces. Saul was at Gilgal, prepared to march against the enemy, but could not do so until the customary sacrifices had been offered up by the Prophet Samuel. For seven days he waited in vain, and at last, waxing impatient, he offered up the sacrifice himself. At this juncture Samuel appeared, and denounced him for having violated the law of God, predicting that the sovereignty should pass away from his house. It is not difficult to perceive the tremendous political importance which attaches to this act of Saul. The Hebrew nation was to owe obedience to God alone, and to be governed by the laws directly promulgated by Him and expounded by the mouth of His priests and prophets. When the aged Samuel yielded to the entreaties of the people, and chose for them a king, it was with the understanding that his functions should be merely civil and military, and he was as much bound as any of his subjects to observe the Law and to respect the Mosaic constitution. By assuming such priestly functions, he was directly violating that constitution, and striking at the very root of theocratic government; and, had such an act of even unwitting arrogance been permitted to pass unquestioned, it would have been equivalent to a complete nullification of the Mosaic ordinances.

Saul received the reproof with meekness and resignation, and occupied himself solely with the military duties which the present crisis imposed upon him. With a small band of 600 ill-armed men he occupied the fortress of Gibeah, with apparently but little prospect of success against the numbers of the enemy that already began to overrun the country. A daring exploit of Jonathan, who was attempting to pass through the enemy's outposts and join his father at the fortress, caused a panic in the Philistine ranks, and Saul, rushing down from the heights of Gibeah, fell upon them when the confusion was at its height, and, being joined by multitudes of Israelites, who were concealed in hiding-places in the neighbourhood, he completely routed the enemy. The defeat might have been more decisive, but for an ill-timed vow of the king, who swore that none of his men should taste food until the close of the day. The soldiers were consequently unable from sheer exhaustion to pursue the advantage they had gained, and when the evening came they fell upon the spoil with such avidity that they ate the slaughtered animals " on the blood," Heathen fashion, in direct diso-

G

bedience to the Mosaic precept. Jonathan, who, in ignorance of the order, had tasted a little honey with the end
of his staff, would have been put to death by his stern
father for breach of discipline had not the people risen to
forbid the sacrifice. Saul's military career continued successful after this; but a fresh act of disobedience again
brought upon him the awful denunciation of Heaven, and
hastened his downfall.

The fierce Bedawi hordes of the Amalekites were the
hereditary foes of Israel, and, so long as they should
continue to harass the borders of Palestine, the safety of
the country was continually jeopardised. A war of extermination was therefore declared against them, by Divine
command, and the very flocks and herds were to be included in the general ban.*

Disregarding these injunctions, Saul, having conquered
the Amalekites, saved the best portion of the spoil, and
spared the life of Agag their king. Samuel publicly
rebuked the king, and with his own hand hewed the
captive Amalekite in pieces; after that, Saul and Samuel
parted, to meet no more in life.

These continued displays of unconstitutional tendencies,
as well as his vacillating character, alternating between
meek submission to, and contemptuous impatience of, the
Divine commands, proved Saul no longer worthy of the
high trust reposed in him; and Samuel, by God's direction,
anointed the youthful David as his successor. Saul, no
longer supported by Divine aid, sank into the condition of
a moody and fitful tyrant, and developed symptoms of that
most terrible of all maladies, insanity.

David was born at Bethlehem, and was a son of Jesse,
and grandson of Ruth and Boaz, whose story is so affect-
ingly told in the Book of Ruth. The history of his early

---

* The only sure method of repressing the atrocities of Bedawín tribes
in the present day is found to be the depriving them of all their flocks
and herds, a process which strikes at the very root of their existence,
quâ Bedawin. See Note to p. 69.

life is romantic in the extreme. After being anointed by Samuel, he appears to have resumed his pastoral occupation; but before long the well-known incident of his conflict with Goliath, the giant of Gath, brought him prominently forward, and secured for him not only the notice of the king, but the lasting affection of his son Jonathan.

In the meantime Saul's malady had become gradually worse, and David was again summoned to the court, to try the effect of music in quieting the perturbed mind of the monarch. At first the attempt was successful; but ere long the jealousy which Saul appears to have conceived, in consequence of the renown which David had acquired by his conflict with Goliath, returned with re-doubled vigour, and he twice attempted the young hero's life. After this, we find the king, with the true inconsistency of a madman, alternately promoting David to the highest military rank in the kingdom, next to his own and that of his son Jonathan; and driving him an outlaw from his presence. On one occasion, the emissaries sent to arrest David find him in the School of the Prophets, who, with Samuel at their head, are engaged in their customary religious exercises. The contagious enthusiasm affects the messengers, who, instead of executing the orders of the king, themselves join in the inspired song and dance. Three times does the same thing occur, and at last, when Saul goes in person to arrest his rival, the prophetic instincts of his own early training gain the mastery over him, and he, too, casts off his royal robes, and joins the prophetic choir. A fresh attempt upon his life having been warded off by the prudence and devotion of his friend Jonathan, David fled from Saul, and came to the Benjamite town of Nob, where the priest gave him the sword of Goliath which was kept there as a trophy, and even allowed him to refresh himself with the sacred shewbread, which it was unlawful for any but a

G 2

Aaronite to touch. From Nob he fled to Gath, but, being there recognised, and in danger of his life from the Philistines, he escaped in the disguise of an idiot to the Cave of Adullam, where he assembled a few brave but desperate adventurers, and lived for some time the life of a freebooter.

The service rendered by Abimelech, a chief priest of Nob, to David having been reported to Saul by one Doeg, an Edomite, Saul vowed terrible vengeance against the whole priesthood; and, by the agency of the unscrupulous in-

SHEWBREAD.

former, caused no less than eighty-five of them to be put to death.

We need not relate the details of David's exile, and of his narrow escapes and romantic adventures. It will be sufficient here to note that the state of Israel had been gradually growing worse under the Philistine yoke, and that Saul, deserted alike by God and man, determined at last to risk everything on a decisive battle. Deprived of the Divine counsel, he sought an oracle from a female necromancer at Endor, and heard from the lips of the shade of Samuel the sentence of his approaching doom. A few hours later the battle was over ; Israel's hosts were routed ; Jonathan, with all Saul's other sons save one, were among the slain ; and the wretched monarch, together with his faithful armour-bearer, fell each upon his own sword and died.

When David heard the news, he lost no time in claiming the kingly office to which Samuel had anointed him ; and, raising his standard in Hebron, he was soon surrounded by a large following, and by common consent elected to the throne. An attempt to set up Ishbosheth, Saul's only surviving son, as a rival was quickly suppressed ; the disaffected or indifferent chieftains were gained over by David's power and influence ; and, merging their private differences once more in the common cause, all Israel hailed him as king.

After reigning for seven years and a-half at Hebron, David began to turn his attention to Jerusalem, the strong citadel of the Jebusites, which, from its almost impregnable position, offered the most favourable site for the establishment of a permanent seat both of government and religion.

Jerusalem is constantly alluded to in the Bible as "a mountain city," and such it eminently is. The surrounding country consists of a succession of flat-topped hills, intersected here and there by narrow gullies. The rock is of limestone, and the flat strata wear away so as to form regular steps or terraces upon the hill-sides, where vines, olives, &c., are grown.

The city of Jerusalem itself stands upon a tongue of land between two deep ravines, the easternmost of which is called the Valley of Kedron, and the western the Valley of Hinnom. The latter, after running a little distance southward, sweeps round to the east, and, forming the southern limit of the tongue of land, joins the valley of the Kedron. These two ravines commence as mere depressions in the surface of the ground, but as they run southward they sink rapidly, and the sides become very steep. A sort of natural moat thus surrounds the southern half of the city, and when the steep banks were still further strengthened by artificial escarpments, Jerusalem became absolutely impregnable on three of its sides, while the north side was fortified, as Josephus tells us, by "three distinct lines of wall." Besides the two principal ravines of which I have spoken, a third, called the Tyropean Valley, splits the tongue of land into two unequal portions; of these, the eastern is called Mount Moriah, and the western, Mount Zion. Such are the main features of the site of Jerusalem, and students of the Bible would do well to bear them in mind, for by this means very much in the Bible which would be otherwise unintelligible, and therefore uninteresting, will assume an aspect of intense reality, and many a lesson may be gained.

Jerusalem was, as we have seen, besieged soon after the death of Joshua, when the Lower City was taken and burnt (Judges i. 8). The citadel on Mount Zion itself appears to have held out, and to have continued in the hands of the Jebusites up to the period of which we are treating. This fortress David now determined to attack; but the Jebusites, relying upon the natural strength of their city, answered the summons to surrender by placing their halt, maimed, and blind in insolent mockery upon the walls. When David, enraged at the insult, offered a reward to any one who would scale the walls, the challenge was answered by Joab, afterwards chief captain of the host. The steep escarpments and the walls were scaled, and the citadel taken.

Having thus secured and taken possession of the capital city, David's next care was to have the Ark removed thither; it was brought with due solemnity from Kirjath-jearim, attended by 30,000 men, with David at their head.

When the pavilion which had been prepared for its reception was in readiness, the king made a great feast for the people, at which he himself ate, and casting aside his royal robes, joined in the song and dance, as he had erewhile been wont to do amongst the company of the prophets. His wife Michal, the daughter of Saul, presumed to question his conduct, as inconsistent with the kingly dignity, and was justly rebuked for her pride and want of sympathy with the national religion. David would fain have built a suitable temple for the reception of the Ark of Jehovah, and the plan was at first approved of by the prophet Nathan. But the glorious task was reserved for his son Solomon, and God Himself declared, "Thou hast shed blood abundantly, and hast made great wars; thou shalt not build a house unto My name, because thou hast shed much blood upon the earth in My sight" (1 Chron. xxii. 8).

Abiathar, the son of the priest Abimelech who had aided David in his flight from Saul, and who had escaped the general slaughter of the priesthood, was now appointed to conduct the services; and the sacerdotal order was restored to its ancient dignity. Later on, Abiathar was deposed in favour of Zadok, in whose line the office of the high priest afterwards descended. David rapidly increased in power, was everywhere victorious over the enemies of Israel, and extended the borders of his kingdom to the utmost limits of the Promised Land. Philistia, Edom, Moab, and even the countries east of Damascus, bordering on the Euphrates, felt the force of his arms; while on the north and west the borders of the kingdom were secured by an alliance with the kings of Hamath and Tyre.

David was at the height of his prosperity when a war broke out with the Ammonites; but, though this war was brought to a successful issue, for the king himself the period was the commencement of a long series of disasters and misfortunes. Uriah, the bravest man in David's army,

was absent, conducting the siege of Rabbah, the capital of
Ammon ; in an unhappy moment the king looked on the
fatal beauty of Bathsheba, the general's wife, and sullied
the unexampled brightness of his hitherto glorious career
with the heinous sins of adultery and murder. A dark
cloud of misery now rested over David's house ; his sons
violated the most sacred ties ; incest, fratricide, and rebellion against him who had given them birth, drove the king
an exile from the city he had founded ; and when, later on,
he was reinstated upon the throne, it was at a frightful
cost—the death of his rebellious, but much-loved son.
" O my son Absalom," cried the bereaved father, "my
son, my son Absalom ! would God I had died for thee ; O
Absalom, my son, my son !" (2 Sam. xviii. 33).

Worse than all, the northern tribes felt themselves ag-
grieved because the men of Judah had restored the king
without consulting them. Fresh rebellions followed, and
those seeds of discord were sown which ultimately bore
such fatal fruit, and led to the disruption of the kingdom.
The Philistines, too, taking advantage of the enfeebled
state of his military resources consequent upon all these
civil wars, again made head against him, and were only
repressed with great difficulty and sacrifice of life. At
last, David, having shown himself penitent for his sins,
and submissive to the chastisement brought upon him,
recovered all his former power and dominion.

Whether from pride, or from a longing to extend his
dominions at some time by foreign conquest, David instituted a census of the people. This proceeding not only
offended the Law, but called down a direct expression of
Divine displeasure, and the king was bidden to choose between three evils : seven years of famine ; three months
of defeat in war ; or three days' pestilence. David wisely
left the issue in the hands of God ; the plague came, and
seventy thousand people were destroyed. When the
epidemic had reached Jerusalem itself, the angel of the

Lord appeared to the king on the threshing-floor of Araunah, king of the Jebusites, on Mount Moriah, and the progress of the disease was arrested. On the spot where the angel had stood David built an altar to the Lord; this was the site of the future Temple.

Although David was not permitted himself to build the house of the Lord, yet he made active and costly preparations for the undertaking. Towards the latter end of his life, fresh troubles began to arise in his own household.

THRESHING-FLOOR.

Adonijah, the brother of Absalom, aspired to the throne, and was supported by Joab and the priest, Abiathar; and in order to bring matters to an issue he summoned all his partizans to a feast. When David heard of the movement, he commanded Nathan the prophet, Zadok the priest, and Benaiah, one of his generals, to take Solomon, the offspring of his marriage with Bathsheba, down to Gihon, and there to anoint him king. This promptitude was successful in its results. The people hailed the young

king with acclamation; the party of Adonijah was completely broken up, and the succession of Solomon uni-
versally recognised.

Solomon was twelve years old when his father died.
His first act gave evidence of unusual wisdom and vigour,
even before that superhuman wisdom, which more than
his wealth has made his name famous, was bestowed upon
him. Adonijah having showed signs of an inclination to
renew his pretensions to the throne, he caused both him
and Joab to be put to death, suspended Abiathar from his
office of High Priest, and thus nipped in the bud a
threatened civil war. Shimei, who had cursed David in
his flight, and whose hostility to Solomon himself was
ill-concealed, was spared, on condition that he should
never leave Jerusalem. Three years afterwards he broke
his parole and perished.

Although Solomon's reign was the culminating point of
the prosperity of Israel, its story may be told in few words.
The internal affairs of the kingdom were administered with
such sagacity and justice that "Judah and Israel dwelt
safely every man under his vine and under his fig-tree,
from Dan even to Beersheba, all the days of Solomon"
(1 Kings iv. 25). Foreign treaties wisely contracted, the
construction of mercantile fleets, and the opening up of
well-made and well-guarded roads throughout the country,
made it the highway of nations and the emporium of the
commerce of the world. Incalculable wealth thus flowed
into the country, and the magnificence of the Hebrew
monarch exceeded that of any of the most opulent and
luxurious courts of the ancient world. The vast and
almost fabulous resources which Solomon possessed were
well and wisely applied; the largest share was appropriated to the building of a fitting temple for the abode of
the God of Israel; and if incredibly large sums were
lavished on the king's own tastes for luxurious indulgence
and oriental display, his treasures were bestowed with an

equally ungrudging hand upon the construction of public works of utility or beauty.

Besides the magnificent Temple of which the Bible gives us so graphic a description, Solomon constructed many noble and useful public works, some of which, as the Pools of Solomon near Bethlehem, from which, by a splendid aqueduct, Jerusalem was supplied with water, remain to the present day, as lasting monuments of his divinely-inspired wisdom and his power.

SOLOMON'S POOLS.

But there was a dark side to the picture. The corrupt influence of unbounded wealth and irresponsible power had tarnished the brightness of that Divine Wisdom which had been vouchsafed to him, and Solomon was guilty of many and flagrant violations of the law of God and of the Hebrew constitution. With a clear perception of the danger, both moral and political, of foreign conquest,

Moses had forbidden Hebrew kings to multiply chariots and horses, to accumulate gold and silver, and to marry many foreign wives. Solomon had done all these things, and the result was that which the inspired lawgiver had foreseen. His military displays raised up against Israel many and formidable foes, his lavish expenditure laid heavy burdens upon his subjects, and his strange wives seduced him from the worship of God to follow the vain and filthy idols of the surrounding peoples. Troubles began to gather round him ; Adad, the Edomite prince, organized a revolt against his authority ; an adventurer named Rezon seized Damascus, caused himself to be proclaimed king there, and interrupted the communications between Tadmor and Palestine ; and worse than all, one of his own officers, Jeroboam, conspired against him, and on being forced to fly, found an asylum with Shishak, king of Egypt ; his subjects, moreover, were beginning to murmur, for his despotism curtailed their liberty, and his extravagance increased their pecuniary burdens. At last, after a reign of forty years, Solomon died. He had raised the Jewish kingdom to the very pinnacle of greatness, but, failing to give God the glory, he had undermined the fabric which he had raised, and henceforth the decline of the monarchy was as rapid as its rise.

Solomon was not only distinguished as a monarch and a statesman, but as a writer and philosopher. Besides the collection of Proverbs, the Book of Ecclesiastes, and the Song of Songs, he was, we are told, the author of numerous philosophical and poetical works, and several treatises upon natural history. His attainments in the latter science were so extraordinary, and were so much in advance of his time, that a very ancient tradition perpetuated in Mohammedan writings has ascribed to the great king of Israel a knowledge of the language of birds and beasts.

One Arabic epigram, in which this legend is embodied,

is so striking that I am tempted to quote it; the author is
an Egyptian poet of the thirteenth century, named Zoheir:

> " A foolish atheist, whom I lately found,
>   Alleged philosophy in his defence;
>   Said he, ' The arguments I use are sound.'
>   ' Just so,' said I, '*all sound* and *little sense*.'
>
> " ' You talk of matters far beyond your reach;
>   You 're knocking at a closed-up door,' said I.
>   Said he, ' You do not understand my speech.'
>   ' I 'm not King Solomon !' was my reply."

Rehoboam, Solomon's son, next ascended the throne,
but, as the loyalty of the other tribes was more than doubtful, it was determined to hold a solemn assembly at Shechem, at which he should be anointed king before all
Israel. The rebel chieftain Jeroboam was amongst the
crowd assembled on the occasion, which was an extremely
critical one, equivalent, in fact, to taking a *plebiscitum*
which should decide the fate of the monarchy. The people,
before giving in their allegiance, demanded, by their spokesman Jeroboam, some alleviation of the burdens which
Solomon had placed upon them, and some guarantee that
he would respect the constitution. Rehoboam's older and
wiser counsellors would have persuaded him to give the
necessary promise, but the haughty and hot-headed youth
would not listen to their advice, and, acting at the sug-
gestion of the younger members of his council, addressed
the assembled multitude in the well-known speech, " My
father made your yoke heavy, and I will add to your
yoke : my father also chastised you with whips, but I will
chastise you with scorpions " (1 Kings xii. 14). This was
the signal for immediate revolt. " To your tents, O
Israel ! " cried the infuriated throng, and the assembly dis-
solved in the utmost confusion. Judah and Benjamin
still remained faithful, but the other ten tribes renounced
Rehoboam's authority, stoned Adoram, his tribute-collector,
and forced him to seek safety in a hurried flight. Jero-

boam, who had distinguished himself as a popular leader in Solomon's time, had been already designated by the prophet Ahijah as ruler over the ten tribes whose defection he predicted. This fact, added to the enormous influence which his private wealth and his connection with Shishak, king of Egypt, gave him, made him one of the most prominent men of the time; and when he appeared at Shechem as the champion of the people and defender of their liberties the revolted tribes unanimously chose him for their king. Rehoboam was not inclined to yield his empire without a struggle, and as the honour of the haughty tribe of Judah was at stake, he found no difficulty in raising a force to send against the rebels. An army of 180,000 men was equipped for service. The warning voice of the prophet Shemaiah was raised to prevent the civil war, and the mighty host dispersed. Rehoboam and his rival then began fortifying their respective borders, and the rupture of the kingdom was complete. The struggle was not one between two rival aspirants to the throne, nor did Rehoboam's impolitic speech alone cause the separation; the contest was really between north and south, between the inhabitants of the two great divisions of the country,* the mountain districts of Judah and Ephraim. These two tribes had, in fact, become the representatives of the nation, and had, politically speaking, absorbed all the rest.

The southern kingdom thus comprised the amalgamated tribes of Judah and Benjamin, Simeon having long before lost its independent existence. The northern kingdom was headed by Ephraim, and the remaining tribes were so subordinate that Ephraim and Israel became henceforth synonymous terms; and, after this great division, Israel became an equivalent for the kingdom of the north as distinguished from the southern kingdom of Judah. It is instructive to note how exactly the geographical divisions

* See page 52.

of the country represent the position of the two opposing parties. The southern portion of Palestine appears on reference to the map like an intrenched camp, with Benjamin pushed forward to guard the lines. The northern half of Palestine, on the contrary, appears like a large advancing army; Ephraim leads the van, and opposes a compact front to the enemy.

CHAPTER VI.

ONE thing was evident—that, so long as Jerusalem continued the seat of the national worship, it would always
form a rallying-point, and might at any time lead to the
re-establishment of the supremacy of Judah. To avoid this
contingency, Jeroboam determined to establish a separate
worship and priesthood, and he accordingly set up two
golden calves, one in Bethel, venerated as " the House of
God," and the other in the city of Dan, which, as we have
seen,* already contained a sanctuary. This direct viola-

* See page 67. It is curious to see how history repeats itself.
When, in the early history of Mohammedanism, two rival caliphs contended for the throne, Abd el Melik, to "weaken his rival's prestige,
conceived the plan of diverting men's minds from the pilgrimage to
Mecca, and of inducing them to make the pilgrimage to Jerusalem instead."—" Besant and Palmer's Jerusalem," p. 78.

tion of the Divine commandment called down a special rebuke from the Most High ; and as Jeroboam was officiating at his altar of incense, the prophet of the Lord appeared before him and pronounced a curse upon him and upon his house. When the king would have seized upon the unwelcome messenger, the hand which he stretched forth was withered, but at the prophet's prayer was soon restored again.

A grievous misfortune now fell upon the kingdom of Judah, and it is impossible to acquit Jeroboam of instigating, or at least conniving at it. Shishak, the king of Egypt and Jeroboam's old patron, came up against Jerusalem with such an overwhelming force that Rehoboam, by the advice of the prophet Shemaiah, submitted without a struggle. By his surrender Jerusalem was saved from utter destruction ; but the temple and palace of Solomon were stripped of their accumulated treasures. The conquest was rendered all the easier in consequence of Rehoboam, yielding to the influence of his Ammonitish mother, having exceeded his father in the licence allowed to idolatry, so that the corrupting tendencies of the foreign habits thus introduced had undermined the temporal as well as the spiritual power of Judah.

Rehoboam, having reigned seventeen years, was succeeded by his son Abijah. His first act was to make war upon Jeroboam, whom he defeated with great loss, effectually humbling his power, and capturing Bethel, the sacred city of Israel. Abijah died after a reign of three years, during which short period he had done much towards recovering the ancient glory of Judah. His son Asa followed up the advantage his father had gained, not by extending his conquests, but by restoring the purity of the national faith, crushing out idolatry, and strengthening the defences of the country. This wise policy enabled him to repel a formidable invasion by one Zerah, an Ethiopian, whom he defeated in the valley of Zephathah,

H

and pursued into Gerah.* Meanwhile the rival kingdom of Israel enjoyed no such prosperity. Jeroboam's young son, the heir to his kingdom, lay sick, and his mother, an Egyptian princess, wrapped in a close disguise, sought the aged prophet Ahijah, and implored him to pray that her child might live. The prophet, old and blind as he was, at once detected the wife of Jeroboam, refused her unhallowed gifts, and pronounced the awful doom that should befall his devoted race. The sick child, said he, must die, but he shall rest in a peaceful grave, and all Israel shall mourn for him ; but for the rest of the descendants of the idolatrous king, " Him that dieth of Jeroboam in the city shall the dogs eat ; and him that dieth in the field shall the fowls of the air eat : for the Lord hath spoken it " (1 Kings xiv. 11).

The dreadful curse was speedily and literally fulfilled. Nadab, Jeroboam's son, succeeded him upon the throne ; but in the second year of his reign, Baasha, a man of the tribe of Issachar, attacked him while he was besieging a Philistine city, and put him to death, together with all the house of Jeroboam, till not a single soul of that wretched family was left alive. Baasha, having succeeded to the vacant throne of Israel, at once made war upon Asa ; and the latter, to counteract the energetic measures which his rival was taking, formed an alliance with Benhadad, the now powerful heathen king of Damascus ; and while Asa harassed the southern frontier of Israel, Benhadad descended upon the northern province of Naphthali. Baasha died in the twenty-fourth year of his reign, and was succeeded by his son Elah, who was murdered by Zimri, captain of the guard, who thus became possessed of the kingdom.

Zimri utterly exterminated his master's family ; but the army who were still besieging the Philistine town of Gibethon chose Omri, their general, as king. The monarch

* See page 34.

elect at once raised the siege and proceeded to Tirzah, where Zimri had fixed his residence; and the latter, being unable to hold out against his enemy, set fire to the palace, and perished in the flames.

Another pretender to the throne now arose, in the person of Tibni, but Omri in the end prevailed, and founded a new dynasty of Israelitish kings. For six years Omri was content to dwell at Tirzah, at the expiration of which time he bought of one Shemer a fertile hill in the mountains of Ephraim, and there founded the city of Samaria, where he died and was buried, being succeeded by his son Ahab.

Ahab was himself a feeble monarch, but he had married Jezebel, daughter of the king of Sidon, a fierce and unscrupulous woman, who had obtained unbounded control over him. So completely did she contrive to hold the reins of government in her own hands that she obtained the formal abrogation of the worship of Jehovah in favour of that of Baal and Ashtaroth, the gods of the Phœnicians, whose temples and altars rose throughout the length and breadth of the land. The prophets raised their voices against this awful desecration, but in vain. The merciless and vengeful queen instituted a terrible persecution against them, and all the order were put to death, except one hundred, who escaped by concealing themselves in a cave.

Amidst their barbarian splendour in the ivory palace at Jezreel, the imbecile king and his inhuman consort were startled by a strange and ominous apparition. A rude herdsman from the mountains of Gilead, "an hairy man and girt with a girdle of leather about his loins," suddenly stood before the king, and exclaimed, "As the Lord God of Israel lives, before whom I stand, there shall not be dew nor rain these years, but according to my word." Having uttered this fearful prediction, Elijah the Tishbite, for he it was, withdrew, and, guided by the Spirit of the Lord, hid himself by the brook Cherith, a wády which falls into the Jordan.

Here he dwelt, miraculously supplied with food brought him every morning and evening by ravens.*

When his prophecy began to be fulfilled and the brook became exhausted by the general drought which fell upon the land, the prophet Elijah fled to Sarepta in the kingdom of Sidon, the very seat of that idolatry which he had denounced ; here he sojourned with the widow woman whose son was restored to life, and whose little store of flour and oil was rendered inexhaustible at his intercession.

EAST END OF CARMEL.

For three years the drought and famine wasted the land, and at the expiration of that period Elijah again appeared before the king, having first sent the trembling Obadiah to announce his approach. Ahab at once went out to meet him, and in words which betokened the awe and terror with which the prophet had inspired him, exclaimed, "Art thou he that troubleth Israel ?" And Elijah answered, " I have not troubled Israel ; but thou and thy

* Some of the Jewish commentators understand by the word ravens עֹרְבִים either " Arabs," or " merchants." Cf. Oreb and Zeb, page 70.

father's house, in that ye have forsaken the commandments of the Lord, and thou hast followed Baalim. Now
therefore send, and gather to me all Israel unto Mount
Carmel, and the prophets of Baal four hundred and fifty,
and the prophets of the groves four hundred, which eat
at Jezebel's table" (1 Kings xviii. 17—19). The challenge
was accepted. The prophets of Baal four hundred and
fifty, and the prophets of Astarte four hundred, assembled
on Mount Carmel, and Elijah, alone and single-handed,
stood forth to confront them, in the name of Jehovah, the
God of Israel.

The priests of Baal first chose their victim and placed
it on the altar, and as the sun, Baal himself, rose in the
east, they hailed him with solemn invocations, and bade
him kindle the fire beneath the offering and vindicate his
majesty. At noon the orb was at its meridian, and louder
and louder grew the cry, " O Baal, hear us !" but no
answer came. Slowly, as the day wore on, the sun
descended towards the western horizon, heedless of the
frantic invocations of his worshippers, who leapt about in
wild excitement and gashed their bodies with the sacrificial
knives. Meanwhile the stern prophet mocked their efforts
and taunted them with the indifference of their god.
" Cry aloud," said he, " for he is a god ; either he is
talking, or he is pursuing, or he is in a journey, or peradventure he sleepeth, and must be awaked " (1 Kings
xviii. 27). At last the sun sank down beneath the waves
of the western sea, and as the last ray faded from their
sight the priests of Baal knew that their hope was gone.
Then Elijah rose and set up an altar of twelve stones to
the Lord, and laid the victim on it, and filled the trench
around it with water ; and when the time for evening
sacrifice came, he said, " Lord God of Abraham, Isaac,
and of Israel, let it be known this day that Thou art God
in Israel, and that I am Thy servant, and that I have
done all these things at Thy word " (1 Kings xviii. 36).

Swift and awful was the answer to that prayer: "The fire of the Lord fell, and consumed the burnt sacrifice, and the wood, and the stones, and the dust, and licked up the water that was in the trench. And when all the people saw it, they fell on their faces: and they said, The Lord He is the God; the Lord He is the God. And Elijah said unto them, Take the prophets of Baal; let not

WEST END OF CARMEL.

one of them escape. And they took them: and Elijah brought them down to the brook Kishon and slew them there" (1 Kings xviii. 38—40).

To this day the memory of the event is preserved, as well as the local names attaching to the spot; the eastern end of Carmel's ridge is known as El Mahrakah, "the burning;" and the Arab peasant still speaks of the

Kishon as Nahr el Makatta, "the river of slaughter." *
After this, Elijah foretold the cessation of the drought,
and that same evening a storm of rain burst over the
thirsty land.

Thus was the worship of Jehovah re-established in the
land; but Jezebel remained impenitent; and when she
heard how Elijah had slain the prophets with the edge of
the sword, and humbled her country's gods, she swore that
before another day had passed she would make his life as
one of theirs; but Elijah eluded her vengeance and fled,
first to Beersheba, and then, passing through the desert, he
came to Horeb, the Mount of God. This is the first
recorded instance of the Mount of God having been re-
visited by one of the Hebrew nation since the first delivery
of the Law from its rocky brow. Here Elijah received a
direct revelation from God, by Whom he was commanded
to return by the wilderness of Damascus, there to anoint
Hazael king over Syria, and Jehu, the son of Nimshi, king
of Israel, and to anoint Elisha, son of Shaphat, to be his
own successor in the prophetic office.

Nothing can exceed in sublimity the description of the
revelation of the Most High to Elijah on Mount Sinai;
"Behold the Lord passed by, and a great and strong
wind rent the mountains, and brake in pieces the rocks
before the Lord, the Lord was not in the wind; and
after the wind an earthquake, the Lord was not in the
earthquake; and after the earthquake a fire, the Lord was
not in the fire; and after the fire a still small voice." To
Moses God had manifested Himself in the fire, the earthquake, and the tempest, in all the terrors of the Divine
majesty; but to Elijah He came not amid the mighty
forces of nature, but in the still small voice of mercy and
love with which He speaks to the human conscience and
the human heart. To Moses He gave the Law in all its
severity, and to Elijah He revealed a glimpse of the

* See page 53.

higher law of Divine love of which the first was but a foreshadowing; but it was not until Moses and Elias stood side by side with the glorified Saviour on the Mount of the Transfiguration that the full measure of God's love and justice was known.

Since the abolition of idolatry had removed the curse of famine from the land, Israel had prospered. A long war, undertaken with some reluctance at first, against a confederacy of Syrian kings, who, with Benhadad at their head, had invaded the Holy Land, had terminated successfully, and Ahab the king lived in greater pride and magnificence than ever. Near his palace at Jezreel was a vineyard which Ahab desired to purchase, but Naboth, the proprietor, respected the Mosaic law, which prohibited the alienation of land, and refused to sell the plot of ground. The proud and remorseless Jezebel could but ill brook this display of independent spirit from a Hebrew peasant, and at her instigation the king suborned witnesses and contrived that the contumelious subject should be con- victed of blasphemy, and stoned. When, after this foul murder, Ahab went to take possession of the place, he was again confronted by the awful figure of the Tishbite prophet, who fearlessly denounced the vengeance of the Lord upon him, his queen, and all his house. Nor was the fulfilment of the prophecy long delayed. Asa, king of Judah, after a peaceful and prosperous reign of forty-one years, had been succeeded on the throne by his son Jehoshaphat. With the latter Ahab had concluded an alliance, and he had given his daughter Athaliah in marriage to Jehoram, the heir-apparent to the throne of Judah. Yielding to the advice of the false prophets, who were his counsellors, and heedless of the warning voice of Michaiah, who prophesied his impending fall, Ahab set out upon an expedition against Ramoth-Gilead, which was then in the occupation of the Syrians, and summoned Jehoshaphat, his ally, to aid him in the enterprise. The result was a₃ Michaiah had predicted. Avoiding the king of Judah and his troops, the Syrians concentrated their attack upon Ahab himself. He fell, pierced by an arrow, and was carried back to Samaria dead; and as they washed his blood-stained chariot in the pool of Samaria, " the dogs licked up his blood," according to the word of the Lord by Elijah.

Ahab was succeeded by his son Ahaziah. His reign was short, and signalised by only two memorable events, namely, his own death, foretold by the prophet Elijah, and the destruction by fire from heaven of two companies of his soldiers, whom he had sent to compel the prophet to come down from the mountain where he dwelt and to accompany them on an idolatrous mission, in the king's behalf, to the shrine of Baal-zebub, the Philistine god of Ekron.

Jehoram, Ahaziah's brother, next ascended the throne. In his reign the king of Moab threw off the Israelite yoke, in conjunction with the Ammonites. This people had some time before made an effort to regain their independence, and had made an incursion upon Engedi, in the territory of Jehoshaphat. The attempt had proved a failure, and while the army of the king of Judah were engaged in solemn religious rites, a panic had broken out in the invaders' ranks, causing them to disperse and leave a rich booty behind. They now turned their attention to the northern kingdom, and determined to try their strength with the king of Israel. This revolt of the king of Moab is told in the Bible in few words, and has never until quite recently been regarded as a prominent event in the history of Israel. Lately, however, a circumstance has occurred which has drawn unusual attention to the incident; I mean the discovery of the " Moabite stone."

"The inscription on this stone commemorates the reign of a certain Mesha, king of Moab, and records the triumphs obtained by him over Israel in the course of a long and sanguinary struggle. It begins by setting forth his name and titles, and briefly recounts his successful effort to throw off the yoke of the king of Israel; then follows a list of bloody battles fought, of towns wrested from the enemy, and of spoil and captives fallen into his hands. For these conquests he returns solemn thanks to Chemosh his god— 'the abomination of Moab' (1 Kings xi. 7)—and glories with a religious fervour, that sounds strangely to our ears, in having despoiled the sanctuary of Jehovah. The inscription concludes by setting forth the names of towns rebuilt or fortified by the Moabite king, of altars raised to Chemosh, of wells and cisterns dug, and other peaceful works accomplished. This portion of the records is a most valuable addition to our knowledge of sacred geography; for the names, as given on the Moabite stone, engraved by one who knew them in his daily life, are, in nearly every case, absolutely identical with those found in the Bible itself, and testify to the wonderful integrity with which the Scriptures have been preserved. So far, we have the history of King Mesha's rebellion from his own Moabite point of view, and so far we read of nothing but his success; but if we turn to 2 Kings iii. 5—27, we may look upon the other side of the picture. In that passage we have a concise but vivid account of the rebellion and temporary successes against Israel of this same monarch. There we learn how the allied kings of Israel, Judah, and Edom went against the rebellious prince; how they marched by way of Edom, that is, round by the southern end of the Dead Sea; how they devastated the land of Moab, and drove their foeman to take refuge in his fortress of Kir-Haraseth in Wády Kerek. Then comes the awful tragedy with which the history ends: Mesha, hemmed in and driven to despair, made one last furious effort to burst through the besieging lines; he failed, and ' then he took his eldest son, that should have reigned in his stead, and offered him for a burnt offering on the wall.'

THE MOABITE STONE.

The concluding portion of this verse is curious, for it goes on to say : 'And there was great indignation against Israel, and they departed from him and returned to their own land.' Can it be that, goaded to madness by this supreme act of grim devotion and despair, the men of Moab rose up to avenge their king and drove the invaders from the land ? If so, we have in this inscription, so strangely rescued from the oblivion of three thousand years, the sequel to the Biblical account; and we can understand the tone of mingled reverence and dread with which King Mesha seems to look upon the dark divinity, who, he believed, had sold him victory at such a fearful price. The passage quoted above speaks of the author of the Dhibán inscription in the following terms : 'And Mesha, king of Moab, was a sheep-master, and rendered unto the king of Israel an hundred thousand lambs and an hundred thousand rams with the wool.' Here, again, the Bible receives fresh confirmation from geographical facts ; Moab, with its extensive grass-covered uplands, is even now an essentially sheep-breeding country, although the 'fenced cities and folds for sheep,' of which mention is made in the Book of Numbers (xxxii. 36), are all in ruins. But in its palmier days, when those rich pastures were covered with flocks, no more appropriate title could have been given to the king of such a country than that he 'was a sheep-master.'" *

On the death of Jehoshaphat, his son Jehoram ascended the throne, so that we have a king of Judah and a king of Israel of nearly the same name. Jehoram, king of Judah, had, as we have seen, married Athaliah the daughter of Ahab and Jezebel. This princess proved herself worthy of her parentage, and on her husband's accession to the throne she induced him to put all his brethren to death in order to secure the succession to her own offspring. From murder she quickly led him on to idolatry, until at length

* "The Desert of the Exodus," pp. 495—497.

the measure of his crime was complete. Divine judgment
overtook him; one by one the tributaries of his kingdom
fell away; Edom revolted against him, took his seaport
of Elath on the Red Sea, and cut off the commerce of his
dominion; the Philistines and Arabians invaded the
country, and penetrated even to his palace, and slew all his
sons but one; and he himself at last perished of a dreadful disease, and sank into an unknown and dishonoured
grave.

Joram, king of Israel, had in the meantime renewed
the quarrel with the king of Damascus. The prophet
Elijah had disappeared in the whirlwind and chariot of
fire; but his mantle rested on his servant Elisha, and to
him the nation looked for counsel and for aid. Unlike his
great master, the prophet Elisha affected not desert soli-
tudes, nor a strange wild garb and mode of life; he dwelt
amidst the men of Israel, and the fame of his miracles and
prophetic power had spread far and wide, even to the
capital of Syria, where Naaman, a great Syrian general,
had been cured of leprosy by the intervention of the
prophet. The king, Benhadad, finding himself foiled
at every point in his campaign against Israel, endeavoured to surprise and capture Elisha, whom he suspected to be the main instrument in causing his failure.
The plot failed, the soldiers who had been sent to take
him being miraculously smitten with blindness. At last
the whole of Benhadad's forces were concentrated upon
a blockade of Samaria, the capital of Israel, and the
besieged were driven to such extremities that the
filthiest offal was sold for a large price, and mothers
devoured their own children. One case of this kind,
in which two women had agreed to slay and eat their
children together, came under the king's notice. On hear-
ing the ghastly story, the king rent his clothes, and the
people, as he passed along, saw that he was wearing sack-
cloth next his skin, in token of his deep humiliation. In

the madness of despair, the king turned against Elisha, and swore to take his life, but the prophet announced to the messenger, who had come to execute the king's commands, that on the morrow the famine and suffering should be changed to plenty and deliverance. The prediction was literally fulfilled, for a sudden panic fell that night upon the Syrian army; sounds as of multitudes of horsemen and chariots were heard on every side, and the besieging army, believing that the Egyptians, or some other powerful allies, were upon them, took to flight, and left their well provisioned camp a booty to the famished Samarians. One of Jehoram's military officers, who had derided the prophecy, was trampled to death in the gates of the city as the eager crowds pressed out towards the deserted camp, a fate which the prophet had declared should overtake him for his disbelief.

We next see the prophet journeying towards Damascus, where the king, Benhadad, lay sick. Hazael, one of the chief officers, met him with a magnificent present, borne on forty camels, and inquired of him if his master would recover. Elisha answered that the sickness was not mortal, but that the king's end was near; and with this he burst into a flood of tears, for he knew that Hazael would conspire against his king and slay him, and that when he had usurped the throne he would become a formidable enemy to Israel. The prophecy was literally fulfilled. Hazael returned to Benhadad, and told him that he would recover from his sickness, and that very night he suffocated him in his bed, and seized the throne.

The usurper's first act was to declare war both against Judah and Israel. Joram, king of Israel, and Ahaziah, who had succeeded his father Jehoram as king of Judah, prepared to resist the invader. A bloody battle took place at Ramoth in Gilead between the united forces of the two Hebrew monarchs and those of Hazael the usurping king of Syria; in this Jehoram was wounded, and retreated to Jezreel, where Ahaziah came to meet him. In the meantime Elisha had sent a young man, a prophet, to the camp at Ramoth, to anoint Jehu, one of the captains of the army, king over Israel. The king-elect was not slow to seize upon the kingdom thus unexpectedly offered him. The army at once espoused his cause, and he himself set out for Jezreel. Driving furiously, he reached the city, and was met by Joram and Ahaziah in the vineyard of the

DAMASCUS.

murdered Naboth. "Is it peace, Jehu?" demanded Joram. "And he answered, What peace, so long as the whoredoms of thy mother Jezebel, and her witchcrafts, are so many?" (2 Kings ix. 22.) Joram, on this, took to flight, exclaiming, "There is treachery, O Ahaziah!" but an arrow from Jehu's bow pierced him through the heart, and the body was cast out in the vineyard of Naboth for the dogs to eat. Ahaziah was also taken and slain, but his body was carried to Jerusalem, where it received an honourable burial. Jehu then drove into the city of Jezreel, where Jezebel, with painted face and gaily-tired head, looked out upon him from the window of her palace. If she had calculated upon fascinating him by the queenly attractions which she still possessed, the hope was soon dispelled by Jehu's stern demeanour, and she proceeded to reproach him for his treachery, saying, "Had Zimri peace, who slew his master? And he lifted up his face to the window, and said, Who is on my side? who? And there looked out to him two or three eunuchs. And he said, Throw her down. So they threw her down, and some of her blood was sprinkled upon the wall, and on the horses: and he trode her under foot" (2 Kings ix. 81—83). Later on in the day, while the conqueror was at a banquet given him by the obsequious citizens, he consented to the burial of the queen; but the men despatched to perform the task could find nothing but the skull, the feet, and the palms of the hands, for "the dogs had eaten the flesh of Jezebel in the portion of Jezreel."

There were still seventy sons of Ahab left in Samaria; and the crafty Jehu sent to command the elders of the city to set the ablest and best of the princes upon the throne. But the citizens were too wise to oppose the usurper; they gave in their ready allegiance to him; the heads of the seventy sons of Ahab were sent to him in baskets to Jezreel, and Jehu himself was able plausibly to exculpate himself from complicity in their murder: "Behold," he said to the assembled people that crowded round the gate, "behold I conspired against my master and slew him; but who slew all these?" The remaining members of the family of Ahab, together with all their friends and adherents, were next indiscriminately slaughtered; the house of Ahaziah shared the same fate, and the massacre of the entire priesthood of Baal completed the list of horrors amidst which Jehu, the son of Nimshi, ascended the throne of Israel.

But in the meantime, although Israel was freed from the house of Ahab, Athaliah, Jezebel's daughter, had usurped the throne of Judah, and had put to death all the members of the royal house of David, with the exception of one child, Joash, who had been concealed in the Temple by his aunt Jehosheba, wife of the high priest. For six years she continued to reign, but in the seventh the people, led by the priesthood, rose up against her and put her to death, proclaiming the young Joash king in her stead.

As the young king was still but a child, Jehoiada, the high priest, acted as regent, and by his command Mattan, the priest of Baal, was slain in his own temple, and the idolatrous worship of Jezebel's Sidonian deities once more gave place to that of God Most High.

Under Jehu and his successor, Jehoahaz, the kingdom of Israel rapidly declined, for the promise of energy and religious zeal which the son of Nimshi had displayed at the outset of his career was not borne out by his subsequent conduct. The worship of Baal was, it is true, abolished, but the scarcely less idolatrous cult, instituted by Jeroboam, still stood its ground, corruption and effeminacy crept into the morals of the court, and the result was defeat and disgrace. Hazael, the king of Damascus, fulfilling Elisha's prophecy, had reduced Israel almost to the condition of a tributary province; and when Jehoash commenced his reign in Jerusalem, the Syrian monarch was already advancing upon the Holy City from the south, having already got possession of the Philistian city of Gath. Jehoash was unable to cope with the formidable invader. He had shown himself utterly unworthy both of his royal lineage and of the high trust reposed in him; for when Jehoiada, the aged high priest, died, he had yielded to evil counsel and had forsaken the true faith for Baal, and had even sanctioned, or instigated, the murder of

I

Zachariah the prophet, whose voice was raised against the general apostacy and depravity. When Hazael, therefore, stood before the gates of Jerusalem, and demanded the surrender of the city, Joash purchased his retreat at the expense of an immense tribute, to raise which he plundered the sacred treasures of the Temple. But ere long the vengeance of an offended God overtook him, and after lingering for some time on a bed of sickness, a prey to anguish and remorse, he died a miserable death, murdered by two of his own servants.

Amaziah, his son and successor, was a man of a different stamp. He commenced his reign by vigorous operations against the Edomites, who had revolted against his authority, and obtained signal victories over them. Amongst the army he had raised for this campaign were 100,000 merceraries from Israel. These, however, he dismissed, by the command of a prophet, and the discontented troops, as they returned homewards, revenged themselves by surprising certain cities in the territory of Judah. Irritated at this aggression, and flushed with his recent conquests in Edom, he declared war against the king of Israel. Hazael was now dead, and Jehoash, who had succeeded to the throne of Israel, had successfully made head against the Syrians, and restored the independence of his country. The king of Israel made light of Amaziah's threats, and prepared for war. A battle took place at Beth-shemesh, in which Judah was completely routed; the king of Israel at once marched on to Jerusalem, took Amaziah himself captive, threw down the walls of the Holy City, and carried the treasures of the temple off to Samaria.

Joash died in his own city, and his rival, Amaziah, fifteen years afterwards, perished at Lachish, whither he had fled from a conspiracy of the priesthood, whom he had offended by his idolatrous tendencies.

Amaziah was succeeded by his son Azariah, or Uzziah.

For fifty-two years he ruled Judah well and wisely, recovering many of her lost possessions abroad, and strengthening and improving her resources at home. At last, in an evil moment, he ventured to usurp the priestly office; but as he took the censer in his hand, to burn incense in the temple, he was smitten with the loathsome disease of leprosy, and was compelled, by the rigid provisions of the law, to abdicate, and to exchange a palace for a lazar-house, where he died.

In Israel, Jeroboam II. had succeeded his father Joash as king. His military successes were even greater than those of his father, and the frontier of the kingdom was never more extended than during his reign, the whole of the trans-Jordanic provinces having been re-conquered, and Damascus, Ammon, and Moab brought under complete subjection. After a brilliant reign of forty-one years, he died, and for ten years the kingdom was given up to anarchy and confusion; but at last, Zachariah, Jeroboam's son, was seated on the throne. He did not long enjoy his dignity, but was assassinated by Shallum, who was in turn put to death by one Menahem of Tirzah. Menahem, a barbarous and tyrannical prince, ruled Israel for ten years. During his reign, Pul, the Assyrian conqueror, invaded the country, and Menahem was obliged to purchase immunity for himself and people by the payment of an enormous tribute.

He was succeeded by his son Pekahiah, who, after reigning ten years, was murdered by one Pekah, the son of Remaliah. In the second year of Pekah, Jotham became king of Judah, in place of his father Uzziah, who, as we have seen, was smitten with leprosy, and consequently forced to abdicate the throne. After a reign of sixteen years, in which he materially strengthened the capital as well as the frontier towns of Judah, he died. He was succeeded by his son Ahaz.

In the meantime the Assyrians were advancing to uni-

versal conquest, with gigantic strides; race after race, and
tribe after tribe were absorbed or swept away, and the
Hebrew prophets of Israel were already raising their voice
to warn the chosen people that even they must pay the
penalty of disobedience to God, and fall before the advancing scourge.

A fratricidal struggle between the two kingdoms of
Judah and Israel hastened their impending fall. Pekah
entered into an alliance with Rezin, king of Syria, and in-

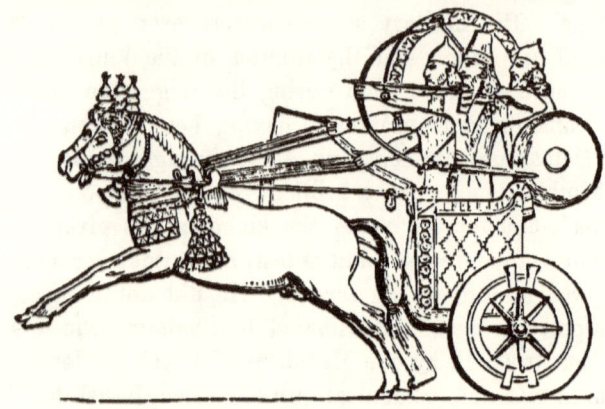

ASSYRIAN BAS-RELIEF OF A KING IN HIS CHARIOT.

vaded Jerusalem. The first attempt was unsuccessful;
but the confederate monarchs returned to the attack. Ahaz
was worsted in a bloody battle, and the port of Elath, on
the Red Sea, was seized by the Syrians. At the same
time, the Philistines and Edomites revolted from the
authority of the king of Judah. In his extremity, Ahaz
sought the powerful aid of Tiglath-Pileser, king of Assyria.
The Assyrian monarch at once recognised the immense
advantages of obtaining a hold upon Judea, and lost no
time in coming to Ahaz's assistance. He marched straight
upon Damascus, and took it, putting Rezin the king
to death and carrying the people into captivity. But it

'was no part of the ambitious Assyrian's policy to aid Judah in regaining her independence. Against her southern foes, the Philistines and Edomites, he sent no aid, knowing that they would continually harass the kingdom, and so effectually prevent any interference from that quarter with his own aggressive plans; in the meantime, he exacted a heavy tribute, to pay which, Ahaz not only oppressed his people, but robbed the sacred treasury of the Temple.

The infatuated king of Judah seemed now bent upon undermining the national faith and hastening the dreadful

KING WORSHIPPING.

catastrophe that was to follow. He paid public worship to the gods of Syria, set up a heathen altar in the Temple itself, and even practised the inhuman rites of Moloch, sacrificing his own son to that deity by making him "pass through the fire in the valley of Hinnom." Idolatry was rampant throughout the land, and especially that particular form of it, the worship of the heavenly bodies, for which the Jews continually manifested so strong a predilection. Horses dedicated to the sun were placed at the gate of the Temple, and altars for astrological observation and worship were placed everywhere on the roofs of the houses.

At length Ahaz died, and was succeeded by his son Hezekiah, who, abhorring the evil practices of his father, set himself to purge the land of idolatry, and thus for a time averted the destruction of his kingdom. But the end of the kingdom of Israel had already come. Pekah had been slain at the instance of Hoshea, who thus obtained possession of the throne of Samaria. Tiglath-Pileser had been succeeded by Shalmanezer. This monarch was even more ambitious and powerful than his predecessor. He had already advanced as far as Phœnicia, and Israel was only able to avoid final subjugation by payment of tribute. Relying upon the promised aid of So, or Sevechus, king of Egypt, Hoshea ventured to refuse payment of this impost, and thus incurred the anger of Shalmanezer, who poured down his countless hosts on Israel, cast the king into prison, and, after a terrible siege of three years, took the capital city of Samaria. The Assyrians, in all their conquests, pursued a novel and ingenious policy. The mass of the inhabitants of the countries conquered by them was transplanted to the central provinces of their empire, and Assyrian colonists were sent to take their place. Thus all disaffection in the newly acquired border-lands was effectually prevented, and peaceful agricultural populations were brought to settle in districts which had hitherto been overrun by savage nomad hordes. In accordance with this policy, the flower of the ten tribes who formed the independent kingdom of Israel were carried away into captivity. The trans-Jordanic tribes had been already swept away by Pul and Tiglath-Pileser, and Shalmanezer now carried off the rest ; and from this moment the ten tribes of Israel disappear from history. What was their ultimate fate, whether they were absorbed by the nations amongst whom they settled, or whether, as some have imagined, their descendants still exist, though no longer retaining the tradition of their Hebrew birth, can be only a matter of speculation.

In Judah, Hezekiah had proceeded thoroughly with the work of reformation, and Jehovah was once more recognised and worshipped as the true God. The king was aided by the faithful counsel of the inspired prophet Isaiah, who, throughout the reign of his father Ahaz, had continually protested against the wickedness and depravity of the age. His object appears to have been to consolidate the Hebrew kingdom, and to induce all of the race to rally round the altar of Jehovah. He restored the Temple and the priesthood with great magnificence, and sent into the neighbouring kingdom to invite all Israel to a solemn celebration of the Passover. Ephraim, then under the rule of Hoshea, scorned the summons, but many of the smaller tribes obeyed it. He next distinguished himself by taking most energetic measures against the Philistines, the implacable and ever restless enemies of Judah. At last, he even ventured to throw off the Assyrian yoke. For a time, the conquest of Israel and of Tyre occupied the attention of the Assyrians, and averted the threatened calamity; but at length, Sennacherib, Shalmanezer's successor, appeared before Jerusalem, and Hezekiah was compelled to sue for pardon. This was granted him on the payment of an enormous tribute, for which Hezekiah was compelled completely to strip both his own palace and the Temple. But at that moment he was detected in secret correspondence with the king of Egypt, and Sennacherib, who was encamped in Lachish, within the territory of Judah, sent three of his generals to demand the unconditional surrender of the place. Rabshakeh, the spokesman of the three officers, delivered the message in insulting terms, taunting the people with their reliance on God, and depicting vividly the hopelessness of resisting the mighty monarch of Assyria.

The king and the people listened with sad misgivings, and began to waver in their resolution to defend the city; but Isaiah encouraged them to defy the foe, and to trust in the Lord in spite of the Assyrians' insulting taunts. And soon the deliverance came : the Assyrian army encamped

SENNACHERIB.

before Jerusalem, but that very night the Angel of the Lord smote them, and the morning light revealed to the astonished people of the city a deserted camp strewn with dead bodies. All those who had escaped the pestilence fled, Sennacherib himself to his own city of Nineveh, where he was murdered by his own sons.

The Assyrian empire had reached its culminating point; its greatness now began to wane, and the hitherto unknown nation of Chaldeans, or Babylonians, emerged from obscurity. Hezekiah had been miraculously cured of a mortal sickness, and Merodach-Baladan, the first king of Babylon, sent an embassy to Jerusalem, ostensibly to congratulate the king upon his recovery. Hezekiah imprudently displayed all his treasures to the strangers, and thus excited their cupidity. Isaiah sternly rebuked him for his ostentation, and predicted that these very people should destroy the kingdom of Judah and carry the people into captivity.

The remaining years of Hezekiah's life were passed in peace and prosperity, for Assyria was too much distracted by internal dissensions to prosecute her foreign aggressions. Many noble and useful works were carried out during his reign. The fortified cities of Judah were strengthened; Jerusalem itself was furnished with a magnificent aqueduct; and agriculture was fostered and improved. At length he sank into an honoured grave, mourned by all the people, for with him died the glory and independence of Judea.

Manasseh, who succeeded him, ascended the throne at the age of twelve years. Evil counsellors and an evil disposition made this king a monster of iniquity by the time that he had attained his maturity. Former kings of Judah had been guilty of idolatrous practices, but Manasseh surpassed them all, and not even the abominations of Ahaz could be compared with the superstitions practised by this insane prince. To these vices he added the political crimes of tyranny and oppression, and when Esar-haddon, the then king of Assyria, invaded Judea, Manasseh was unable to offer any resistance, and was carried captive to Babylon; there, however, he so humbled himself, and repented, that he was shortly restored to his throne.*

* The captivity and restoration of Manasseh is not mentioned in the older account, recorded in the Book of Kings.

His son Amon succeeded him, and followed the same idolatrous courses as his father had done. Fortunately for the nation, his reign was but short ; he was murdered at the end of two years by some of his own officers, who had conspired against him.

Josiah, his son, was a mere child of eight years old at the time of Amon's death ; but he was, nevertheless, proclaimed king. Josiah proved himself zealous for the cause of true religion and the welfare of the state. He thoroughly extirpated idolatry from the land, reformed all the abuses that had crept into the government, and repaired the oft-desecrated Temple. During the progress of the repairs, a copy (said to be the original copy) of the Law was found amidst the rubbish. And thus the Mosaic precepts, which had become neglected and almost forgotten in Israel, once more became known to the people in their integrity. The young king was supported in his work of reformation by earnest and able counsellors, amongst whom were Zephaniah, Habbakuk, and Jeremiah. The virtues of the young king, and his wise administration, appeared likely for a time to avert the fall of the Jewish kingdom, especially as Assyria was weakened by the inroads of the Scythians and the attack of the Babylonians, and therefore compelled to leave Judea in comparative peace.

Josiah found his position a difficult one, and it required no ordinary statesmanship to avoid embroiling his own kingdom in the conflicts of the rival empires. But when the kingdom of Egypt for a time regained its independence, and still further complicated matters by invading Mesopotamia, the king of Judah felt that the crisis had arrived. Bound both by policy and gratitude to his Assyrian masters—for he had been permitted to add the desolated city of Samaria to his dominions—Josiah refused to allow Necho a free passage through Judea, and appeared in person amongst his troops, to dispute the advance of the

Egyptian army. Though disguised as a common soldier, to prevent recognition by the Egyptian archers, who would have made him a special object of attack, a chance shaft laid him low and destroyed the last faint hope of Israel.

Necho's expedition against the Assyrians was completely successful, and on his return Jerusalem yielded without resistance, and Jehoahaz, younger son of Josiah, who had been hastily chosen by the people, was deposed and imprisoned.

Jehoiachin, a weak and idolatrous sovereign, next ascended the throne. In spite of the warnings and remonstrances of the prophet Jeremiah, he was mad enough to attempt to cope with Nebuchadnezzar, who, at the head of the armies of Assyria and Babylon, having completely crushed the Egyptian power and wrested from Necho II. all the conquered territory from the Euphrates to the river of Egypt (Wády el 'Arísh), was now advancing upon Judea. At first, Jehoiachim was induced to submit, and for three years he paid a tribute to Nebuchadnezzar. The latter at once sent an army to suppress the rebellion, and collected troops from Ammon, Moab, and other tribes unfriendly to the Israelites. In the meantime Jehoiachim died. Jehoiachin, his son, next ascended the throne ; but when, a few months afterwards, an invading army, with Nebuchadnezzar himself at its head, appeared before the walls of Jerusalem, the city surrendered, and the king and all his family, together with the treasures of the Temple and the flower of the army and the nobility of the land, were carried off to Babylon.

Zedekiah, a son of Josiah, was allowed to assume the name and office of king. But in the ninth year of his reign he was infatuated enough to assert his independence, in direct opposition to the warnings and predictions of Jeremiah. This rash movement was encouraged by Hophra, the then reigning king of Egypt, who was enabled to make some stand against the tide of Babylonian conquest, and who now came in person, with a large army, to the assistance of his Jewish ally. The event fully vindicated the wisdom of the prophet's advice ; for Hophra was defeated, and compelled to retire, and Jerusalem was left to its fate ; famine soon compelled the city to surrender, and Zedekiah, who had attempted to escape towards his ally the king of Ammon, was seized on the plain of Jericho ; his children were put to death before his eyes, after which he himself was blinded, and in this piteous condition was carried captive to Babylon.

JEWISH CAPTIVES.

The prophet Jeremiah witnessed the accomplishment of the dreadful doom which he had foretold, and in his unrivalled elegy he has left us a record of what his feel-ings were as he witnessed the final desolation. Jerusalem was reduced to a mass of ruins ; the remaining treasures of the Temple, even to the two brazen pillars which stood before the gate, were carried off to Babylon. The great mass of the Hebrew people were removed to Babylon, but a wretched few were still permitted to remain, under the command of Gedaliah, a lieutenant of the Babylonian monarch. Jeremiah still clung fondly to his native land, and elected to remain with Gedaliah at Mizpah, where the seat of government had been fixed. Shortly after, Gedaliah was murdered by one Ishmael, who endeavoured to supplant him in his inglorious dignity; and the Chaldean garrison, who had been left to support him, were massacred. The murderer escaped to Ammon, but Johanan, who had attempted to revenge the death of Gedaliah, knowing how severe an account Nebuchadnezzar would exact for the murder of his soldiers, fled with the remnant of Israel to Egypt. There Jeremiah the prophet died—stoned to death, it is said, by his own countrymen, for venturing to reprove them for their idolatry.

Of the actual condition of the Israelites during their captivity in Babylon we know but little. The pathetic strain of the well-known psalm, " By the waters of Babylon we sat down, and wept when we remembered thee, O Zion," shows how keenly they felt their degradation, and how they yearned after the Holy Land from which they had been so ruthlessly torn; but it does not appear that they were treated with harshness or oppression by their conquerors; and many of them appear to have attained to high rank in their new home, and to have become possessed of considerable property. They were also permitted to exercise their religion without let or hindrance. Prophets, too, flourished among them, and the books of Daniel and Ezekiel belong to the period of the captivity. Daniel's high position at the Babylonian Court, and the respect which his fearless obedience to the commands of God extorted from the king himself, made him a fitting representative of, and a powerful intercessor for, the whole nation, whose prospects were thus, no doubt, considerably improved. Daniel maintained his eminence, not only during the lifetime of Nebuchadnezzar, but in the reigns of his successors, Evil-Merodach and Belshazzar; and when, in accordance with his own prediction, the sceptre was wrested from the hands of the last-named monarch by Darius the Median, the Hebrew prophet still prospered. With Belshazzar the Chaldean dynasty ended ; but it is doubtful whether Darius the Mede was Cyaxares, the uncle of Cyrus, or whether he was the founder of a fresh dynasty, who in turn yielded to Cyrus. Certain, however, it is that the Babylonian empire was at last overthrown, and that, as the seventy years of their captivity drew towards the close, the Jews saw the Medes and Persians pouring over the eastern world in countless and victorious hosts, with Cyrus, the predicted deliverer of Israel, at their head.

The following chronological table, borrowed from Milman's " History of the Jews," will be found of great service to the student :—

FIRST PERIOD.

KINGS OF JUDAH.	Years.	B.C.	KINGS OF ISRAEL.	Years.
Rehoboam..reigned	17	979	Jeroboam...........reigned	22
Abijah...............	3	962		
Asa.....................	41	959		
		957	Nadab...........................	2
		955	Baasha..........................	23
		932	Elah.............................	2
		930	Zimri, Omri..................	11
		919	Ahab............................	22
Jehoshaphat.........	25	918		
		897	Ahaziah........................	2
		895	Joram..........................	12
Jehoram...............	8	893		
Ahaziah...............	1	885		

SECOND PERIOD.

KINGS OF JUDAH.	Years.	B.C.	KINGS OF ISRAEL.	Years.
Athaliah	6	884	Jehu	28
Jehoash...............	40	878		
		855	Jehoahaz	14
		841	Joash..........................	16

SECOND PERIOD—*continued.*

KINGS OF JUDAH.			KINGS OF ISRAEL.	
	Years.	B.C.		Years.
Amaziah	29	838		
		825	Jeroboam II	42
Uzziah or Azariah	52	809		
		781	Interregnum	11
		770	Zachariah and Shallum	1
		769	Menahem	10
		759	Pekahiah	2
		758	Pekah	20
Jotham	16	757		
Ahaz	16	741		
		737	2nd Interregnum	9
		728	Hosea	9
Hezekiah	29	726		
		719	Samaria taken.	
Manasseh	55	697		
Amon	2	642		
Josiah	31	640		
Jehoahaz .....3 months } Jehoiachim .... 11 }		609		
Jehoiachin } or Coniah } 3 months } Zedekiah.............. 11 }		598		
Jerusalem destroyed...		587		

POST-BIBLICAL HISTORY;

FROM

THE CAPTIVITY OF BABYLON TO THE TAKING

OF

THE CITY BY TITUS.

PART THE SECOND.

CHAPTER VII.

THE RESTORATION.

The return from captivity—Rebuilding of the Temple; opposition by the Samaritans, its completion—Esdras and Nehemiah—First establishment of synagogues—Effect of the captivity upon the national religion—Restoration of the primitive form of government—State of the country after the death of Nehemiah—Murder of Joshua by his brother Johanan, the high priest, in the Temple—Invasion of the country by Darius Ochus—Alexander the Great; his visit to Jerusalem; favours the Jews—Schism of the Samaritans —Division of Alexander's empire—The Jews carried into captivity by Ptolemy, king of Egypt—The Alexandrian Jews—Simon the Just—The Jews under the Ptolemies—Antiochus the Great; prosperity of the Hebrew nation under his rule and that of his successor—Seleucus makes an attempt on the treasures of the Temple—Antiochus Epiphanes desecrates the Holy City; enormities of his creatures Jason and Menelaus—The persecutions under Antiochus Epiphanes.

AFTER a captivity of seventy years—the exact period predicted by the prophet Jeremiah—the Jews were restored to their country by Cyrus the Great, king of Persia, who issued a royal decree, permitting them to return to Palestine and rebuild the Holy City and Temple of Jerusalem. This permission was eagerly seized upon by certain members of the tribes of Judah and Benjamin, while the

K

remainder, who preferred to stay in Babylon, assisted them from their private resources. Re-established in their native land, they occupied themselves with unremitting ardour in the restoration of their worship and holy places. The Samaritans were very desirous of participating in this national work, but the jealousies existing between the two communities were too strong, and their offer of co-operation was refused, under the pretext that the decree of Cyrus extended only to the house of Israel. This was an additional cause of ill-feeling, and from that day forth an implacable hatred sprung up between the Jews and Samaritans, which has never ceased to exist, even to the present time. The Samaritans now set themselves to oppose the plans of their rivals, and succeeded so well that the reconstruction of the Temple was for a long time suspended; a subsequent decree of Darius, however, confirmed the privileges which Cyrus had granted, and provided that the Jews should continue the building without molestation. In the sixteenth year of the reign of Darius, the building of the new Temple was completed, and the inauguration was solemnised with great rejoicing and general thanksgiving. The Old Testament ends with the restoration of the Jews to Palestine and the reconstruction of the city and Temple, during the high-priesthood of Esdras' and the government of Nehemiah.

Esdras and Nehemiah, as we learn from the inspired books which they have left us, laboured unceasingly to reform the abuses which had crept into the government of the Jewish community, and to restore the primitive simplicity of the Mosaic law.

It was after the return from the captivity at Babylon that the Jews first began to establish synagogues, that is, buildings consecrated for religious meetings and prayer. Before the captivity, the only place available for *public* worship was the Temple itself at Jerusalem: the great body of the people, thus left to themselves, without authorised religious instruction, lapsed, as was to be expected, into superstitious and idolatrous observances in their own homes, and the law was practically unknown, or misunderstood. The evils arising from such a system of neglect became even more apparent than before, for the captivity had brought too plainly before their eyes the possibility of the separation of large bodies from the community, and had, in a measure, prepared them for that general dispersion of the people which was one day to take place. To prevent the recurrence of such a state of things, the scheme of establishing synagogues was devised; the great ceremonies of religion, and especially the sacrifices, were still confined to the ministration of the Temple; but the synagogues drew together the members of local communities, for the purpose of daily prayer, and of the reading and expounding of the law.

So long as the Jews had remained domiciled in Palestine, so long as the Temple, with its precious relics of the Mosaic age, remained intact, and so long as the daily worship held therein perpetuated the worship in the Tabernacle, as instituted in the wilderness, there was no room or opportunity for the admission of heretical doctrines into the Jewish creed, and no possibility of open or avowed schism. Whatever ill effects the intercourse with idolatrous nations, or the sumptuous extravagances of the later monarchy may have had upon the tendencies of individuals, no one had openly dared to attack the ordinances of the law itself. The spell once broken, and the people dispersed, the position of affairs was of course changed: a sojourn of seventy years amongst a nation of idolaters, a nation, moreover, professing that very form of idolatry, sun-worship, which from the primitive age of Job down to our own day has always possessed such a mysterious attraction for the Semitic races, could not fail to exercise a pernicious effect upon their belief. The very fact that Esdras and Nehemiah laboured so strenuously to restore the primeval simplicity of the law is of itself a sufficient proof that there were numerous heretical abuses which needed to be reformed. In effect, we find henceforth springing up in Judaism different sects, all differing more or less widely from the spirit of the law, and embodying in a greater or less degree the superstitious dogmas and practices of paganism. The law, written by the finger of God on Mount Sinai, and delivered to Moses for Israel's guidance and government, became obscured by a cloud of tradition; plain precepts became distorted from their original signification by the addition of subtle glosses and interpretations, and the simplicity of the ancient history itself was destroyed by the addition of mythical details and allegorical expositions. Thus arose that second and spurious law which is embodied in the Rabbinical writings, and which, though speciously pretending to be an exposition of the Word of God, in reality substitutes for that Holy Word the vain imaginings of men.

The position of the Jews after the return from captivity, and under the first kings of Persia, was by no means secure; they were objects of jealousy and dislike to the surrounding people, and especially to their neighbours the Samaritans. The history contained in the Book of Esther indicates plainly how precarious was even the very existence of the nation, subject as they were to the caprice of Persia's despotic sovereign. This episode, the details of which need not be repeated here, enables us also to form an estimate of the immense numbers of Jews scattered through the Persian dominions. The weak-minded and vacillating Ahasuerus has been identified by later scholars with Xerxes, the celebrated invader of Greece.

After the restoration, Jerusalem had recovered, it is true, the shadow of its former glory, and strangers once more flocked to the Holy City to lay their offerings before the altar of the sanctuary. Even the primitive form of

government which existed in Joshua's day had been restored, and the affairs of the Jewish nation were administered by the high priest and a council of seventy-two
elders, called the Sanhedrin. But the national independence had gone, the zeal for religion had died out, and
with it the glory of Israel had departed. Judea, after the
death of Nehemiah, became, what it is at the present day
under the Turkish rule, a mere appendage to the prefec-
ture of Syria; and the high priests held their authority
from the prefect. Avarice and ambition now appeared to
be the only incentives to action; the basest means were
resorted to to obtain the high priesthood, and the office
was made by its possessors a mere instrument for extortion
and injustice.

In the forty-third year of Artaxerxes Memnon, the
high priest Jehoiada was succeeded in that office by his
son Johanan; the latter, not long after his election,
received a visit from his brother Joshua, who informed him
that Bagoas, governor of Syria, had promised to confer
the honour of the priesthood upon him; an angry dispute
at once arose between the two brothers, which resulted
in the murder of Joshua within the very porch of the
Temple. The heathen governor Bagoas administered a
severe and well-merited rebuke to the Jews for having
permitted the desecration of their holy temple by so
dastardly an act, and he condemned the high priest to
pay a heavy fine, which was not remitted until the death
of Artaxerxes. In the reign of his successor, Darius
Ochus, many fresh troubles and dangers threatened the
Jews. After conquering the greater part of Phœnicia, that
monarch marched upon Judea, captured Jericho, and took
a large number of the inhabitants into slavery. Ten years
after, Johanan died, and was replaced by his son Jaddua.

Two hundred and eight years after the fall of Babylon,
the prediction of the inspired prophets came to pass, and
the kingdom of Persia was extinguished by Alexander of

Macedon. Though experiencing many vicissitudes, the
Jewish nation owed much to the kings of Persia, and they
evinced their gratitude and loyalty to the last of that race,
by refusing to aid the Greek conqueror at the siege of
Tyre. Alexander, enraged at their partisanship, turned
his victorious arms against Jerusalem. As the dreaded
invader marched upon the Holy City, the minds of all
within were filled with consternation and despair; but
Jaddua the high priest offered supplication and sacrifices
to the God of Israel. The prayer was answered in the most
unexpected manner, and the threatened calamity averted
by an incident so marvellous that its truth has been
repeatedly attacked, though not, it would seem to us,
upon sufficient grounds. Inspired by a vision, Jaddua
the high priest sallied forth to meet the conqueror. He
was dressed in his full sacerdotal habits, the priests who
accompanied him wore their richest vestments, and the
people, clad in white robes, marched forth in his train.
Alexander, at the sight of this imposing procession, was
affected with an uncontrollable sentiment of awe, and, to
the astonishment of his followers, prostrated himself suddenly upon the ground before the high priest, adoring
the holy name inscribed upon the golden frontlets which
the latter wore. In explanation of his strange conduct,
Alexander declared that, while yet in Macedonia, he had
beheld in a dream the very figure of the Jewish priest
before him, encouraging him to make war against the Persians, and promising him success in the name of the God of
the Jews, of Whose protection he said he could no longer
be in doubt, and Whom he now honoured in the person
of His priest. Accompanied by the whole of the *cortège*,
Alexander the Great made his entry into Jerusalem, offered
up sacrifice in the Temple, and was shown in the book of
the prophet Daniel the prophecy of his own conquest and
empire. Alexander, after this, regarded the Jews with
great favour, released them from the tribute which they

had been obliged to pay every seven years, and permitted them to exercise their religion and to govern themselves according to their own laws. Many of them he established in his newly founded city of Alexandria, in Egypt, where he accorded them all the privileges of Macedonian citizens.

After the conquest of the Persian empire by Alexander, the Samaritans endeavoured to conclude a civil and religious alliance with the Jews; with this object, Samballat, governor of Samaria, gave his daughter in marriage to Manasseh, brother of the high priest Jaddua, and his presumptive successor. Until such time, however, as Manasseh should succeed to the dignity, Samballat was obliged to take his son-in-law under his protection, for the Jews, and especially the Sanhedrim, were very indignant at an alliance which they regarded as unholy and profane. He applied for, and obtained, permission to build a temple upon Mount Gerizim, and appointed Manasseh to be the high priest. Many Jews and priests who had contracted similar alliances joined the Samaritan community. The construction of this rival temple, and the defection of so large a number of their own body, exasperated the Jews beyond measure, and the animosity which existed between the two parties became more violent than before, and gave place to frequent hostilities.

At the death of Alexander, his empire was divided amongst four of his generals. The dissensions amongst these potentates involved the whole of the civilised world in war and revolution. Egypt and Syria were necessarily the chief centres of these disorders, and Judea, being situated midway between the two kingdoms, was exposed to trouble on both sides.

It was at first governed by Laomedon of Mitylene, one of Alexander's captains, but this prince was subsequently conquered by Ptolemy Soter, king of Egypt. The Jews refused to renounce their allegiance to Laomedon, and

Ptolemy, irritated at their resistance, marched upon Jerusalem. Knowing how strictly they observed the Sabbath, he selected that day for the attack, took the city by surprise, and carried a hundred thousand of the inhabitants into captivity. Ptolemy was, however, too good a politician not to appreciate and turn to account the loyalty which was so natural to the Jewish character, and which they had so often evinced towards former conquerors. He accordingly treated them with great consideration, appointed them to important military commands, and confirmed all the privileges which Alexander had accorded to their nation. Some of the captives he established in Libya, and others in Cyrenaica; from these last were descended the Jews of Cyrene, who are mentioned in the New Testament.

The year after the battle of Ipsos died Onias, who had for twenty years held the office of high priest under Ptolemy and Antigonas, and had, during the whole of that stormy period, conducted the administration with much prudence and decision. He was succeeded by Simon, whose virtues, piety, and learning were so remarkable that they earned for him, even from his contemporaries, the honourable title of the Just. Simon's memory is held in loving veneration by the Jewish nation, even to the present day, who regard him as the last and worthy representative of the grand council that was instituted in the days of Nehemiah, to administer the civil and religious affairs of Judea. When Ptolemy took the city of Jerusalem, Simon the Just was then in office, and this circumstance exercised a most beneficial influence over the future of the nation.

Ptolemy, a good and wise ruler, was, as we have before hinted, predisposed to favour the Jews, and as their own chief magistrate was a thorough patriot, and an able, as well as an honest, politician, the good intentions of the Egyptian king were able to be realised to their fullest extent. Ecclesiasticus (chap. 50, entitled the praise of Simon, son of

EBAL AND GERIZIM.

Onias) commemorates the restoration and fortification of the Temple by this excellent magistrate, and is devoted entirely to a eulogy of his public and private virtues.

Philadelphus, successor of Ptolemy Soter, maintained and even extended the privileges of the Jews. It was by his order that the first Greek version of the Old Testament was prepared, and deposited in the public library of Alexandria. This version, known as the Septuagint, served to propagate the Jewish religion among the Gentiles, and the Temple received in consequence many costly and magnificent offerings from neighbouring monarchs. The Jews were also specially favoured by Seleucus Nicator, king of Macedonia and Syria, who allowed them to settle in all the towns which he had founded in Asia Minor, and accorded them the same privileges as those enjoyed by his Greek and Macedonian subjects.

Under the Egyptian monarchs, the affairs of Judea preserved a favourable aspect until the reign of Ptolemy Philopater, during whose reign the nation suffered many vicissitudes. The Samaritans made constant incursions into the Jewish territory, and caused no small annoyance and loss of life and property. At this same epoch, too, Antiochus, king of Syria, made most determined efforts to obtain possession of Palestine, but was repulsed by the Egyptian sovereign. The latter paid a visit to Jerusalem, and offered up thanksgiving and sacrifice to the God of Israel for the victory which he had achieved. This visit resulted in disastrous consequences, for Ptolemy, actuated by an irresistible curiosity, attempted, in spite of the remonstrances of the priests and the cry of the people, to penetrate into the Temple. At the moment that he was about to push his profane curiosity to the extreme, and violate the sanctuary itself, he suddenly fell to the ground, we are told, stricken by an unaccountable terror, and was carried out in an almost lifeless condition. Whether he was irritated by the threatening murmurs which his attempt excited amongst the people, or whether he suspected some unseen human agency in the shock which he had received, and which had baffled him at the very moment when he appeared on the point of accomplishing his desire, certain it is that he exhibited from that day a violent animosity against the Jews. On his return to Egypt, he commenced a system of persecution against those who inhabited that country, revoked all their privileges, degraded them to the rank of the meanest of his subjects, and even condemned many of them to slavery and death. Although compelled subsequently to modify his sanguinary decrees, the Jews were, never, during the whole of his reign, restored to the full enjoyment of their rights.

When, after the death of Philopater, Antiochus invaded Cœle-Syria and Palestine, the Jews, whose fidelity to the Egyptian throne had been shaken by the capricious injustice of its last possessor, openly threw off their allegiance, and offered to place themselves at the disposal and under the protection of Antiochus. The Syrian monarch gladly accepted the offer, and, in return for the zeal and fidelity which they evinced, restored to Jerusalem its ancient privileges, granted from his own treasury a considerable sum of money for the restoration of their temple and worship, set at liberty all those who had been carried off captive in his dominions, and, in order to increase the stability and prosperity of the city, he issued a decree that all Jews, dispersed in different countries, who chose to return to their capital, should be exempt from all imposts for the space of three years.

The privileges accorded by Antiochus were maintained by Seleucus, his son and successor, who, moreover, decreed that the expenses of the sacrifices of the Temple should be defrayed from the royal treasury.

Intestine strife now began to endanger, and ultimately put an end to, the long and almost uninterrupted prosperity of the Jewish people. A fatal quarrel arose between Onias III., the high priest, and Simon, governor of the Temple; and the latter, actuated by a spirit of revenge, reported to the prince such an exaggerated account of the riches of the Temple, that, the cupidity of Seleucus becoming aroused, he determined to appropriate a part of the treasure to himself. Heliodorus his treasurer was commissioned to proceed at once to Jerusalem, and instructed to carry back with him the treasures to Antioch. The high priest endeavoured, but in vain, to dissuade him from executing the unjust decree, and protested that the greater part of the funds was destined only for the succour of the widows and orphans of Israel, and that some of it belonged to a private person named Hyrcanus. As Heliodorus continued inflexible, the priests and people fervently implored the God of Israel to protect His sanctuary. Nor were their prayers without effect; for Heliodorus, pursued by a terrible dream, hastened to quit the city, and declared to his royal master that he dared not further resist the power of the God Who protected it. Simon, furious at the failure of his infamous design, accused the high priest of having worked upon the imagination of the treasurer; but Onias succeeded in justifying himself before Seleucus, and the perfidious governor was driven into exile.

Shortly after the events we have just recorded, Antiochus Epiphanes ascended the throne of Syria. Jason, the brother of Onias, repaired to Antioch, and obtained from the king the office of high priest, by a bribe of 360 talents; he at the same time obtained an order against Onias, sentencing that just and excellent magistrate to exile and perpetual imprisonment at Antioch. This impious and treacherous priest exercised the functions of his sacred office in a manner worthy of the means by which it had been acquired. He first broke through the national exclusiveness, and violated the sanctity of the Holy City, by establishing therein a gymnasium, or public place for athletic exercises, after the Greek model; and then, pro-

ceeding to still greater enormities, he openly encouraged
the people to adopt the pagan superstitions and idolatrous
practices of their conqueror. From that time forth,
apostacy became the order of the day, and the Temple services were utterly neglected. After enjoying his ill-gotten
power for a few years, Jason was supplanted in the high
priesthood by his own brother, Menelaus, who employed
the self-same means for obtaining his end. Menelaus
offered 300 talents more than his brother had given, and
sold the holy vessels of the Temple in order to pay the
amount ; he moreover conciliated the favour of the courtiers
by large bribes, obtained by the same sacrilegious means.
Onias, who protested-against these outrages, was put to
death, and Menelaus proceeded to Jerusalem, to enter upon
the high priesthood, and at once expelled his brother Jason
from the city. The enormities which the latter had committed were eclipsed by the outrageous conduct of Menelaus, who openly renounced his faith and profession, and
adopted, together with his followers, the rites and habits
of the Greeks. At last his tyranny and oppression became
unbearable to the people, and a revolt at last broke out
in Jerusalem.

Antiochus was at this time making war on Egypt, and, a
false report of his death having been spread abroad, Jason
placed himself at the head of a thousand men, and marched
upon Jerusalem, where he inflicted severe chastisement
upon the partizans of Menelaus. The king of Syria, hear-
ing of this revolt, and irritated beyond measure at the rejoicings which had been manifested on the occasion of his
supposed death, hastened to Jerusalem, and gave up the
city to be sacked and pillaged by his soldiery for three
consecutive days. It is reported that more than 40,000
persons were massacred, and as many more sold into
slavery. The traitor Menelaus aided and abetted Antiochus
in his outrages, and, to crown his treachery, introduced
the Syrian tyrant into the very sanctuary of the Temple.

The Temple was robbed of all its treasures, including the
sacred vessels, and a pig was sacrificed upon the altar of
burnt offerings. Having thus desecrated the holy places,
and made the city flow with blood, the impious prince returned to Antioch, having entrusted the office of governor
of Jerusalem to a Phrygian named Philip, and that of
high priest to the perfidious Menelaus. As for Jason,
he had taken to flight on the first news of the approach of
Antiochus, and died miserably in exile some time after.

About two years after the events we have just described,
Antiochus sent Apollonius, the governor of Syria, to
Jerusalem, at the head of twenty thousand men, with orders
to destroy the city, to put the male inhabitants to the
sword, and to sell the women and children into slavery.
Arrived at Jerusalem, Apollonius disguised his designs
until the Sabbath, when he executed the barbarous commands of his master. The town was delivered over to
pillage, the houses set on fire, and the walls demolished;
the Temple itself was spared, but the Syrian soldiery
erected a fort before it, and prevented all persons from
coming thither to worship. Not content with these enormities, Antiochus determined to abolish altogether the
Jewish religion, and, if possible, entirely to exterminate
the race. With this intention, he issued an edict throughout his dominions, calling upon all the nations who were
subject to his authority to renounce their religion and
worship his gods, and this order he enforced with the most
severe pains and penalties. The Jews were the only
people who ventured to disobey the edict, whereupon,
Antiochus ordered them to be treated with the utmost
rigour, and sent to Jerusalem an old man named Atheneas,
who was well versed in the rites of the Greek worship, as
commissioner, to enforce obedience to his commands.

This old pagan dedicated the Temple to Jupiter Olympus,
and placed a statue of that false deity upon the altar of
burnt offering. This desecration was not confined to

Jerusalem, for everywhere throughout the Syrian empire groves and temples were dedicated, and statues and altars erected, to the heathen deities, and the worship of the true God was everywhere prohibited, and punished as the worst of crimes. That the chief fury of Antiochus's impious rage was directed against the Jews is evident from the fact that, whilst a general edict was published, condemning to death or torture all those who refused to worship the idols, a special decree was promulgated, by which it was made death to offer sacrifices to the God of Israel, observe the Sabbath, practise circumcision, or indeed to conform in the smallest degree to the precepts of the Mosaic law. Every effort was also made to destroy the copies of the Holy Scriptures ; and persons refusing to deliver them up were punished with death.

In this terrible distress, many of the Jews abandoned their homes and took shelter in the wilderness, where " they lived in the mountains after the manner of beasts, and fed on herbs continuously lest they should be partakers of the pollution " (2 Macc. v.). Of those who remained behind, some few yielded to the temptation, and saved themselves by apostacy, but the majority remained faithful to the God of their forefathers, Who, in His own good time, hearkened to the prayers of His people, and sent them a deliverer.

CHAPTER VIII.

THE MACCABEES.

Mattathias—Judas Maccabeus; defeats the Syrian forces—Miserable death of Antiochus Epiphanes—Antiochus Eupator continues the war; his forces under Lycias defeated by Judas—Siege of Beth-zura—Onias IV. builds a temple, and establishes a priesthood in Egypt—Failure of second Syrian invasion under Nicanor—Judas Maccabeus concludes a treaty with the Romans—Defeat and death of Judas Maccabeus—The Hassidim—The Syrians evacuate Judea—Jonathan reorganises the government; defeats Apollonius in Philistia; is taken prisoner and treacherously murdered by Tryphon— Simon—John Hyrcanus—Aristobulus I. proclaimed King of Judea—Alexander Jannai—Civil war brought about by the Pharisees—Alexandra— Disputes between Hyrcanus II. and Aristobulus; they appeal to Pompey; the latter besieges and captures the city—Machinations of Antipater— Death of Aristobulus and his son—Licinius Crassus.

A LEARNED and venerable priest named Mattathias, of the family of the Asmoneans, withdrew himself, together with his five sons, to Modin, his native city, in order to escape the persecutions which were desolating Jerusalem. When one of the royal commissioners arrived at Modin, with orders to compel the people to conform to the decrees of Antiochus, Mattathias and his five sons stoutly and manfully withstood him, and refused to sacrifice to the idols, or to renounce the law of their fathers. For some time they confined themselves to a verbal protest, but presently, a Jew having come forward to offer up the sacrifice required of him by the authorities, Mattathias, in conformity with the law of Moses (Deut. xiii. 9), killed him on the spot with his own hand. This daring act so inflamed the patriotic ardour of the bystanders that they fell upon the commissioner and his followers and put them all to death ; then, running through the city, Mattathias and his sons called upon all who loved their country and were zealous for the law of the Lord to strike for the defence of Israel. Numbers flocked to his standard and sought refuge in the wilderness of Judea. Here they were followed by the army of Antiochus, who, knowing their religious scruples, attacked them on the Sabbath, when many of them perished without making any resistance. After this disaster, a decree was made and sanctioned by the priests, permitting the people to defend themselves upon the Sabbath; and this permission was secretly communicated to all the Jews of Palestine and its vicinity.

The result of this dispensation soon made itself felt: the next time Mattathias and his friends were attacked upon a Sabbath, they defended themselves with desperate valour, and the soldiers of Antiochus, who had not ex pected any resistance, were taken by surprise and ignc miniously defeated. This gave fresh impetus to the cause, and their numbers were daily increased; in less than a year, they had completely gained the mastery in Palestine, the idols were once more broken down, and the worship of the true God and the practice of the law were re-established. Unhappily, in the midst of this glorious career, Mattathias was surprised by death; but, before breathing his last, he earnestly exhorted his sons to follow in his footsteps, and to devote their lives to the service of their God, their country, and their law.

Mattathias was succeeded by his son Judas, surnamed Maccabeus, one of the noblest heroes of Jewish history. With his devoted little band of 6,000 men, he reduced the principal fortresses of Judea; made himself formidable to the Syrians and Samaritans; routed the apostates, and offered an asylum to all Jews who would range themselves under his banner. Antiochus Epiphanes in vain attempted to stifle the rebellion. Judas bravely encountered the armies sent against him, and in less than a year had conquered in no less than five battles. In the last of these, Lysias, governor of Syria, with an army of 60,000

L

men, was completely routed and put to flight. This
victory completely established the power and reputation
of the Maccabeans, who at once marched upon, and
took possession of, Jerusalem. They could not drive
the Syrians from the fortress of Mount Acra, which overlooked the Temple, but they fortified the sacred enclosure ;
and, having defended it by a strong garrison, proceeded to
the restoration of the services and the purification of the
desecrated spots. Jealous of these successes, the neighbouring nations made common cause with the Syrians
against the Hebrews, and endeavoured to check their advancing power ; but it was in vain, for Judas and his
brethren gave them battle, and defeated them with great
slaughter.

Antiochus, who was just returning from an unsuccessful
expedition against Persia, was frantic with rage when he
heard of the revolt of the Jews and the total defeat of his
forces in Palestine. He swore that he would utterly exterminate the Jewish nation, and abolish the worship of
their God ; but, scarcely had he uttered this blasphemous
oath, when he was attacked by a loathsome and incurable
disease. Recognising, when it was too late, the folly and
wickedness of which he had been guilty, he expressed the
most lively sorrow, and desired to appease the offended
God of Israel by repairing the Temple and enriching it
with costly offerings. But his disease rapidly grew worse ;
and, as the author of the Book of Maccabees tells us,
" Thus the murderer and blasphemer, having suffered
most grievously, as he entreated other men, so died he a
miserable death in a strange country in the mountains."
He was succeeded by his son, Antiochus Eupator, who continued the war against the Jews.

Shortly after the death of Antiochus, Judas Maccabeus
laid siege to the fort of Acra, to which we have before
alluded as commanding the Temple. The young king,
with his guardian Lysias, at once led a large army into

Judea, consisting of 100,000 foot, 20,000 horse, 50 elephants, and 300 war chariots, determined, once and for all, to crush the rebellion. Judas Maccabeus immediately raised the siege of Acra, and hastened to meet the advancing foe. By a skilful manœuvre he surprised the enemy by night, killed a large number of them, and, having thrown the camp into confusion, retired in good order to Jerusalem.

The Maccabeans had placed a strong garrison at Bethzura, relying mainly upon the strength of this frontier fortress to withstand an invading force. To this the army of Antiochus now laid siege ; and, having gained possession of the stronghold, they marched without impediment to Jerusalem and commenced the blockade of the city. The garrison defended themselves with heroism, but, being badly provisioned,* they were not able to withstand a protracted siege. Providentially, the rumour of an insurrection in Syria compelled the besiegers to conclude a peace upon advantageous terms.

The king had no sooner entered into the city than, in open violation of the treaty to which he had sworn, he commanded the fortifications to be destroyed.

Menelaus, the apostate high priest, had accompanied the Syrian army into Judea, and Lysias, the commander-in-chief, now accused him of having instigated the war. Upon this charge, he was put to a cruel death ; and Antiochus conferred the high priesthood upon one Alcimus, of whose previous history we know but little, but who proved himself by his subsequent acts a worthy successor of the detestable Menelaus. The Jews, however, were well acquainted with his disreputable character, and refused to allow him actually to exercise the sacerdotal functions.

* This was in consequence of the year being the Sabbatical one, during which time the land was allowed to lie fallow. and all agricultural operations were suspended.

When Menelaus died, Onias, son of Onias III. who had
been murdered at Antioch, expected to succeed to the
dignity. The appointment of Alcimus having disappointed
his hopes, he retired in disgust to Egypt; there he
sought and obtained from Ptolemy Philometor and Queen
Cleopatra permission to erect a temple for the Jews in
their dominions, alleging as a pretext that the prophet
Isaiah had predicted that there should be an " altar to
the Lord in the midst of the land of Egypt " (Isaiah
xix. 19). Sufficient funds being placed at his disposal, and
a site being granted him at Heliopolis, he erected a temple
after the model of that at Jerusalem, though of smaller proportions, where he exercised the functions of high priest;
and, in concert with priests and Levites of his own ordain-
ing, carried on the services of the Temple in precisely the
same manner as in the capital of Judea.

Alcimus, when he found that the Jews would not receive
him, had no alternative left but to betake himself to
Antioch and lay his case before the king. But, on his
arrival, he found that Demetrius, son of Seleucus Philo-
pator, and brother of Antiochus Epiphanes, and consequently legitimate heir to the crown, had put Antiochus
to death, and seated himself upon the throne. Demetrius, however, espoused his cause, and sent a large army
into Palestine, under the command of Bacchides, governor
of Mesopotamia, and of Nicanor, governor of Judea.

Nicanor, on his arrival before Jerusalem, was unwilling
to commence hostilities against Judas, by whom he had
been already defeated, and whose prowess he feared, and
he accordingly adopted a temporising policy. His whole
energy was concentrated upon a scheme for entrapping
Judas and his immediate followers, and for this purpose
he abstained for some time from hostilities, and when the
suspicions of the people were completely disarmed, he
invited the Maccabean general and his brethren to a conference, with the ostensible object of concluding a final

peace. Being foiled in this attempt, and his treachery having been discovered, he was forced to give Judas battle, and an engagement took place at Caphar Salameh, near Jerusalem, in which the Syrian army was completely routed, and Nicanor himself forced to take refuge in the City of Zion. Penetrating into the Temple itself, he swore that he would burn it to the ground unless Judas were delivered into his hands. But his impious threat was never destined to be carried into effect; for, having encamped shortly afterwards at Beth-horon, he was attacked by Judas with a reinforcement of 3,000 men ; his army was completely routed, and he himself perished miserably in the combat.

Not long after this, Judas concluded a treaty of alliance with the Romans, who had already once used their influence at the court of Antioch on behalf of the Jews. But, before his ambassadors returned from Rome with the proclamation of the senate in favour of the Jews, Demetrius sent Bacchides into Judea, at the head of 22,000 of his picked troops, to avenge the death of Nicanor, and re-establish Alcimus in the high priesthood. Judas's little band of 3,000 men was cowed by the presence of this gigantic force ; all but 800 of them fled in terror, and the Maccabean leader was left with this handful of soldiers to withstand the army of the idolaters. Such a contest could have but one result. The little band of heroes fought with the courage of despair ; at one time they even seemed to be gaining the advantage, for they turned the enemy's right and pursued them as far as Mount Azotus, but the left wing quickly turned and fell upon their rear. Hemmed in on every side, the Maccabeans were speedily overcome ; a few only managed to cut their way through the enemy's ranks, the rest were left dead upon the field, and Judas Maccabeus himself was amongst the slain.

On the death of Judas, Bacchides took possession of Jerusalem without resistance, and established Alcimus in his office with much pomp. Now that a Greek general and a Grecianized Jew were masters of the Holy City, the apostates, who during the lifetime of Judas had not dared to set foot within it, returned in large numbers; those who remained faithful to the law, and especially the immediate partizans of the Maccabees, were soon left in the minority, and subjected to a bitter persecution. The members of the patriotic party, and particularly the association of men, under the name of Hassidim, by whom the Maccabean movement had been supported and maintained, were hunted down and put to the most shameful and cruel deaths. The worst impieties of Jason's and Menelaus's time were enacted over again, and the epoch was a darker one for the fortunes of the faithful in Israel than even the Babylonian captivity itself had been. But the warlike spirit of the Maccabees was not yet extinct; Jonathan, the brother of Judas, still lived, and in him the Jews had found a worthy successor. This leader prosecuted the war against the Syrians with so much success that, distracted as their kingdom was by internal dissensions, they were compelled ultimately to evacuate Judea.

Jonathan then devoted himself to the establishment of a regular form of government on the ancient model of that of the Judges of Israel; he restored the fortifications of Jerusalem, and executed other important public works, so that, under his sway, the Holy City began to assume something of her ancient glory. By the unanimous vote of the people he was invested with the dignity of high priest, an office which had not been filled up since the death of Alcimus, seven years before. The fame of Jonathan's deeds soon travelled beyond the limits of Judea, and even such powerful nations as the Romans and Lacedemonians found it to their interest to have the Maccabean priest for their ally.

The affairs of Syria itself were at this time in a most

disordered state, and in the year 153 B.C. a youth named
Balas was encouraged by certain political parties who
were intriguing at Rome to personate Alexander, a deceased son of Antiochus Epiphanes, and lay claim to the
throne of Syria. Jonathan, remembering the injuries
which Demetrius had heaped upon his nation, declared
for the pseudo-Alexander, and mainly contributed to the
success of the pretender, who shortly after ascended the
throne of Syria. But Alexander, or Balas, did not long
enjoy his usurped power, and a few years after, Demetrius,
son of the deposed monarch, regained the paternal throne.
The new king appointed Apollonius his general, and the
latter, collecting a large force, immediately advanced against
Jonathan, to punish him for the hostility which he had
displayed towards his master's family.

Apollonius had encamped at Jamnia, from whence he
challenged Jonathan to come out from his rocky stronghold and give him battle in the open plain. Jonathan,
without hesitation, accepted the challenge, and marched
from Jerusalem to Joppa, which place he wrested from the
hands of Apollonius's garrison. The Syrian general then
proceeded to Ashdod, whither he was pursued by Jonathan,
and the latter would have probably succumbed to an am-
buscade which had been prepared for him on the way,
had he not been opportunely reinforced by the troops of
his brother Simon, who had come up to the rescue.
The united Jewish forces completely routed Apollonius's
army, who took to flight, many of them seeking refuge
in the Temple of Dagon at Ashdod. But the sanctuary of
a heathen god was of little avail against the soldiers of the
Lord of Hosts, and the Jews attacked the temple, burnt
it to the ground, and slew 8,000 of the Syrian refugees.
The town of Ashdod itself was also destroyed by fire ; the
neighbouring city of Ascalon surrendered ; and Jonathan
returned in triumph to Jerusalem. Subsequently to the
events which we have just related, Jonathan entered into

ASHDOD.

an alliance with King Demetrius, and rendered him important services; but, finding him unfaithful to his engagements, he seceded from his cause. Deprived of the powerful support of the Maccabean leader, Demetrius II. was, in his turn, dethroned by Antiochus VI., a son of Alexander Balas. The young king found in Jonathan a faithful and powerful ally, and Tryphon, a Syrian general, who had mainly contributed towards establishing Antiochus on the throne, but who now was plotting his destruction, saw in the very faithfulness of the Hebrew leader a fatal obstacle to the success of his schemes, and accordingly resolved upon his destruction. With this object, he decoyed him into the fortress of Ptolemais (now St. Jean d'Acre), and there detained him a prisoner, and murdered his escort.

Tryphon then prepared to march upon Jerusalem, but, as the people had been exhorted by Simon, the younger brother of Judas and Jonathan, to fight for their country and their God, he found the city strongly fortified and garrisoned against him; instead, therefore, of storming the city, he demanded of Simon a hundred talents of silver and two of his children as hostages, promising that, if these demands were agreed to, he would deliver up the captive Jonathan. Simon, although putting but little faith in Tryphon's word, was yet unwilling to let a chance go by of saving his brother's life and restoring him to freedom. The money and hostages were accordingly handed over to Tryphon, who, as Simon had expected, withdrew without performing his part of the agreement. Proceeding into Gilead, he basely murdered Jonathan, after which he returned to Syria. Simon, however, recovered his brother's body, and buried it in the family mausoleum at Modin.

After the death of Jonathan, Simon was unanimously chosen to succeed him in the office of high priest. His rule was distinguished by the same valour and discretion which had rendered that of his brother so famous and so fortunate for Judea. He repaired the fortresses of Judea, took and destroyed the tower of Acre, and renewed the treaties with the Romans and Lacedemonians. He also took advantage of the internal dissensions of the Syrian kingdom to augment the power and importance of his own nation, and espoused the cause of Demetrius, who was then contending for the sovereignty with Tryphon— for the latter had murdered his young *protégé* Antiochus, and usurped the disputed crown. Demetrius gladly accepted Simon's proffered assistance, and in return granted him the title and privileges of an independent prince. Under his reign, Judea once more enjoyed prosperity and peace. It is true that this tranquillity was from time to time threatened, particularly by the fall of Demetrius, and by the accession of his son Antiochus, who, unlike his father, displayed a spirit of hostility against the Jews: but Simon had taken advantage of the times of peace to so strengthen the defences and resources of the country that it was enabled to withstand the invasion of foreign foes. Alas! it was shortly destined to experience a severer and more insidious attack from treachery within. Ptolemy, the son-in-law of Simon, who had been promoted by him to the post of governor of Jericho, himself aspired to the priesthood, and, having invited Simon to a banquet, caused him to be treacherously murdered. Thus, after a short but brilliant reign of eight years, died Simon, the last of the sons of Mattathias, the deliverer of Israel.

Antiochus Sidetes, who was then king of Syria, took advantage of the death of Simon once more to invade Palestine, and this time with complete success. The Jews were forced to lay down their arms, to demolish the fortifications of Jerusalem, and to submit to the payment of an annual tribute. But the death of Antiochus (which happened not long afterwards in an expedition against the Parthians), and the internal dissensions in Syria which followed that event, enabled Hyrcanus, Simon's son and successor, to cast off the foreign yoke. The career of this prince was distinguished by a series of brilliant successes. He made war upon the nation of the Idumeans, reduced them to complete subjection, and compelled them to forsake their idolatry and embrace the Jewish faith. The Samaritans in turn yielded to his arms, and their temple on Mount Gerizim was destroyed. After a prosperous reign of twenty-nine years, Hyrcanus died, amidst the universal regrets of the nation. He was succeeded by his eldest son Aristobulus, who assumed the office of king in addition to that of high priest, being the first since the Babylonian captivity who had assumed that title.

Although successful against foreign enemies, Aristobulus was a cruel and extortionate tyrant to his own people; to his other crimes he added that of matricide, and died, after a short reign, a prey to the bitterest remorse.

His death raised his brother, Alexander Jannai, from a prison to the throne. This prince was also of a warlike disposition, and achieved signal successes against the Philistines, and the people of Arabia, Gilead, and Moab. But his reign was a turbulent and unhappy one. The Pharisees, against whom his father, John Hyrcanus, had issued the most stringent laws, found in him an implacable enemy. Their intrigues soon excited a rebellion against his authority, and a civil war followed, which lasted six years, was equally disastrous to both parties, and cost the lives of more than 50,000 men. The party of Alexander, however, at last triumphed in a decisive battle. He died in the twenty-seventh year of his reign, leaving the sovereignty and the guardianship of his children to his wife Alexandra.

Acting on the last advice of her husband, the queen adopted a conciliatory policy towards the Pharisees, entrusting some of the most important offices of state to the chiefs of this sect. But even this did not tend towards

the peace of the kingdom, for she shortly found herself
embroiled with the opposing sect of the Sadducees. She
died, after a reign of nine years, and was succeeded by her
eldest son, Hyrcanus II., who already exercised the functions of high priest. Hardly had he mounted the throne,
when his brother Aristobulus, with a large army, made
head against him, and forced him to resign both offices.
Antipater, governor of Idumea, and father of Herod the
Great, espoused Hyrcanus's cause, and having obtained
the assistance of Aretas, king of Arabia, the three allies
assembled a large army and besieged Aristobulus in Jerusalem. The latter now called in the assistance of the
Romans, and induced them by rich presents to favour his
cause. Aretas was commanded by the senate to evacuate
the country, and did not dare disobey the order, whereupon,
Aristobulus, being the stronger of the two, appeased his
vengeance by a massacre of the adherents of Hyrcanus.
The two brothers now resolved to commit their dispute to
the arbitration of Pompey the Great, commander-in-chief
of the Roman forces in the East.

The Roman general, having heard the arguments on
both sides, promised to consider them carefully and to
pronounce a speedy decision ; but Aristobulus, impatient of
the delay, and probably not feeling much confidence in
the justice of his own cause, occupied the interim by
making preparations for war. The implied insult to
Pompey's integrity irritated him beyond measure, and,
casting Aristobulus into prison, he marched for Jerusalem
with all his army.

The partizans of Hyrcanus opened the gates for him and
his troops, while the followers of Aristobulus ensconced
themselves in the Temple enclosure, and there awaited a
siege. After a siege of three months, the Romans made themselves masters of the stronghold. The too strict and superstitious observance of the Sabbath again caused the defeat
of the Jews ; for, although the decree issued at the com-

mencement of the Maccabean period allowed them to defend themselves when actually attacked on the holy day, they did not consider themselves justified in taking the offensive, when the Romans, taking the advantage of the Sabbath, planted their engines against the walls, and made every preparation for an assault.

The carnage which ensued was frightful; more than 12,000 persons fell by the enemy's sword, or perished by their own hands, while the priests allowed themselves to be butchered without resistance, in the very act of offering up the sacrifices. The day on which the Romans gained possession of Jerusalem was the very one which had been set apart as a solemn fast, to commemorate the taking of the city by Nebuchadnezzar.

Pompey, like all its former conquerors, was curious to examine the interior of the Temple, and penetrated into the sanctuary in company with several of his officers. Unlike his predecessors, however, he respected the sanctity of the place, and commanded that the sacrifices and other services should be resumed.

On the day when the Roman general took Jerusalem, the independence of the Jewish nation was at an end. Hyrcanus, it is true, regained the dignity of high priest and the title of prince; but he reigned as the mere tributary and vassal of the Roman Senate. Pompey, indeed, pro- vided against any future struggle being made by the Jews to regain their freedom; for he destroyed the walls of Jerusalem, freed Samaria and the cities of the sea- coast, took from the people all the places appertaining to Cœle-Syria of which they had become possessed by con- quest, confined the limits of their territory to the strict boundaries of Judea Proper, and made it an express con- dition of the treaty that they should attempt no further conquests.

Judea was now a prey to civil discords. Alexander, the son of Aristobulus, had found means to escape from Rome, whither he had been carried by Pompey with his father and brother, and appeared in Palestine at the head of a numerous army. Hyrcanus had abandoned the reins of government to Antipater. This minister appears to have been a most designing and ambitious man, and, recognising that whatever power existed in Judeá was held from the Romans, he lost no opportunity of ingratiating himself with that people, and with their assistance easily

POMPEY'S PILLAR.

suppressed the rebellion. Aristobulus himself shortly afterwards escaped from captivity, and joined the disaffected party; but his attempt was likewise unsuccessful, and he himself was retaken prisoner. A few years later, he was set at liberty by Julius Cæsar, who hoped by his means to bring the Jews over to his side, to aid him in his contest with Pompey. The partizans of Pompey, however, put the unfortunate ex-monarch and his son Alexander to death.

Licinius Crassus was now appointed by the Roman Senate governor of Syria. Before setting out for the East, he obtained a decree, empowering him to make war against the Parthians, and was invested with all the power and authority necessary for raising men and money to carry out the undertaking. On his way, he passed by Jerusalem, and made use of his authority to strip the Temple of all the treasures which Pompey had left untouched; the amount of plunder thus obtained exceeded 10,000 Attic talents (nearly two-and-a-half millions of pounds sterling). Crassus's expedition against the Parthians came to a disastrous end; his army was completely routed, whilst he himself and his only son were slain.

The power and influence of Antipater was now daily increasing. After the death of Pompey, Cæsar rewarded him for his services in Egypt by conferring upon him the privileges of a Roman citizen, and naming him his lieutenant in Judea; he also confirmed Hyrcanus in the dignity of high priest.

CHAPTER IX.

THE HERODIAN FAMILY.

Judea under Julius Cæsar—Death of Antipater—Intrigues of Hyrcanus—Herod escapes to Rome; is proclaimed king of Judea; captures Jerusalem—Character of Herod; his crimes; he rebuilds the Temple—THE BIRTH OF OUR LORD —Death of Herod—Archelaus—Roman governors—Pontius Pilate—Herod Antipas—Accession of the Emperor Caligula; he proposes to set up a statue of himself in the Temple; his death—Herod Agrippa; his blasphemy and awful end—Agrippa II.—Cuspius Fadus—Tiberius Alexander—Cumanus—Collision between the Roman soldiers and the Jews—Felix—Symptoms of the revolt—Anti-Christs—"The Zealots"—Troubles at Cæsarea—Albinus—Gessius Florus.

UNDER Julius Cæsar, the Roman yoke pressed lightly on the Jews, for they were allowed to rebuild the fortifications of Jerusalem which Pompey had destroyed, and were granted numerous other privileges. Antipater, though nominally second to Hyrcanus the high priest, now exercised the supreme power in Judea, in his capacity as Roman procurator. His unbounded influence and his Idumean extraction provoked the jealousy of the national party, who conspired to murder him and his four sons, amongst whom the afterwards notorious Herod was most conspicuous; for the latter he had obtained the government of Galilee, and for his eldest son, Phazael, that of Jerusalem. Hyrcanus would willingly have rid himself of this troublesome family, but found it impossible to extricate himself from the meshes which they had thrown around him. The troubles in Rome, consequent upon the death of Julius Cæsar, enabled Antigonus, nephew of Hyrcanus, to carry partly into effect the designs of the national party, of which he was the head. Antipater was poisoned. Hyrcanus was dethroned, and, together with Phazael, thrown into prison. Herod sought safety in flight, first betaking himself to Egypt, and then to Rome, where he pleaded for assistance against Antigonus : Mark Antony, who was then at the summit of his power, declared him king of Judea, upon which he returned at the head of a numerous army to Palestine, and made himself master of Galilee.

Jerusalem for some time resisted the force of his arms, but by the aid of reinforcements sent him by Sosias, governor of Syria, he succeeded in reducing the city after a siege of six months. The usual scene of carnage ensued upon the taking of the city, and Antigonus, the last prince of the illustrious house of the Asmoneans, perished in the general slaughter.

The Idumean Herod now ascended the throne of Judea. This prince, one of the most detestable tyrants of which history makes mention, commenced his reign by a series of murders, and a horrible system of persecution directed against the partizans of Antigonus. All the richest and most influential among their number fell victims to his cupidity and hate. The aged Hyrcanus, who had taken refuge among the Parthians, was induced by the most solemn promises of protection to return to Jerusalem, and was then assassinated. Aristobulus, the grandson and successor of Hyrcanus in the priesthood, was suffocated in a bath, and the beautiful Mariamne, a daughter of the house of the Asmoneans, whom Herod had espoused, fell a victim to her husband's blind and senseless jealousy. It seems as though Herod had nourished the national enmity against the Jews for which his race was distinguished, and had determined to make use of his power, to revenge the forced conversion of his country to Judaism, by heaping contempt and disgrace upon the Jews, their religion and their law. He deprived the high priests of the right of hereditary succession, appointing and removing them according to the caprice of the sovereign ; he abolished the authority of the Sanhedrin ; destroyed the archives of the Jews ;

M

raised temples and statues to the heathen deities ; set aside days to be kept as holy days in honour of Augustus ; constructed an amphitheatre for the disgusting and inhuman exhibitions of gladiatorial combats ; and, in a word, conformed in every particular to the manners and customs of Pagan Rome.

But with all his brutality, and his contempt for all laws human and Divine, he was sufficiently foresighted to perceive that, without conciliating in some way the favour of the masses, his power, and consequently his means of indulgence, must be of short duration. He therefore maintained his open profession of the Hebrew faith, and even displayed considerable zeal for the restoration of the glories of the Holy City. Thanks to his unscrupulous exactions, his treasury was so amply filled that his wealth appeared inexhaustible, and he accordingly determined upon rebuilding the Temple in a style of magnificence which should rival that of Solomon himself; for in this work was a ready means of at once gratifying his ambition and taste for display, and of strengthening his power by conciliating the people—and all this at little or no sacrifice to himself.

The following is Josephus's account of the Temple of Herod, as he himself beheld it :—

" Herod accordingly, at an incalculable expense, and in a style of unsurpassed magnificence, in the fifteenth year of his reign, restored the Temple, and breasted up with a wall the area around it, so as to enlarge it to twice its former extent. An evidence of its sumptuousness were the ample colonnades around the holy place, and the fort on its northern side. The colonnades he reared from the foundation ; the fort, in nothing inferior to a palace, he repaired at an immense cost, and called it Antonia, in honour of Antony."—*Bellum Judaicum*, book i., chap. 21. (Traill's translation.)

" The Temple, as I have said, was seated on a strong

hill. Originally, the level space on its summit scarcely sufficed for the sanctuary and the altar, the ground about being abrupt and steep ; but King Solomon, who built the sanctuary, having completely walled up the eastern side, a colonnade was built upon the embankment ; on the other side the sanctuary remained exposed. In process of time, however, as people were constantly adding to the embankment, the hill became level and broader. They also threw down the northern wall, and enclosed as much ground as the circuit of the Temple at large subsequently occupied. After having surrounded the hill from the base with a triple wall, and accomplished a work which surpassed all expectation, they built the upper boundary walls and the lower court of the Temple. The lowest part of the latter they built up from a depth of 300 cubits, and in some places more. The entire depth of the foundations, however, was not discernible, for, with a view to level the streets of the town, they filled up the ravines to a considerable extent. There were stones used in the building which measured 40 cubits."

" The entire circuit of the cloisters, including the Antonia, measured six furlongs."—(Book v., chap. 5.)

After centuries of wars and rumours of wars, the earth was now at peace, and the Temple of Janus was closed for the first time since the idolatrous nations of the earth had bowed down before the arch-idolater Rome, and the conquering eagles been raised in mocking pride over the very sanctuary of the one true God.

The world thus at peace, Cæsar, yielding to the intoxication of irresponsible power, allowed himself to be addressed by titles appropriate only to the Deity, and boastingly ascribed the universal peace to himself; but a greater than Cæsar was to come, and while his star had already passed its meridian, and was even now verging on its decline, the never-setting star of Bethlehem arose, and heralded the advent of the Prince of Peace.

M 2

ВиѲлеемъ.

A year after the birth of our Lord, Herod, that monster of cruelty, died of a painful and horrible disease. Knowing full well that his death would be hailed with general joy and satisfaction, he seized upon the heads of all th' chief Jewish families, and gave orders that they should all be put to death as soon as he himself had expired, for he was determined, he said, that the nation should mourn his decease. These iniquitous orders were fortunately never carried into effect. After the death of Herod, Augustus divided the kingdom of Judea amongst the sons of the late king.

For some years the brothers governed Palestine with equity and moderation; but Archelaus, having later on obtained half the kingdom, under the title of Exarch, behaved with such tyranny and injustice that the Jews and Samaritans combined to accuse him before Augustus; and in consequence of this appeal, Archelaus was deposed and sent into exile. From this moment, Judea became both nominally and actually a Roman province, being governed by prefects appointed according to the caprice of the emperor. The Jewish authorities were no longer permitted to exercise their functions, and justice was administered in the name of the Romans and according to their laws. The taxes were collected by the process known as "farming," which is still practised in Turkish dominions. Each district, instead of being accurately assessed, was sold to the highest bidder, who was empowered to levy taxes in the name of the government; and so long as the amount stipulated for was paid into the imperial treasury, the Roman authorities troubled themselves but little as to the amount actually levied by the collector, or the means employed by him to extort it: these tax-farmers were called *publicani*, the "publicans" of the New Testament.

The Roman governors of Judea professed a great contempt for the Jewish religion and worship, and lost no opportunity of displaying it. Pontius Pilate introduced into the Holy City all the emblems of pagan worship and authority, and, under the pretext of constructing an aqueduct to Jerusalem, committed fresh depredations upon the treasures of the Temple.

Seven years after the crucifixion of our Lord, the retribution came, and Pontius Pilate, as Josephus tells us, was at last called to account for his tyrannical and dishonest policy in Judea. Condemned by the Roman authorities, he was sent into exile, and perished miserably by his own hands, some say at Vienne in France, others on a mountain in the neighbourhood of Lucerne, which still bears his name.

The flickering flame of Jewish independence was soon to be extinguished for ever. But, before that moment came, it flared up for a short time into something of its former brightness. Herod Agrippa, a grandson of Herod the Great, had been educated at Rome, and had obtained the favour of the Emperor Caligula, by whom he was appointed to the tetrarchy of Philip, with the title of king.

His uncle, Herod Antipas, was also soon afterwards deprived of his tetrarchy of Galilee in favour of Agrippa.

It was during the reign of the latter that the infamous and crazy Emperor Caligula issued a decree which commanded that Divine honours should be paid to him throughout the Roman dominions. A special order was sent to the governor of Jerusalem to erect a statue of the emperor in the sanctuary of the Temple. Touched by the piteous prayers of the people that they might be spared this supreme desecration, Petronius, the governor, and King Agrippa, who was in great favour at the Roman court, pleaded for a revocation of the decree. The emperor was with some difficulty induced to consent, and his death, which happened shortly after, insured the non-violation of his promise.

On the death of Caligula, Claudius ascended the throne, and it was mainly to the assistance of Herod Agrippa that he owed his elevation. To requite him for these services, the emperor added Judea, Samaria, and Idumea to the dominions which he already possessed, so that his kingdom was really greater in extent than that of his grandfather Herod. Although a Roman by education, he was strongly attached to the national religion, and, in order to gain some additional popularity amongst his fellow-countrymen, he commenced a series of cruel persecutions against the now fast-increasing sect of Christians. Having once entered upon his evil courses, his arrogance and impiety knew no bounds, and he even allowed some deputies from the cities of Tyre and Sidon to address him as a god.

He had determined to commence hostilities against the two places in question, and these men were sent to dissuade him from the proposed expedition, and to obtain terms. The scene which took place on the occasion, and the speedy and tragical punishment which followed upon Herod's impious assumption of Divine honours, are briefly but graphically told in the New Testament: "And upon a set day, Herod, arrayed in royal apparel, sat upon his throne, and made an oration unto them. And the people gave a shout, saying, It is the voice of a god, and not of a man. And immediately the angel of the Lord smote him, because he gave not God the glory : and he was eaten up of worms, and gave up the ghost " (Acts xii. 21—23).

His death was deeply deplored by his Jewish subjects ; for, with all his faults, his attachment to the national cause had been steadfast and sincere ; but the non-Jewish inhabitants of the country had regarded him with feelings of anything but affection. At Cæsarea, the Roman garrison gave expression to their satisfaction at the event in so extravagant and indecent a manner that the Emperor Claudius determined to remove the cohorts from Palestine. Unfortunately, as we shall presently see, he was induced to abandon this intention.

On the death of Herod Agrippa, Judea was again

reduced to the name and condition of a Roman province. His son, Agrippa II., was too young to be entrusted with so important a position, and his uncle Herod was appointed superintendent of the Temple and Treasury, with the title of King of Chalcis, while Cuspius Fadus was sent as governor to Judea.

Cuspius Fadus was succeeded by one Tiberius Alexander, an apostate Jew, and a nephew of the celebrated Philo, the historian of Alexandria. He held office for two years, during which King Herod of Chalcis died. Agrippa II. (the King Agrippa of the Acts of the Apostles) succeeded him in his titles and office.

It was under the next governor, Ventidius Cumanus, that the spirit of discontent and rebellion which had so long smouldered in the bosoms of the Jewish people, as one by one their privileges were snatched away, at last burst out into a flame of open revolt.

Shortly after the arrival of Cumanus, the festival of the Passover was celebrated at Jerusalem; and as on these occasions immense multitudes were assembled in the city, the Roman procurator sent for some additional troops, to maintain order amongst the worshippers. By a singularly unlucky chance, the cohorts thus brought to Jerusalem were the very same which had been censured by the authorities for their extravagant exhibition of animosity against the Jews at Cæsarea. The fortress of Antonia, in which the garrison was quartered, overlooked the Temple area, and during one of the public services some of the Roman soldiers expressed their contempt for the proceedings by indecent gestures. The enthusiasm of the people, already inspired by the solemnity of the service, was suddenly changed into the uncontrollable fury of fanaticism, and they declared that Cumanus had himself instigated the affront. The Roman governor behaved with great moderation, and, being unable to appease the people, ordered the rest of the soldiery into the fort. The crowd, misunderstanding the manœuvre, and imagining that they were about to be attacked, were seized by a sudden panic, and in endeavouring to escape from the Temple area they trampled each other to death by thousands in the narrow outlets.

Frequent collisions now took place between the Jews and the Roman authorities, and the Samaritans, taking advantage of the growing impatience of the latter, commenced a series of outrages upon their Galilean neighbours ; Cumanus, as was to be expected, sided with the Samaritans, but, upon appeal being made to Rome, a decision was given in favour of the Jews, and the procurator was recalled.

Felix, an emancipated slave, and an infamous creature of the Emperor Claudius, was the next governor of Judea. His public career was marked by the worst vices of Oriental despotism. His rapacity and injustice drove the people to madness, so that in their despair they listened to the voice of every impostor who promised them deliverance. As our Lord had predicted, false prophets and antichrists continually appeared, attracting crowds of deluded followers to their banners, only to furnish fresh victims for the stern military despotism of Rome.

One of these antichrists, an Egyptian Jew, who had led a disorderly band into Palestine, succeeded in assembling no fewer than 30,000 men upon the Mount of Olives, promising that at his command the walls of the city should fall down, and that the people, freed for ever from the Roman yoke, should triumphantly enter in. The misguided mob were attacked by Felix's troops, and nearly all were either cut to pieces on the spot or taken prisoners. These continued disasters weakened the national party, and hastened the catastrophe that was so surely to come. Another fatal blow to Judaism was the introduction of the Sicarii into the city of Jerusalem. Jonathan the high priest had continually besought Felix to mend his

ways, reminding him that it was through his influence that
the Roman governor had obtained his appointment. In
order to rid himself of so troublesome an acquaintance,
Felix determined to have recourse to assassination, and
the instruments were ready to his hand in the Jewish
order of the " Zealots." This association had grown out
of the Maccabean movement, and the name by which they
were known, and the principles which they professed, were
derived from the last words of Mattathias, "Be ye zealots
for the Law, and sacrifice your lives for it." They bound
themselves by a terrible oath to observe the following
tenets : To acknowledge God as the sole spiritual and
temporal King of the nation ; to ignore all temporal
authority ; cheerfully to sacrifice their own lives and those
of all who were near and dear to them, in the cause of the
Law and of the liberty of the Jews ; to consider all means
lawful in order to compass this end ; and lastly, to grant
no quarter, either to the Romans, or to those unworthy
Jews who upheld their sway.

Amongst the members of such an association as this, it
was easy for the tyrant to find instruments to carry out
his project ; and, having impressed upon a certain number
of them the fact that Jonathan had shown himself favourable to the Roman rule, he bade them join the crowd of
worshippers who were going up to the Temple. The "Zealots," who carried daggers concealed beneath their garments
(from which circumstance they were known by the name of
Sicarii), soon made an end of the high priest Jonathan ;
and, knowing that they would receive immunity at the
hands of the Roman governor, whatever atrocities they
might commit, they proceeded to murder all who were
obnoxious to them, even within the hallowed precincts of
the Temple itself.

A period of perfect anarchy had now set in ; no man's
life or property was safe from open violence or treacherous
attacks ; and the very priests were affected by the general

demoralisation, so that the chief priests appropriated all the tithes and left the poorer ones to starve. Two parties presently grew out of the disorder, and for some time a deadly feud raged throughout the city. A dispute which occurred at Cæsarea brought matters nearer still to a crisis. This town had been founded by Herod, and enriched with many noble buildings and temples, all, however, in the Greek style and devoted to Pagan worship. The Greek and Syrian inhabitants of the town insisted that the maintenance of their institutions should be paramount; the Jews, on the other hand, contrary to the manifest intentions of the founder, claimed pre-eminence for themselves, their worship, and their laws, on the ground that the founder of their city had been himself a Jew by birth. The dispute was at last referred to Rome, and the Emperor Nero decided against the Jews. Portius Festus, who replaced Felix in the government, made some effort to stem the tide of lawlessness and bloodshed, but, unfortunately, death struck him down in the midst of his reforms.

Albinus, who succeeded him, had but one passion in life, and that was cupidity. Under his rule, the imposts were exorbitantly increased, and any act of crime was overlooked and connived at, if only the criminal had means to satisfy the rapacity of the governor. To add to the general discord, the works of the Temple were now just finished, and 18,000 artisans were suddenly thrown out of work. We who live in these days of strikes may form some idea of the effect which such a mob, idle and starving, would have upon a crowded city, already torn by civil dissension, and groaning under an oppressive foreign yoke. The more orderly portion of the inhabitants besought Agrippa to find these men work to do, by rebuilding the eastern cloisters of the Temple, a magnificent piece of work, which had originally been built by Solomon.

Agrippa, however, who had studied the signs of the
times to some purpose, and was already preparing for
himself a comfortable place of refuge at Beyrout, required
all his money for the palaces, baths, and theatres which
he was building in the latter city; he was, nevertheless,
with some difficulty persuaded to pave Jerusalem with
stones, so that temporary employment was found for a
large number of the workmen, and an immediate outbreak
was thus deferred.

NAZARETH.

Albinus was at last recalled, and Gessius Florus ruled
in his stead.   Florus was a stern, uncompromising man;
and while he displayed as much rapacity as any of his
predecessors, he did not, as they had done, temper his
oppression with any consideration for the habits or religion
of his subjects.   Josephus declares that Florus's avowed
object was to drive the people to a revolt; but this could
hardly have been the case, as the dangerous and stubborn

character of the Jewish nation was well known at Rome. It is more probable that his object was to exact as much as possible from the people, and so to lay up a provision for himself in the case of his own recall or banishment. This policy has always been a favourite one with Eastern governors, and I could name several Turkish pashas who have most successfully pursued it. But, whatever his motives may have been, it is clear that his conduct was mainly instrumental in bringing about the long-threatened calamity. The terrible prediction of our Lord was on the eve of accomplishment, and all the signs which He had declared should presage it began to appear with startling rapidity; even the heathen historian Tacitus bears witness to this, and speaks of the famine, the earthquake, the prodigies, and the awful signs in the heavens, which heralded the fall of the Holy City.

CHAPTER X.

THE first outbreak occurred at Cæsarea, where the efforts of the Greek and Syrian population to carry out Nero's decision caused a fierce and bloody contest. The rebellion quickly spread itself to Jerusalem, and King Agrippa, who was residing in the city at the time of the first commencement of hostilities, implored the people not to enter upon so unequal a contest ; but to spare themselves, their children, and the Holy House. His appeal, supported by the tears of his sister Berenice, a great favourite with the people, was all in vain, and he himself was compelled to seek refuge in flight from the fury of the mob, and to leave the doomed city to itself.

The fire of civil war, once kindled, spread with alarming rapidity, and Judea became a scene of indiscriminate carnage. In Cæsarea, 20,000 Jews were put to the sword ; at Alexandria, 52,000 ; at Ptolemais, 2,000 perished ; and at Jerusalem, the troops of Florus massacred 3,500 people in a single day. The Jews, on their part, were not idle, and an immense number of Syrians and Romans were slaughtered by way of reprisal. In

Jerusalem itself, the revolt assumed formidable proportions. One Menahem, grandson of Judah of Galilee, and hereditary chief of the "Zealots," caused himself to be proclaimed king, and stormed and took the fortress of Antonia. Eleazer, the son of Ananias the high priest, and also a chief of the association, refused to sacrifice for the prosperity of the emperor, and thus formally renounced his allegiance to Rome. All the Roman fortresses in Judea fell one after another into the hands of the insurgents; and the Roman garrison at Jerusalem, which after the capture of Antonia had been compelled to seek refuge in the three strong towers of Hippicus, Phasælus, and Mariamne, were induced to capitulate, on condition that their lives should be spared. No sooner, however, had they laid down their arms, and marched out from the citadel, than the Jews rushed upon them, and murdered them to a man.

At length Cestius Gallus, the governor of Syria, arrived before the walls of Jerusalem at the head of an army of 20,000 men, and besieged the city. For some unexplained reason, he suddenly changed his purpose, broke up his camp, and commenced a retreat. The Jews, who a few hours before had been despairingly contemplating the speedy capture of their city, were intoxicated with delight at the unexpected turn which affairs had taken; and, rushing out of the city, in countless numbers, they assailed the retreating Romans with stones and darts. Harassed by these assaults, and maddened by the insults heaped upon them by the exultant mob, the Roman ranks were thrown into the wildest confusion. Nearly a quarter of Cestius' men perished in this retreat, and he himself was so affected by the disgrace he had brought upon the Roman arms that he shortly after fell sick and died.

Eusebius tells us that at this critical moment the Christians left Jerusalem, in obedience to the word of their Master, Who had bidden them quit the city and flee unto the mountains, when they should " see the abomination of desolation, spoken of by Daniel the prophet, stand in the holy place " (Matt. xxiv. 15). In order to conform to this Divine command, they withdrew to the town of Pella, situated on the other side of Jordan, about forty leagues from Jerusalem; here they remained in safety during the whole of those troublous times.

The defeat of Cestius Gallus increased the obstinacy of the Jews, and, fired with their success, they commenced preparations for continuing the war. The high priest Ananus, and Josephus, son of Gorion, were appointed governors of Jerusalem, and entrusted with the task of repairing the fortifications; the most tried generals were at the same time placed in command of the troops in the provinces. Amongst this number was Josephus, the descendant of the illustrious family of the Asmoneans, and author of the well-known works upon the antiquities and wars of the Jews, to which we are indebted for nearly all our knowledge of these events. During the war, he distinguished himself as a general, but, on being made prisoner by the Romans, he appears to have forsaken the national cause, and to have become the confidant and friend of Vespasian and Titus, the latter of whom he accompanied during the siege of Jerusalem. After the fall of the city, he followed Titus to Rome, where Vespasian bestowed upon him the rights of citizenship, and granted him a pension. At Rome, he studied the Greek language, in which he composed his celebrated history. Josephus died in the year 93 of the Christian era, at the age of 56.

Seeing the active preparations which the Jews were making, and viewing with disquietude the moral effect produced in the East by the defeat of Cestius Gallus, the Emperor Nero sent Vespasian, already known as a brave and skilful general, into Judea. Vespasian at once commenced levying troops, and his son Titus fetched two Roman legions from Alexandria.

At the beginning of the following spring, Vespasian, at the head of 60,000 well armed and disciplined men, marched into Galilee. After carrying the fortress of Gadara at the first assault, they proceeded to lay siege to Jotapata, which place Josephus defended for forty-seven days with great vigour and heroism; but it was at last taken by surprise, and all the inhabitants were either put to the sword or taken prisoners. The number of those who fell on this occasion is estimated at 40,000, and that of the captives at 1,200, Josephus himself being amongst the latter. He had escaped the general slaughter by cutting his way through the enemy's ranks, together with forty of his bravest soldiers, and taking refuge in one of the numerous caverns with which Palestine abounds. Vespasian discovered his retreat, and offered him his life on honourable terms if he would surrender. Josephus was willing to accept the conditions, but his companions would not permit him. Seeing that they were all determined to die rather than fall into the hands of the conquerors, Josephus counselled them to select by lot two of their number, who were first to slay their brethren and then each other, so that they might thus avoid the sin of suicide. Josephus, being of priestly rank, and chief of the party, was appointed to cast the lots. By a lucky chance, if chance it were, the lots fell upon himself and a trusty companion, and the pair at once proceeded to their horrible task. Having completed the butchery of their companions, Josephus and the other survivor easily absolved themselves from their own part of the compact, and at once gave themselves up to the Roman general, by whom they were courteously received. For the particulars of this most suspicious transaction we are indebted to Josephus himself; and indeed it is difficult to review the conduct of the historian during this and the subsequent campaigns without a strong suspicion that he was from the very first unfaithful to the national cause.

N

During the siege of Jotapata, Vespasian attacked a neighbouring city named Japha, which had revolted. After an
obstinate siege, the town submitted, when all the male inhabitants, to the number of 15,000, were put to the sword,
while all the women and children were carried into captivity. A few days afterwards, the Samaritans, having assembled in a riotous fashion upon Mount Gerizim, were
put to the sword.

TIBERIAS.

Joppa, which had been devastated by Cestius, and subsequently re-fortified by some insurgent Jews who had found
a refuge there, was next attacked by the imperial army,
who, without difficulty, effected an entry; many of the inhabitants took to their ships, and put out to sea for safety,
but, a violent tempest arising in the night, the greater portion of the fleet was dashed to pieces against the rocks,
so that the wretched few who had sought safety from
butchery at the hands of the Romans fell victims to the
devouring sea.

After a short rest, Vespasian marched his troops against Tiberias. That city opened its gates to the Roman general, and, at the intercession of Agrippa, the inhabitants were spared. Tarichœa, a strongly fortified place on the Sea of Galilee, was next reduced, after long resistance, and the fall of Gamala and of the mountain fortress of Tabor followed in quick succession. Of all the towns in Galilee, Giscala alone held out, and Titus was sent to reduce it to submission. The principal inhabitants were disposed to submit at once, and so to avoid the slaughter which would inevitably follow upon a protracted resistance ; but John, the son of Levi, chief of one of the factions in the town, succeeded in inducing the populace to prevent this resolution from being carried out.

One Sabbath, he implored Titus to cease from hostilities for the day, and promised to submit himself on that condition ; he, however, took advantage of the truce to withdraw himself, together with a large number of followers, to Jerusalem. The Romans speedily pursued the fugitives, and put 6,000 to death, capturing at the same time more than 3,000 of the women and children. John of Giscala himself, with his immediate adherents, succeeded in gaining the Holy City. The inhabitants of Giscala lost no time in capitulating, and explained that they had had no part in the treacherous movement of John and his companions. Titus believed them, and consented to spare their lives. With the fall of the city, the last stronghold in Galilee fell into the hands of the Romans.

After the events which we have just described, Titus rejoined his father at Cæsarea. The revolutions which were going on in Rome prevented the Roman general from prosecuting the war for the next year with the same vigour with which he had commenced it. This, however, caused him little uneasiness, for he knew that the whole strength of the nation was concentrated in Jerusalem, and that the factions which already reigned in that city were slowly

but surely facilitating its conquest and hastening its destruction.

Two parties existed at this time in Jerusalem. The
more moderate of the inhabitants recognised the hopelessness of contending against the overwhelming power of
Rome, and desired to submit to the conquerors rather than
compass the inevitable destruction of the nation. The
other party, consisting of the lower classes of the population, who had attached themselves to the cause of the
" Zealots," clamoured for an uncompromising resistance,
and were only too glad to avail themselves of the popular
outcry against the Romanisers to pillage the goods and
take the lives of the men who had nothing to gain and
everything to lose by resistance. The party of order,
under the venerable high priest Ananus, were at last
compelled to take up arms in their own defence, and
the " Zealots," after a terrible contest, were forced to
seek refuge within the precincts of the Temple, where
they were closely besieged. John of Giscala, who professed a desire for peace, was sent to induce them to come
to terms, but, instead of fulfilling his mission, he exhorted
them to persevere, and to seek assistance from without.
The Idumeans, a fierce, warlike race, who, as we have
seen, had been Judaised during the reign of Hyrcanus,
were accordingly invited to take part in the defence of the
Holy City; but Ananus, justly suspicious of such allies,
refused to admit them into the city. That night, a terrible storm broke out, and, taking advantage of the darkness and confusion, the " Zealots " forced the gates of the
Temple, and, precipitating themselves into the city,
admitted 20,000 of their Idumean allies. A scene of
horrible carnage ensued, and in the morning 8,000 corpses
strowed the enclosure of the Temple, Ananus, and Jesus
the son of Gamala, being amongst the number of the slain.
The moderate party was thus finally stamped out and
exterminated.

The "Zealots," having rid themselves of all who were obnoxious to them, turned their arms against each other. Simon ben Gioras, a dangerous and ambitious leader, declared against the authority of John of Giscala, and established his headquarters at the fortress of Masadah, and by specious promises succeeded in attracting large numbers to his standard. With this army he successfully invaded Idumea, and ultimately laid siege to Jerusalem itself. Within the city the "Zealots" were committing the most horrible atrocities, while both these, and the few who still dared to lift up their voices in favour of the cause of order, were equally opposed to the tyrannous rule of John of Giscala. The latter threatened to set fire to the city unless his authority were obeyed, and in an evil moment the despairing citizens consented to throw open their gates and admit Simon. A fierce civil war went on between the partizans of the two rival chieftains, and the city was the scene of one fierce and uninterrupted struggle up to the very moment when Titus appeared before the walls.

In the meantime, Vespasian had been elected emperor of Rome, and his son Titus assumed the command of the forces in Palestine, and commenced active preparations for the siege of Jerusalem.

In April of the year 70 A.D., he set out on his march from Cæsarea. His army consisted of four legions, amongst which was the 12th, the same which had suffered so disgraceful a defeat under Cestius Gallus; to this formidable force of regular troops was added a large number of auxiliaries, and, comparing various accounts, we may estimate the force under his command at not less than 80,000 men.

Titus marched from Cæsarea to Jerusalem without encountering any opposition, and arrived before the walls on the 11th of April. Within the city, the civil dissensions had gone on from bad to worse. "John, Simon ben Gioras, and Eleazar, each at the head of his own faction, made the streets run with blood. John, whose followers numbered 6,000, held the Lower, New, and Middle City; Simon, at the head of 10,000 Jews and 5,000 Idumeans, had the strong post of the Upper City, with a portion of the third wall; Eleazar, with 2,000 Zealots, more fanatic than the rest, had barricaded himself within the Temple itself. There they admitted, it is true, unarmed worshippers, but kept out the rest. The stores of the Temple provided them with abundance of provisions, and while the rest of the soldiers were starving, those who were within the Temple walls were well fed and in good case. This was, however, the only advantage which Eleazar possessed over the rest. Their position, cooped up in a narrow fortress—for such the Temple was—and exposed to a constant shower of darts, stones, and missiles of all sorts from John's men, was miserable enough. John and Simon fought with each other in the lower ground, the valley of the Tyropœon, which lay between the Temple and Mount Zion. Here were stored up supplies of corn, sufficient, it is said, for many years' consumption. But, in the sallies which John and Simon made upon each other, all the buildings in this part of the town were destroyed or set on fire, and all their corn burnt; so that famine had actually begun before the commencement of the siege." *   To add to the miserable condition of the besieged, their numbers were enormously increased by the country folk, who, on the first approach of the Romans, flocked in multitudes into the city.

The appearance of the Romans before the walls united for a moment the conflicting parties, who resolved to band together against their common foe. Their first sally was so vigorous and desperate that the Roman army was compelled to abandon its position, and to take refuge in the mountains. Instead of following up the advantage thus gained, the Jews seized the opportunity afforded by

* Besant and Palmer's "Jerusalem," p. 21.

the temporary withdrawal of the enemy to renew their own faction fights. John having treacherously murdered a great number of the partizans of Eleazar, and reduced the others to submission, there remained now but two factions in the city; these, however, carried on an incessant and bloody conflict. In the meantime, the Romans were making preparations for an attack. All the neighbouring forests were cut down for the construction of their engines of war; the fosses around Jerusalem were filled up; and walls and towers began to rise round the doomed city, from which terrible and destructive missiles could be hurled at its defenders.

A CATAPULT.

The sight of these operations once more recalled the infatuated Jews to their senses; again they ceased from their internecine contest, to defend themselves against the besieging force. They had the engines which had been captured from Cestius Gallus, and these they directed against the Roman works; but their want of practice rendered their artillery almost useless, while that of the Romans did terrible execution. A breach was soon effected, the Romans entered the town, and the Jews

withdrew within the second wall. Titus thus became
master of Bezetha, in the new town, forming about a
third of the city. The conquerors lost no time in attack-
ing the second wall, and their battering-rams soon destroyed one of the towers, so that they were enabled tc
effect a breach. The defenders fought with the fury of
despair, but nothing could withstand the steady advance of
the well armed and well disciplined Roman legions, and in
a few days the whole of the lower town was in Titus's
hands.

And now, the dense masses of people which the city
contained being compressed within narrower limits, and
the provisions, scanty enough from the first, having been
entirely consumed, all the horrors of a famine were
added to those of the siege. Josephus, an eye-witness of
the events which he describes, gives us all the ghastly
details ; how the " Zealots " rushed from house to house,
to search for food, and murdered men, women, and children for the morsels which they were in the very act of
swallowing ; how the wretched inhabitants crept out of the
city by night, to search for food in the valley, and were
either caught and crucified by Titus's soldiery, or robbed
by the sentinels at their own gates of the miserable roots
which they had hoped to bring home to their starving wives
and children. These horrors have been described over and
over again, and it is not my purpose to dwell upon them
here ; suffice it to say that the sufferings of the Jews
during this memorable siege have never been equalled in
the history of the world.

All Titus's efforts to induce the people to capitulate
were in vain ; and at last, weary of the protracted siege,
he resolved upon a decisive attack. Three days sufficed
for his soldiery to raise a wall of circumvallation round the
city, and a strict blockade was established ; thus was fulfilled the prediction of our Lord : " For the days shall
come upon thee that thine enemies shall cast a trench

about thee, and compass thee round, and keep thee in on every side " (St. Luke xix. 43).

Cut off from their last feeble resource—that of gathering roots in the valley—the horrors of the famine were redoubled, and under such suffering even the obstinacy of the Jews at last gave way. One Judas, who was in command of a tower in the Upper City, conspired, with ten of his men, to admit the Romans. Titus, who had too often been deceived by similar proposals, allowed the opportunity to slip by ; the plot was discovered, and Judas, with his accomplices, was thrown over the ramparts.

In twenty-one days, the Romans made the preparations for their assault, and the Jews were too feeble to prevent them. When all was completed, the battering-rams and other engines were brought to bear upon the walls, and at night, when darkness compelled both sides to desist, the wall, which had been grievously battered, fell of its own accord. The soldiers of Titus rushed in, but, to their dismay, found yet another wall, behind which the defenders had retreated in anticipation of this catastrophe, and which they were now preparing to defend as obstinately as the first. Two days afterwards, a few Roman soldiers effected an entry by a successful *ruse*, and the fortress of Antonia fell into their hands. Nothing now remained to the Jews but the Temple itself, and this the Jews stoutly defended, still hoping against hope that the God of Israel would not desert His sanctuary, but would at the supreme moment bring them some miraculous deliverance. As the enemy approached, the defenders commenced to destroy portions of the Temple with their own hands ; and Titus, willing to save the noble edifice from destruction, sent Josephus, to make a last appeal to John ; he was repulsed with bitter taunts and insult. The end was drawing nigh. It was now the 9th of August, the anniversary of the burning of the first temple by Nebuchadnezzar, and the Jews nerving themselves for a decisive effort, made a sortie from the walls; but, after five hours' fighting, they were driven back into their stronghold.

Titus now retired into Antonia, and determined that the next day should decide the fate of the city. The Jews, however, being unwilling to wait so long, made another sortie, their last and ineffectual struggle. They were easily beaten back, closely pursued by the Roman soldiers, when one of the latter, without having received any order, found means of setting fire to one of the apartments immediately adjoining the sanctuary, by throwing some burning materials through the windows.

The Jews now thought that God had, indeed, abandoned His sanctuary, and, rushing with frantic cries to the spot, many of them precipitated themselves into the midst of the flames, and perished in their attempt to save the "holy of holies." Titus himself, with his staff, hastened to the scene, and endeavoured to rescue a portion of the "holy of holies," with his own hands beating back the soldiers. But all was in vain; one of the soldiers threw a torch upon the gateway of the Temple, and in a few moments the entire edifice was enveloped in flames. The Roman soldiery, maddened with rage against those who had resisted them so long, intoxicated with the sudden success, and excited by the scene, behaved with unbridled license, and commenced a butchery too horrible to describe; let Josephus himself describe the scene which presented itself to his eyes.

"One would have thought that the hill itself on which the Temple stood was seething hot, full of fire in every part; that the blood was larger in quantity than the fire, and those that were slain more in number than those that slew them, for the ground nowhere appeared visible, for the dead bodies that lay on it; but the soldiers went over heaps of these bodies as they ran after such as fled from them." *

* Josephus, vi., v., 1.

The Temple of Herod was destroyed. But the last act
of the tragedy was yet to come. The fighting men had cut
their way through the carnage, and ensconced themselves in
the Upper City, where they still held out.

Titus demanded a parley, and, standing on a bridge
which connected the Temple with the Upper City, or Zion,
offered terms to the insurgents for the last time.

The remains of this bridge still exist, and the spring of
the arch (called, from its discoverer, Robinson's Arch) is

SPRING OF ROBINSON'S ARCH.

one of the great sights of modern Jerusalem. The ruined
stones of the opposite pier were discovered by Captain
Warren, eighty feet below the present surface of the
ground.

The clemency of Titus was refused, and the Romans began
to raise engines against the wall, as there was no prospect
of carrying the stronghold by assault. Eighteen days were
consumed in the attack, during which time large numbers

of the Jews succeeded in deserting to the Romans. At first, all who left the city were slaughtered, but the Romans presently grew tired of butchery, and detained the fugitives, to be afterwards sold as slaves.

At last the breach was made, and the wretched garrison, paralysed with despair, awaited the signal for their slaughter to commence. John and Simon, with such followers as they could collect, endeavoured to escape over Titus's wall of circumvallation at the south. In this last hope they were defeated. The leaders sought a hiding-place in the subterranean chambers beneath the city, while the men submitted passively to be put to death. Pouring into the town, the Roman soldiers butchered old and young, and, when satiated with blood, turned their thoughts to plunder. But from this they were compelled to desist, for the houses were filled with putrefying corpses, and, sickened at the loathsome sight, the soldiers dared not enter in.

Thus fell the Holy City. Of all the countless multitudes who had thronged the streets of Jerusalem, and bidden defiance to the power of Rome, but a wretched few remained alive, and these were carried off, to grace the conqueror's triumph, and to end their miserable existence as captives in the mines, or as gladiators.

" Butchered to make a Roman holiday."

John and Simon were not among the slain, nor were they taken prisoners, but after a few days the former gave himself up to Titus. Simon was captured the following October, after Titus had departed from the city with his victorious troops. Driven by starvation from his subterranean retreat, he at last determined upon making an attempt to escape. Dressing himself in a long white tunic, he suddenly appeared before the guards, hoping that they might take him for a supernatural apparition, and in their terror let him get clear off. This somewhat undignified trick was unsuccessful. The matter-of-fact sentinel arrested the ghost, and sent him a prisoner to Rome. In a Roman triumph, the chief of the vanquished leaders was always executed. The post of honour was assigned by Titus to Simon, son of Gioras, who met his death boldly at the foot of the Capitoline Hill, amidst the exultant taunts of the Roman mob. John of Giscala was sentenced to imprisonment for life.

From this moment, Jerusalem ceases to be the centre of Jewish history; but, before taking leave of the Holy City, it

TRIUMPHAL ARCH OF TITUS AT ROME.

will be well to say a few words concerning its topography, in order to make the preceding portions of the history more intelligible to the reader.

The present aspect of the city of course enables us to appreciate the general nature of its position and surroundings. But modern Jerusalem conveys no idea of what the ancient city used to be; that is buried fathoms deep below

the surface of the soil. Thanks, however, to the operations of the Palestine Exploration Fund, the most important facts relating to the topography of the ancient
town have been recovered, and the Society has thus
vindicated its right to the old crusading battle-cry, "The
Recovery of Jerusalem," which they have adopted as their
motto.

Let us see, then, with regard to the many places of
absorbing interest which are gathered together within the
compass of that little tongue of land, how far their position
can be identified, and how far such identification tends to
illustrate and confirm the Bible. First, then, unbroken
and unimpeachable tradition, as well as constant occupation, identify the site of the modern city of El Cuds, or
Beit-el-Mucaddas, with the ancient Jerusalem. The principal object in that ancient town, and at once its pride and
glory, was the Temple.

Traditional evidence points to the enclosure now called
El Haram es Sherif, or the "noble sanctuary," as the site
of the Temple. In the fourth century, the site, though
neglected and dishonoured, was perfectly well known, for
Eutychius tells us that "when Helena, the mother of
Constantine, had built churches at Jerusalem, the site of
the rock and its neighbourhood had been laid waste, and
so left. But the Christians heaped dirt on the rock, so
that that was a large dunghill over it. And so the Romans
had neglected it, nor given it that honour which the
Israelites had been wont to pay it, and had not built a
church above it, because it had been said by our Lord
Jesus Christ in the Holy Gospel, 'Behold, your house
shall be left unto you desolate.'"

Omar, the great Mohammedan conqueror, purified the
site from the dirt and rubbish, and built a mosque there;
and his munificent successor, Abd-el-Melik, erected the
present magnificent structure known as the Cubbet-es-
Sakhrah, or "Dome of the Rock," over the identical spot

MODERN JERUSALEM.

upon which the Jewish altar of burnt offering had stood. Had it not been for the excavations made by the Palestine Exploration Fund upon and around the noble sanctuary, it would have been difficult to realise the descriptions contained in the Bible, and in Josephus's history, of the grandeur and magnificence of the Temple. But the shafts sunk by Captain Warren, and the researches of Captain Wilson, have vindicated the accuracy of those ancient records. For instance, the Bible tells us that the materials for the building of Solomon's temple were prepared by Tyrian workmen at a distance from Jerusalem, and that the massive stones of which the walls were composed, were so carefully hewn and chiselled, that, in putting them together, no mortar was required to make them hold, and neither the sound of axe nor hammer was heard, to disturb the sacred repose of the Holy Mount.

Above ground, there are few, if any, stones which still occupy their original position in the Temple wall, so often have they been thrown down and rebuilt; but below the surface, Captain Warren's shafts and galleries reveal massive stones of immense proportions, fitted together without mortar, and with such extraordinary skill and accuracy that it is impossible to insert a penknife into the interstices; while upon the faces of many of these huge blocks of masonry, the marks of Tyrian or Phœnician characters are still as plainly visible as when they were made by the workmen of Hiram, king of Tyre.

Following out the indications contained in the second book of Chronicles, we should naturally place the palace of King Solomon at the southern end of the Temple enclosure, and somewhat lower down. Excavations at the point suggested have revealed traces of the foundations of an ancient structure; and even relics of pottery, containing inscriptions, were found in the same spot. The inscriptions are in the same character as that of the celebrated Moabite stone, which we know to have belonged to the period of the kings of Israel. These are only a few out of numerous instances in which scientific investigation, such as that prosecuted by the Palestine Exploration Fund, confirms the accuracy of Scripture, even in the minutest details.

But, however grand and glorious the Jewish Temple may have been, there is another sight in Jerusalem which, to a Christian mind, possesses an infinitely greater interest, and that is the tomb of our Lord.

MOSQUE OF OMAR.

The authenticity of the tomb now pointed out as the Holy Sepulchre does not, from the very nature of the case, rest upon such good evidence as that which fixes the site of the Temple ; but there is at least very strong probability in its favour. It was identified, or discovered, by Helena, mother of the Emperor Constantine ; and she was no doubt

o

guided by local tradition, which in so short a time as had elapsed since the event (not more than three centuries) could scarcely have been at fault; since that time, the tradition has been perpetuated without interruption.

There is no doubt but that the tomb in question is a Jewish one, and that in its original state it was a cave cut in a rock; and, from the presence in the immediate vicinity, and under the roof of the very same building, of other rock-cut tombs, we may conclude that the locality was devoted to sepulchral purposes. Recent excavations prove, moreover, that the Church of the Holy Sepulchre lies outside of the city walls as they existed in Herod's time. The situation, therefore, exactly accords with the notices contained in the Gospel; and hence, there is no antecedent improbability in the identification.

However much we may smile at the credulity which has collected within the walls of the Church of the Holy Sepulchre such relics as " the stone of unction," " the pillar of flagellation," and " the stone upon which the cock stood to crow when Peter denied his Lord," few Christians could enter within those hallowed precincts, venerated for so many centuries as the actual scenes of our Lord's sufferings and burial, without feelings of the deepest and most solemn awe.

Of one place at Jerusalem there can be no doubt, and that is of the Mount of Olives. From this hill, which is situated to the east of the city, a view is obtained which embraces the whole of the two eminences, Moriah and Zion, upon which Jerusalem is built. Here at least we know that we are treading in the very footprints of the Saviour; that we are looking over that very Jerusalem which He so loved and so strove to reclaim. His pitying eye beheld it in all its glory and splendour, and wept over its coming fall. We see it humbled in the dust, in the hands of Gentiles and infidels, crushed by a long succession of wars and sieges. As we contemplate this aspect of the Holy City, let us take to heart the awful lesson which it conveys—that, if we reject that loving, long-suffering Saviour, we too must fall like her.

JEWS' WAILING PLACE

MODERN HISTORY;

FROM THE FALL OF THE ROMAN EMPIRE TO THE PRESENT TIME.

PART THE THIRD.

CHAPTER XI.

THE LAST DAYS OF THE ROMAN EMPIRE.

Last struggles for independence—Fall of Masada—Jews in Rome—Separation of the Jews into the eastern and western communities—The Prince of the Captivity and the patriarch of Tiberias—The Talmud—Severity of the Emperor Trajan—Insurrections in Cyrene, Mesopotamia, and Cyprus—Bar-cochebas—The last war of independence—Rabbi Akiba—Jerusalem becomes a Pagan city—Rabbi Judah; the Mishna and Gemara—Antoninus Pius—Marcus Aurelius—The Jews join the Parthians in a war against Rome—Septimius Severus—Another rising in Judea—Foundation of the Academy of Nahardea in the East—Restoration of the Magian Religion in the Persian empire—Zenobia, queen of Palmyra—Heliogabalus—Alexander Severus—The Jews under the last Pagan emperors—Conversion of Constantine—Embellishment of the Holy Places—The Arian disturbances in Alexandria—Julian, the Apostate, invites the Jews to rebuild the Temple; failure of the attempt, and death of Julian—Laws of Valentinian and Valens—Theodosius the Great—Disturbances under Theodosius II.—Collisions at Antioch—St. Simeon Stylites—Cyrill, bishop of Alexandria—Expulsion of the Jews and murder of Hypatia—Pretended conversions in the island of Minorca—A false Messiah appears in Crete—Abolition of the Jewish patriarchate—Fall of the Western empire—Removal of the capital to Byzantium—The Vandals and Goths—The Jews under Justinian—Another pretended Messiah in Palestine—The Babylonian Talmud—The Massorah—Invasion by the Persians.

THREE forts in Judea still held out against the Romans, namely, Herodion, Machærus, and Masada. Lucius Bassus, who was sent by Vespasian as lieutenant-governor of Judea, speedily reduced the first two ; but Masada, being well-provisioned, and, from its natural position, almost impregnable, for a long time held out. At length the Romans erected a causeway on the left side of the fortress, and effected a breach in the walls, by which they determined to take the place by assault. On entering it the following morning, they found that Eleazar, its defender, and the desperate band who had joined him, had preferred death to captivity, and that out of 967 persons only two women and

FORTRESS OF MASADA.

five children remained alive, the rest having all sought a voluntary death, the men first destroying their wives and children, and then turning their weapons against each other, until one only remained, who first set fire to the stores and treasures, and then fell upon his own sword. The wretched women and children who survived to tell the tale of horror had managed to save their lives by concealing themselves in some of the vaults or subterranean chambers of the fortress. The merciless policy of the

Romans had reduced Judea to a howling and desolate wilderness. At first a few old persons and children were alone permitted to dwell in the ruined city of Jerusalem ; but by degrees, no doubt, a number of Jews returned to their former home.

The Emperor Titus sold all the lands of Judea, but expressly prohibited the rebuilding of any of the cities. The Jews were, it is true, still permitted to practise their own religion, but with the grievous proviso that they should pay to the Temple of Jupiter Capitolinus a tax con-

SPOILS OF THE TEMPLE.

sisting of an equivalent sum of money for every amount contributed by each of them towards the maintenance of the Temple.

Domitian, Titus' brother and successor, still more increased their burdens, and involved them in the persecutions which he was then carrying on with great vigour against the Christians.

The Jews profited but little by these bitter lessons of adversity, and a fresh insurrection occurred amongst them at Alexandria. Some of their compatriots who had not joined the outbreak, but who feared the consequences for themselves, betrayed the insurgents into the hands of the Romans, and more than 600 were put to death. The Temple of Onias at Heliopolis was also shut up by order of the emperor. Crowds of Jews now dispersed themselves over the world ; some sought an asylum in Egypt, where a colony had been established since the time of Alexandria ; others went farther east, and joined their brethren who had settled at Babylon. The Jewish nation thus becomes divided into two distinct bodies—the Eastern and the Western Jews ; the former inhabited Babylonia, Chaldea, Assyria, Persia, &c., and were governed by a chief elected by themselves, and bearing the title of the Prince of the Captivity ; the latter, who dwelt in Egypt, Palestine, and the European portions of the Roman empire, were presided over by a national officer, whom they called " the Patriarch."

The Emperor Nerva, who succeeded Domitian, relieved the Jews from many of their imposts and disabilities, and even allowed them to rebuild the city of Tiberias on the Lake of Galilee, as the residence of the patriarch. This last dignity remained hereditary in the family of Gamaliel II., and rose to great importance, both political and religious, for although it does not appear that they exercised any real temporal authority over the various scattered Jewish communities, yet their decrees and their teaching were accepted so far as was necessary to preserve the semblance of a Hebrew commonwealth. The patriarch presided over an assembly which bore the name of the Sanhedrim, but it appears doubtful whether this body had continued its sittings during all the troubles of Judea, or whether it was reconstituted at Tiberias.

The Jews who remained in Palestine founded schools for expounding the Law and preserving what scraps of literature wars, sieges, and dispersions had left them. These ultimately produced the celebrated Talmud of

Jerusalem, while similar academics amongst the eastern Jews produced the Babylonian Talmud.*

For some time the Jews remained in comparative tranquillity ; but the memory of their old wrongs still rankled in their bosoms, and the fierce but smouldering hate which they bore to the Gentiles was at length fanned into a flame by the severity of the Emperor Trajan.   It was in

CYRENE.

Cyrene that the insurrection first broke out.   After several collisions between the Jewish and non-Jewish inhabitants of the town, the latter were compelled to withdraw to Alexandria ; there they revenged themselves by massacring all the Jews ; those of Cyrene retaliated by a frightful slaughter of the Libians ; and the rebels, having spread themselves over the whole of Lower Egypt, com-

* See Chapter VII.

mitted frightful atrocities, and were with difficulty suppressed by Marcius Turbo, whom Trajan had sent against
them. A similar outbreak occurred at Mesopotamia during
the following year, and Lucius Quietus having put down
the rebellion with a strong hand, was appointed governor
of Judea. Another rising took place in the island of
Cyprus, where the Jews are said to have massacred no
less than 240,000 of their fellow-citizens. Adrian, who
was sent to the relief of the inhabitants, drove every Jew
out of the island, and forbade them ever to set foot in it
again ; and this decree has ever since remained in force.
When Adrian came to the throne, he determined, once
for all, to stamp out the turbulent religion, prohibiting
circumcision and all other Jewish observances. These
stern and uncompromising measures, for which, after
Adrian's experience of the Jews at Cyprus, we can
scarcely blame him, exasperated them beyond measure.
But even in the most desperate circumstances, the human
heart will cling to hope, however delusive that hope may
be ; and we need not, therefore, wonder that in this their
darkest hour the rumour should have gone abroad amongst
them that a star had appeared in Jacob, that the long-
looked-for Messiah had come at last. .

Accordingly, when a fierce and determined pretender
arose, styling himself Bar-cochebas, the "son of the star,"
and proclaiming that he was the deliverer whose coming
Balaam had foretold, he found plenty of willing listeners
to his lying words ; and when Rabbi Akiba, the greatest,
the most learned, and the most influential doctor of the age,
warmly espoused his cause and endorsed his pretensions,
the enthusiasm reached its height, and Bar-cochebas soon
found himself at the head of 200,000 men, mad with zeal,
and clamouring for freedom and for vengeance. So well did
the insurgents manage to conduct their preparations, that
before the Romans apprehended any danger, the Jews
had taken advantage of their superior knowledge of the

country and had occupied and fortified fifty important
strongholds and nearly a thousand villages. Rufus, the
Roman governor, could make no head against so formidable
a rebellion, and sent off to Adrian for reinforcements. The
emperor immediately despatched Julius Severus, one of
the most illustrious generals of his age. The undisciplined

CYPRUS.

numbers and courage of the rebels availed them nothing
against the military skill and overwhelming forces of the
Roman general. One by one their strongholds fell ; Jerusalem was taken, and Bar-cochebas himself was slain ; and
at length the fortress of Bither, where the last desperate
band had taken refuge, fell before the Roman arms.

Wild and bloody as this struggle for independence was,
there is something noble in the unflinching patriotism and

steadfast faith exhibited by the Jews when the fortunes of
their country were at the worst. Alas! when He Who
would have saved the remnant of Israel came, they
spurned the proffered aid. How just, but how mournful,
was the retribution, when, their hopes for ever crushed,
they themselves were forced to own their folly and their
crime, and in the bitterness of their disappointment to
change the proud title of their vaunted deliverer Bar-
cochebas, " the son of the star," into Bar-cozibah, " the
son of a lie !"

Rabbi Akiba paid the penalty of his credulity, being
seized and executed by the Roman governor at the commencement of the movement.

Frightful stories are told of the massacres which followed the repression of the revolt; and certain it is that
immense numbers of Jews throughout Palestine perished
by the sword, and that the rest were sold into slavery.
In order to prevent their restoration at any future time,
Jerusalem was re-constructed as a Pagan city, and colonised by strangers ; its name was changed to Ælia Capi-
tolina, and a temple of Jupiter occupied the spot where
the Temple of Jehovah once stood. The Christians had
suffered terribly during the revolt of Bar-cochebas, being
tortured by the Jews, and confounded with the latter by
the Romans. To avoid such fatal confusion henceforward
the Christians determined to separate themselves beyond
all question, and to this end appointed a Gentile convert
named Marcus to be their head. They thus obtained permission to reside within the walls of Ælia, which became
the seat of a flourishing church and bishopric. By this
action the breach already existing between the Jews and
Christians was made irreparable ; and that fierce animosity was established between the two sects which subsequently showed itself in such terrible and relentless persecutions.

The third patriarch of the Western Jews was the

famous Rabbi Judah. Amongst other strange legends concerning him, it is said that he converted the Emperor Marcus Aurelius to Judaism, and that he wrote the Mishna by order of that prince. The Mishna is, as its name implies, the second law, and is not so much a commentary on, as a supplement to, the Pentateuch. It contains in a written form all the decisions upon knotty points of doctrine and observance which had been handed down by word of mouth through a long succession of theologians. As might be expected, the Mishna is a crude, undigested, and contradictory collection, and for all that the Jews professed to believe it little less than inspired, yet their faith did not go so far as to prevent them from subsequently compiling a supplement and commentary to it, which they named the Gemara or perfection.

The edict of Adrian prohibiting the circumcision of infants remained in force until the reign of his successor Antoninus Pius, when the Jews again took up arms to obtain the repeal of such an arbitrary law. The emperor easily and speedily suppressed the revolt, after which he restored to them the privilege, to regain which they had rebelled. Antoninus showed clemency and favour to the Jews in other ways; but he still forbade them to make proselytes. This edict is a curious sequel to the rabbinical fable of the conversion of the emperor Marcus Aurelius, to which we have just alluded.

Adrian, on his accession to the throne, had assigned the Euphrates as the limit of the Roman Empire. The Mesopotamian Jews, therefore, had returned to their old masters the Parthians, and with the exception of such as voluntarily went into Palestine to swell the crowd of victims, they were free from the troubles and miseries which befel their Western brethren. In the reign of Marcus Aurelius, however, they joined with the Parthians in a war against the Romans. The emperor having reduced them to submission, once more put in force the edict of Adrian against circumcision, in order to show his indignation at their conduct; nevertheless, in the remoter provinces it was found practicably impossible to enforce the restriction.

The Jews and Samaritans had been allowed to establish themselves in Galilee, but they were still strictly forbidden to enter Jerusalem itself. But in the reign of Septimius Severus they once more endeavoured to throw off the Roman yoke, and incurred another invasion. The emperor having subdued the malcontents behaved with laudable moderation towards them; for he was not unmindful of their fidelity to his cause when Persenius Niger had disputed with him the imperial throne.

About the commencement of the third century was the period when the doctors amongst the Oriental Jews commenced to make themselves famous, and Samuel Jarchenai, who was celebrated both for his military and astronomical talents, became great and influential, chief of the academy of Nahardea.

The restoration of the Magian religion by that Persian monarchy which had taken the place of the Parthian government in the East occasioned some trouble to the Eastern Jews, and we find them persecuted by Shapur, king of Persia, who was possibly driven to such measures by the jealousy of his subjects at the prosperous and important position to which the Jews had attained. Under Zenobia the Jews enjoyed undisturbed peace and prosperity. But when the Emperor Aurelian destroyed the proud monarchy of Palmyra's queen, her Hebrew subjects were compelled to seek an asylum in Persia.

The Emperor Heliogabalus, amongst his other mad and disgusting freaks, endeavoured to incorporate the Jewish dogmas and practices into that medley of heathen superstitions which he dignified by the name of religion; and he even went so far as to impose the rite of circumcision upon his Roman subjects and to prohibit their use of the

flesh of swine. The Jews and Samaritans naturally refused to accept the emperor's proffered offer of amalga-
mation, and their refusal might have brought serious consequences upon them but for his timely death.

Alexander Severus, the next emperor of Rome, was a
noble and enlightened prince. The time was not yet ripe
for the conversion of a Roman emperor to Christianity ;
but Severus recognised the truth and beauty of our

TEMPLE OF THE SUN AT PALMYRA.

Saviour's teaching, and added His image to his gallery of
men whom he considered worthy of divine honours. The
Jews also were very favourably treated by him, and their
religion and privileges so much respected that the emperor
earned for himself the title of the "father of the synagogue."

Under the succeeding emperors the Jews remained unmolested in the West. Philip, who was born in Arabia,

where a great part of the commerce was carried on by
Jews, had had ample opportunity of making acquaintance
with the people, and, forming a favourable impression of
them, accorded them many privileges. Decius Valerian
and Diocletian, hostile as they were to the Christians, did
not disturb the Jews in the exercise of their religion, and
even permitted them to enjoy the rights of citizenship,
and to participate in the honours of the magistracy,
and synagogues were allowed to be erected in all the
principal towns of the empire. In a word, under the last
Pagan emperors the Jews were entirely exempt from
persecution. But when a Christian sovereign mounted
upon the throne, the bitter and unrelenting hatred felt
for the " enemies of Jesus Christ " began to display itself,
and the troubles of the Hebrew nation began anew.

The fourth century witnessed one of the most important
revolutions in the history of the world—the overthrow of
Paganism, and the formal establishment of Christianity
throughout the Roman Empire. Constantine the Great,
the first Christian emperor, restored the ancient name of
Jerusalem, adorned the city with splendid edifices, and
erected magnificent shrines over the Sepulchre of our
Lord and the other holy places in Palestine. Under the
imperial convert and his immediate successors, the Jews
were deprived of the privileges which they had enjoyed
under the later Pagan emperors, and various laws and
edicts were promulgated, which had for their special object
the humiliation of the Hebrew community.

The Eastern Jews, to revenge the affronts heaped upon
their Western brethren, made common cause with the
Magians, massacred all their Christian neighbours, and
destroyed their churches.

Constantius, who succeeded his father Constantine,
showed a disposition to lighten their yoke ; but one or
two attempts at insurrection in Palestine caused the
emperor to repent of and change his clement policy. In

Alexandria the Jews mixed themselves up in the dissensions caused by the heresy of Arius, and joined the Pagans in committing the most frightful atrocities against the Athanasian bishop and his followers. The accession of Julian, surnamed the Apostate, made a new diversion in their favour. This emperor abolished Christianity in favour of paganism by an Imperial edict, and wishing, doubtless, to obtain the influence of the Mesopotamian Jews on his own side in his campaign against the Persians, he adopted a policy of reconciliation towards the whole of the race.

The Jews were invited to rebuild the Temple of Jerusalem; and his favourite, Alypius, was appointed to carry out the work. Never, perhaps, since the commencement of their captivity had such joyful hopes filled the minds of the Jews, and it seemed as though the restoration of Israel was at hand. From all quarters of the world Jewish money and Jewish labour poured into the Holy City to aid in the work. But scarcely had they commenced to clear the site for the foundations of the new temple, when flames of fire, accompanied by loud explosions, burst forth from the long closed subterranean chambers that lay beneath the rubbish. From what cause the fire proceeded, one cannot at this distance of time exactly decide; but it was probably from the foul gases and " fire-damp " that had accumulated in those subterranean vaults, even if, as has been suggested, human malice did not produce, or at least accelerate, the disaster. Be this as it may, the opponents of the Jews lost no time in turning the catastrophe to their own advantage. The flames were attributed to the manifest displeasure of Heaven at the projected violation of its decrees, and the circumstance was related with exaggerated details and supernatural embellishments.

The Mesopotamian Jews disappointed Julian's hopes, and remained faithful to their Persian masters, and the

P

Apostate himself perished in one of the cities which they
had deserted at his approach, and to which his own soldiers
had set fire.

The policy of Jovian, Julian's successor, was directed
towards undoing all that the latter had done, and was
consequently oppressive to the Jews: but it was too short
to make any sensible difference in their condition. Valentinian, an excessively tolerant prince, restored all their
former rights, and Valens, the next emperor, confirmed
them in the enjoyment of all their privileges, with the
exception of the one most important to them, namely, ex-
emption from the public services.

Under Gratian, Theodosius, and Arcadius, they enjoyed
the protection of the throne, being recognised as useful
and loyal subjects. Some Christians having set fire to a
synagogue, Theodosius the Great commanded them to
rebuild it, and charged the Bishop of Calinicum, in
Osrhoene, to carry out the work. Thereupon Ambrose,
Bishop of Milan, broke out into fiery invective against the
too tolerant emperor, and succeeded in inducing him to
revoke the edict. Later on in his reign the emperor re-
enacted laws which secured perfect freedom and toleration
to his Jewish subjects.

Under Theodosius II. the Jews, emboldened by their
long immunity from persecution, began themselves to
manifest a spirit of intolerance and crime: and at a feast
of Purim, when it was customary to affix an effigy of
Haman to a gallows, they substituted for this part of
the ceremony a crucified figure, which they burnt with
the usual imprecations. The emperor prohibited this
wanton insult to his religion; but the Jews of Dacia and
Macedonia having disregarded the interdict, the Christians
of those countries rose against them, burned their houses
and synagogues, and put many of their chief men to
death. Again the emperor endeavoured to interfere and
put a stop to these disorders, prohibiting the Jews, on the

one hand, from insulting the Christian religion, and forbidding the Christians to burn the synagogues or otherwise molest the Jews.

In Syria the animosity between the two sects was as violent and as openly displayed as ever. At a town called Immestar, between Chalcis and Antioch, a young Christian was crucified by some drunken Jews. The offenders received condign punishment from the Roman authorities;

ANTIOCH.

but this did not satisfy the Christians, who shortly after pillaged a synagogue at Antioch. Theodosius ordered the clergy to make restitution, but was induced to overlook this flagrant violation of law and justice at the intercession of the celebrated St. Simeon Stylites.

This man, mistaking the true meaning of love of God, spent thirty years of his life on the top of a column seventy feet high. The influence which he acquired over

the vulgar mind by this jogi-like performance was enor
mous, and extended to the emperor himself. We have
seen to what purpose it was employed. The revocation of
the emperor's decree encouraged the Christians of the
neighbouring provinces to commit new atrocities against
the Jews. In the meantime, disturbances in connection
with the Jews were going on in various parts of the
empire. In Alexandria the Jews had attained to considerable wealth and influence ; but they were somewhat turbulent citizens, and conflicts between them and the Christian
population were of frequent occurrence.

Cyrill, the Christian bishop, attempted to take the law
in his own hands, and threatened the Jews with exemplary
punishment, and, after a free fight, forced them to leave
the city, and plundered their goods. Orestes, the Roman
prefect, took umbrage at this usurpation of his authority,
and sided with the Jews ; whereupon Cyrill, supported by
a number of armed monks from the Nitrean desert, openly
defied and insulted the prefect, who even received a blow
on the head from one Ammonius. The populace, however,
rose in defence of their prefect, and Ammonius was put to
death.

There lived in Alexandria at the time a lady named
Hypatia, distinguished for her extraordinary learning, and
especially for her acquaintance with the Platonic philosophy, which she taught publicly in the schools. Between
her and Orestes an intimate friendship existed, and, as
she was a Pagan, she was suspected of fostering the feud
between the patriarch and the prefect; thereupon the
adherents of the gentle Cyrill seized upon the unfortunate
lady, and murdered her with the most revolting cruelty in
front of a Christian Church. It has been thought by
some that the bishop himself instigated this dastardly
outrage.

In the island of Minorca the Jews had, under the just
and clement rule of Honorius, risen to great importance.

The Bishop, Severus, longed for an opportunity of changing this state of things, and he accordingly took advantage of the opportune arrival of the relics of St. Stephen to attempt the conversion of the Jews on the island. The relics do not appear to have afforded all the miraculous aid that was expected of them; but the bishop's party had other and equally cogent methods of conversion, and the Jews found it better, on the whole, to submit to baptism.

GLEN IN CRETE.

In Crete the conversion of a large number of Jews was likewise achieved. The attendant circumstances are curious. One Moses, an impostor, if not indeed an enthusiast, succeeded in persuading his compatriots that he could restore them to their native land, and that the sea itself would open to give them passage, as the Red Sea had parted beneath the footsteps of their forefathers. An immense crowd followed him to the sea-shore, and at his command the foremost precipitated themselves into the waves. In the confusion that followed, the impostor managed to escape, doubtless with a considerable booty, and those whom the efforts of Christian sailors had rescued from the waves, either to testify their gratitude to their rescuers, or else from very shame, consented to be baptized.

The patriarch of the Jews subsisted upon a tax levied upon all his western co-religionists. As this impost became at last very exorbitant in amount, the Jews complained to the emperor. The emperor promptly removed the cause of dissension by appropriating the tax himself, and the patriarchate, thus deprived of its means of subsistence, collapsed, and with it the union and national existence of the Jews, who were afterwards governed by local chiefs of synagogues called primates.

The latter part of the fifth century witnessed the eruption of the northern barbarians over the whole of the Western empire. Such a political convulsion as this could not fail to involve the Jews in many evils; but, on the whole, they suffered less than might perhaps have been expected. In one way they were positively the gainers, for commerce had been seriously injured by the invasion, and the new masters of the empire were too much addicted to the arts of war to care for commercial pursuits, which were accordingly abandoned to the Jews, whose immunity from civil services left them ample leisure to cultivate them.

The Vandals left them free to exercise their religion, and Theodoric, the Gothic king of Italy, extended his protection to the despised race, and repressed the violent measures of persecution to which his fanatical Christian subjects were too prone to resort.

In the more vigorous days of the Roman empire the Jews had been recognised simply as followers of another religion, and no persecutions were ever employed against them on merely religious grounds; but as the empire began to decay the power of the Church grew stronger, and was unfortunately exercised in violent measures against all who differed from the established creed.

The Byzantine emperors, Justin and Justinian, deprived the Jews of all their political privileges, and excluded them from every office of dignity and emolument. Many of Justinian's enactments were particularly vexatious, as they dealt with things strictly appertaining to the religious usages of the Jews themselves, regulating their calendar and the worship and conduct of their synagogues, and even prescribing the use of the Greek instead of the Hebrew Scriptures. This last law, could it ever have been permanently enforced, would have been the deadliest blow of all to the Jewish religion, for it would have completely destroyed the authority of the Rabbis, which depended upon, and was inseparably connected with, the knowledge of the sacred tongue.

In Africa the emperor, at the request of the Council of Carthage, formally interdicted the exercise of the Jewish religion, and converted the synagogues into Christian churches. Everywhere throughout the empire the Israelites were forbidden to bring up their children in their ancestral faith.

Such tyrannical laws naturally excited a feeling of hostility against the government, and insurrections of the Jews took place in many portions of the empire. In Palestine one Julian, calling himself as usual the Messiah, collected together a great crowd of followers, and murdered many Christians. Justinian sent troops against the insurgents, and routed them with some difficulty. About twenty years afterwards the Jews of Cæsarea also revolted, and laying aside for once their hereditary animosity to the Samaritans, entered into a league with that people and ravaged the country, slaughtering the Christians and destroying their churches. The governor himself was assassinated in his palace.

In Italy the Jews, who were then under the dominion of the Goths, endeavoured to aid their brethren in the war against Justinian and Belisarius; the latter accordingly besieged Naples, and although the Jews defended one quarter of the town with great bravery, the Romans succeeded in making themselves masters of the place and slew every Jew irrespective of age or sex.

We must now glance at the state of the Jews in the East in the fifth century. It was about the year 407, that Rabbi Asche commenced his grand compilation, the Babylonian Talmud. Like the Jerusalem Talmud, this comprises the Mishna of Rabbi Judah and the Gemara or complement, and is to the present day considered as a complete summary of law, doctrine, and religious observance. Rabbi Asche did not live to complete the work, but left the task to his son Huna and two of his most promising disciples. A violent persecution against the Jews amongst the Persians, instituted by the Magians, retarded the work, which was not finished until the sixth century. It may be well to state, for the sake of clearness, that the Talmud of Jerusalem is composed of the Mishna of R. Judah and the Gemara of R. Jochanan, while the Babylonian Talmud contains the Mishna, slightly altered, of R. Judah and the Gemara of Rab Asche.*

Another work, which was probably commenced about the sixth century, is the Massorah, which has for its object the definite fixing of the text of the Holy Scriptures. The Jews pretend that this art was taught by God Himself to Moses on Mount Sinai, and directly handed down by oral tradition.

Kaicobad, who at the beginning of the sixth century occupied the throne of Persia, decreed that all his subjects should embrace the Magian religion. This ordinance was especially distasteful to the Jews, and a certain rabbi named Meir was hardy enough to raise the standard of revolt; a number of Jews followed him, but the insurrection was speedily put down by the Persian monarch, who

---

* The Palestine title was *Rabbi*; the Babylonian, *Rab*.

marched upon Zutra, where the Prince of the Captivity
resided, pillaged the town and hanged the potentate, together with his tutor R. Chamna.   In the following year,
A.D. 531, Naushirwan the Just, or as he is styled by the
European historians, Chosroes the Great, succeeded to the
throne, and commenced by treating the Israelites with
greater severity.

The Jews of Palestine suffered so much at the hands of

TAK KESRA—CTESIPHON ON THE TIGRIS.

the Emperor Justinian, that the condition of their Babylonian brethren looked quite enviable in contrast with their
own ; they accordingly sent to invite the Persian monarch
to invade Judea, promising to furnish him with a con-
tingent of 50,000 men, and holding out promise of rich
plunder in Jerusalem.

By the payment of a large sum of money Justiniar
contrived to patch up a peace which lasted for seven years,

after which Naushirwan again invaded Palestine; but, having extended his conquests to Antioch, was compelled to retire by the prowess of Belisarius, the general of the Roman emperor. In both these incursions the Jews, who had been prevented by Justinian's prompt measures from giving their promised aid to the invader, suffered most severely, and on the second retreat of the Persians they were abandoned to the tender mercies of the masters they had endeavoured to betray.

Hormuzd, or Hormisdas, Naushirwan's successor, was more just and merciful to his Jewish subjects, and under his reign they regained many of their ancient privileges, and reopened their schools. At his death, Chosroes II., who is by some suspected of the crime of parricide, was prevented from ascending the throne by his own son Bahram, and the Jews supported the usurper in his pretensions. When, later on, Chosroes II., with the assistance of Maurice, the Emperor of the East, regained possession of the throne, the Jews had to pay dearly for their imprudence, and many, especially amongst those of Antioch, were ruthlessly put to death. The persecution was rather a political than a religious one, and the Jews presently returned to their allegiance.

An opportunity soon occurred for putting into execution the long-cherished ambitious designs of Persia. Phocas had risen against Maurice, murdered him and his five sons, and caused himself to be proclaimed Emperor of Byzantium. The Jews in Palestine were furious with the usurper, and rendered all the assistance in their power to Chosroes, who was marching onwards to revenge the death of his protector and friend. Galilee soon yielded to the Persian arms, and Chosroes having made himself master of Jerusalem, recompensed his Jewish allies by giving up to their fury the persons and property of the Christian inhabitants. Whilst Chosroes besieged Constantinople, and all the forces of Syria and Judea were withdrawn to defend the capital, the Jews of Tyre seized the opportunity to concert a plan for the capture of that city, and the slaughter of the inhabitants. Forewarned in time, the Tyrians defeated them and drove them out with great slaughter, not, however, before they had burnt a number of Christian churches in the vicinity.

HARBOUR AND RUINS OF ANCIENT TYRE.

CHAPTER XII.

THE GOTHIC AND MOHAMMEDAN DOMINIONS.

Rise of Mohammedanism ; its attitude towards Judaism—Fate of the Jews in
Arabia—Persecutions under Yezdegird, king of Persia, and the Emperor
Horaclius—Prosperous state of the Jews under the Caliphs—Abd-el-Melik—
El Mansúr—El Mehdi; the "veiled prophet of Khorassan"—Harún-er-Rashíd
—El Mámún—El Wáthik billáh and El Mutawakkil persecute the Jews—Fall
of the Abbasside dynasty—The Caraites—The kingdom of Khozar—The Jews
and the Papacy—Toleration of Pope Gregory the Great—The Jews in Spain
—Reputed antiquity of their settlement in that country—Severe laws of the
Gothic kings against them—Persecutions—Additional penalties enacted by
the Visi-Goth kings—The Jews are accused of a plot to favour the invasion
of Spain by the Saracens—King Wittiza restores the Jews to their privileges
—Conquest of the country by the Saracens—The Jews in France—Ferreol,
bishop of Ugés, deprived of his diocese for favouring the Jews—Chilperic,
"the Nero of France," and Dagobert persecute the Jews—Disturbances in
Languedoc—The Jews in the Western Empire—The Jews in Italy—The appearance of a false Messiah—The Saracens threaten Languedoc—Charlemagne
punishes the Jews for their supposed complicity in the Saracen invasion—
—Louis Débounaire favours the Jews—Charles the Bald—Zedekiah, the
Jewish physician, accused of poisoning the king—Degrading conditions
imposed upon the Jews residing in France.

Scarcely had the world settled down into comparative
peace after the successive revolutions caused by the inroads
of the Goths and Vandals, than another revolution burst
forth and spread with lightning-like rapidity over the whole
of the eastern world.

Mohammed had raised a protest against the prevailing
idolatry and corruption of his people, and the cry " There
is no god but God " rung through the valleys of the Hejjáz.
Hitherto the Arab tribes had been divided into small communities, distracted by petty jealousies, and wasting their
rude strength and warlike energies on border raids and
cattle-lifting excursions.   The eloquent enthusiast with his
new and striking doctrine struck a hitherto untouched
chord in their hearts, and a small number rallied round

his standard, to fight, not for the temporary possession of a coveted pasture ground, nor to revenge some comrade's fall, but to battle for an idea, for a conviction.

Even small successes beget confidence and increased conviction; and the little band of warriors fought more fiercely, more enthusiastically, than before. And then began to dawn upon them a great truth, and they learnt that, like the bundle of sticks in the fable, they could singly be snapped asunder by the weakest hand, but when firmly knitted together by a common bond, no man might bend them; they learnt for the first time that they were a nation; they began to feel their own gigantic strength, and they recognised the fact that disunion and anarchy had alone prevented that strength from displaying itself before. Mohammed was just such a rallying-point as they needed. He himself was a son of the desert, an Arab of the Arabs, and he knew how to make his new doctrine agreeable to them by clothing it in a purely Arab dress, and how to make his forms less distasteful by declaring them to be a simple reversion to the primary order of things.

His religion he declared to be that of Abraham, the father of the Hebrew-Arab races, and he accordingly looked first of all for support and credence from that kindred branch of Abraham's stock, the Jews. Of these, large numbers had settled in Arabia, where, by their industry and commercial talents, they had acquired considerable influence and power. As the Jews, too, indulged in longings after liberty, and aspirations after a restoration of the former glories of their kingdom, it is not to be wondered at that they were at the first rather dazzled by Mohammed's proposals, for we find that at the commencement of his mission a good understanding existed between the prophet and his Jewish neighbours, and that he received important help in the literary part of his undertaking from several of their learned men. But both parties had been deceiving themselves. It was not for the faith of Abraham nor for

MOSQUE AT HEBRON.

the advancement of the Semitic race that Mohammed was fighting ; it was, whether he knew it or not, for the unity and aggrandisement of the Arab race. With this the Jews could never sympathise ; as well might it be that Jew and Gentile should fraternise, as that Isaac and Ishmael should go hand-in-hand.

Finding that his offers and pretensions were refuse Mohammed turned upon the Jews and persecuted them with great rancour.

The Jewish tribe of Kainoka at Medina were the first summoned to profess the new faith or submit to the alternation of death. Notwithstanding that they were unaccustomed to the use of arms, they made a brave resistance for fifteen days, but were at last beaten, plundered of all they possessed, and driven to find an asylum in Syria. Other tribes presently shared the same fate, and Judaism ceased to exist in Arabia Proper, although traces of a Jewish origin may still be noted in certain of the Bedawí tribes, particularly those in the neighbourhood of Kheibar, the last stronghold of which Mohammed dispossessed them.

Under the caliphs, or immediate successors of Mohammed, the conquests of Islam spread far and wide in an incredibly short space of time, and Omar, the second after the prophet, during his short reign of ten years subdued the whole of Arabia, Syria, Mesopotamia, and Egypt. The Jews in these countries had little cause to lament the change of masters, for although they were kept in an inferior position by the " true believers," yet they by no means suffered such active persecution as they were made to do under Christian rule. A Mohammedan mosque rose, it is true, upon the sacred summit of Mount Moriah, but even that was preferable in Jewish eyes to the insult which the Christians had heaped upon the holy site.

The passage from Eutychius, quoted on p. 190, shows what was the nature of those insults ; the Christians, in the first burst of enthusiasm, and in their anger against

those who had crucified the Saviour, were desirous of removing every vestige of the hated race and their religious
observances from the Holy city; and in a misguided wish
to further the fulfilment of the prophecy of our Lord,
" Behold, your house shall be left unto you desolate," had
converted the sacred area of the temple into a dungheap.
The fact that the area of the temple was actually used for
this purpose when Omar entered Jerusalem, strengthens
the ground for our belief in the authenticity of the site.

In Persia they were clearly the gainers by the change.
for while Yezdegird, the last native king of that country,
had instituted a bloody persecution against them, and had
shut up their schools, and given over their synagogues to
the Magians, the caliphs allowed them freely to exercise
their religion on the payment of a simple tribute.

The Emperor Heraclius persecuted the Jews with
unusual animosity, and is even said to have excited other
monarchs to follow the same course. Before Jerusalem
was wrested from him by Omar he had already expelled
the Jews from that city, and the events attending the
Mohammedan conquest were not likely to increase his
goodwill towards them, seeing that they hailed the downfall of the Christian power with joy, and doubtless lent a
willing hand to the iconoclastic Moslems in despoiling
Christian churches.

In the eighth, and part of the ninth, centuries the
Oriental Jews, although disturbed by the dissensions which
continually arose amongst their Mohammedan conquerors,
yet enjoyed perfect civil and religious liberty under the
early caliphs.

During the reigns of Omar and Abd-el-Melik, a Jew had
charge of the important trust of the coinage. In the
reign of El Mansúr, the second of the Abbasside dynasty
and the founder of the city of Bagdad, the Jews enjoyed
great prosperity, and many of their rabbis rose to a high
position at the court of these caliphs, where learning was

always welcomed and rewarded. El Mansúr entrusted the Jews in his dominions with the office of collecting the heavy fines which he levied upon all Christians ; we can imagine how the Jews would exercise their functions, especially upon the " ecclesiastics, monks, hermits, ' those who stood on columns,' " and other fanatics, who are expressly mentioned in the Law.

Under the caliphs the Jewish schools of Súra and Pum·

BAGDAD.

beditha were in their most flourishing condition, and the Princes of the Captivity regained something like their former state, and were recognised as the legitimate representatives of the Jewish people in all intercourse with the government.

El Mehdi, the successor of El Mansúr, forced the Jews either to embrace Mohammedanism or to wear a distinctive dress. It was in his reign that the impostor

Q

Hakím, surnamed El Mokanna, or " the veiled," appeared in Khorassan, and, by his pretended miracles,
drew after him a large number of followers. He is said
to have been a Jew by birth. His story and tragic end
are familiar to the English reader from the version given
by Moore, in " Lalla Rookh," under the title of " the
Veiled Prophet of Khorassan," and which in the main
reproduces the historical circumstances of the case.

Harún-er-Rashíd, the next caliph, is also familiar to us
as the hero of many tales in the " Arabian Nights," and as
the ally of Charlemagne. This prince was a great patron
of letters, and particularly favoured the Jews, one of
whom, named Isaac, was actually chosen ambassador
between the caliph and the court of France.

El Mámún was the greatest patron of literature and
learning amongst the Mohammedan sovereigns. Under
his auspices all the principal Hebrew works were translated into Arabic. During his reign the famous Jewish
impostor Músa appeared, claiming to be the great Hebrew
legislator himself risen from the dead.

El Wáthik billáh showed himself less tolerant than his
predecessors, and humiliated the Jews by certain degrading
regulations which he imposed upon them, as, for instance,
that they should wear a leathern girdle and not be allowed
to ride upon horses, but only upon asses or mules.

El Mutawakkil, brother and successor of El Wáthik,
treated the Jews with even greater severity, and imposed
upon them even more ignominious conditions, many of
which have not been removed, even to the present day.

The successors of El Mutawakkil continued to treat
their Hebrew subjects with the same harshness and contempt until Ahmed Ibn Túlún, governor of Egypt, revolted
in the year 868, and gave the death-blow to the 'Abbasside
dynasty, already weakened by defections in other parts of
the empire. But, with the exception of such vexatious
enactments as those of the later 'Abbasside caliphs, the

Jews enjoyed unexampled prosperity under the rule of their Mohammedan masters. The effects of this long interval of peace and security soon began to show itself in the expansion of their minds and their greater freedom of thought and inquiry. Talmudical decisions and Rabbinical authority began to be called in question, and the sect of Caraites, who reject all but the Law of Moses pure and simple, began to assume formidable dimensions; they have been aptly called the Protestants of Judaism.

The Caraites ultimately settled at Jerusalem, where a flourishing community of them exists at the present day; branches of the same sect are also found widely spread over various countries of the world, especially in Poland and the east of Europe.

Jewish writers tell a strange story of the rise of a Jewish kingdom on the west of the Caspian Sea during the eighth century. The name of the country was Khozar, and was inhabited by a Turkoman tribe, which, having exchanged nomadic life for agriculture and commerce, had attained to considerable importance. One of the kings, Bulan, became a convert from heathenism to Judaism, and his dynasty lasted for two centuries and a half. The whole question is, however, involved in considerable obscurity, and many writers doubt even the existence of the kingdom.

Several of the popes of Rome showed a toleration towards the Jews strangely in contrast with the bigoted violence of the secular sovereigns contemporary with them. Pope Gregory the Great is a notable instance of this clemency towards the oppressed nation, and though he earnestly sought after their conversion, he endeavoured to bring it about by conciliatory and legitimate measures.

In Sicily he ordained that such Jews as would consent to receive baptism should be excused a third of their imposts; and he everywhere exhorted the clergy to set before them an example of Christian moderation, and to

Q 2

seek to win them over to the fold of Christ by the exercise
of those virtues which the blessed Saviour had inculcated.
Persecution and misguided zeal he denounced in the
strongest terms; and he even went the length of repri-
manding the Bishop of Terrcina for having interfered
with certain Jews of his diocese in their possession of
a synagogue authorised by law. Against one practice he

THE ESCURIAL.

firmly set his face, and that was, the holding of Christian
slaves by Jewish masters. The laws against this nefarious
traffic he put in force with great vigour, and decreed that
all Jewish slaves who embraced Christianity should, *ipso
facto*, become free.

The history of the Jews in Spain would require a

volume of itself to do the subject justice, and I can only briefly glance at its principal features. At the period which we are now discussing an immense colony of Jews existed in the Spanish peninsula, the origin of which is involved in considerable obscurity, and Jewish writers pretend to trace it back to as remote a date as the reign of King Solomon, and profess to have discovered at Seguntum, in the fifteenth century, the sepulchre of Adoniram, with an inscription containing the following words, in the Hebrew language and characters: "The Sepulchre of Adoniram, the servant of King Solomon, who came hither to collect the tribute." *

Recared, the first Gothic king, found them a prosperous and wealthy community, and he did all in his power, by the promulgation of cruel and unjust laws, to humiliate and ruin them. They were forbidden to exercise any of the distinctive rites of their religion, and were declared incapable of bearing witness against Christians. The last measure was, of course, equivalent to giving a general licence to maltreat and pillage them, and they could not obtain redress, because they were incompetent to testify to their wrongs. These laws did not at first come into active operation, the Jews having, it appears, bribed the king largely to suspend them.

Sisebut, the fourth king after Recared, sternly enforced them, and even added other and more grievous clauses. Without consulting the bishops, and even in spite of their remonstrances, he commenced a fiery persecution against the Jews, imprisoning all their chief men and confiscating the property of all who refused to be baptized. It is said that the Spanish king was instigated to this barbarous conduct by the Emperor Heraclius, to whom it had been predicted that his empire should fall by the hands of the circumcised, and who, being ignorant of the Mohammedan movement which was shortly to fulfil the prophecy, cherished

* 1 Kings iv. 6, v. 13.

an unrelenting severity against all the Hebrew race. The Jews attempted to remonstrate with the sovereign, and a strange controversy took place between the suppliants and their royal oppressor, the details of which have come down to us.

The Israelites adduced the example of Joshua, who, they said, did not enforce the Canaanites to embrace the Mosaic law, to which the king replied, " That all those who were not baptized would perish everlastingly, and he was determined to avert such a calamity as far as possible." The Jews humbly represented that just as the Jews who had despised the Promised Land were sufficiently punished by being excluded from it, so his majesty might, in their case, be content with the punishment of exclusion from eternal life, which upon the whole they would prefer to risk rather than submit to the terms proposed to them. Upon this, Sisebut, as a last clinching argument, threw them all into prison. It is said that 90,000 persons consented to become nominal Christians to save their lives and property, while others made their escape into France and Africa, in the former of which countries they were promptly robbed, tortured, and murdered, with a similar benevolent motive.

The Spanish clergy strongly disapproved of these harsh and brutal measures, and Isador, Bishop of Seville, and President of the Fourth Council of Toledo, declared such laws to be contrary to the true spirit of Christianity. After reprobating forced conversion in no measured terms the council somewhat illogically ordained that all those whom persecution had compelled to become Christians should be kept to the profession of their new religion. Suintila renewed the persecution, and in order to bring the clergy over to his views and obtain their co-operation, he convened the Sixth Council of Toledo. The worthy ecclesiastics thus assembled praised the zeal of Suintila and prescribed a form of oath by which every king on his accession bound himself, under pain of anathema, to

execute the laws against the Jews. The successive sovereigns of Spain obeyed this edict only too well, and a new
decree of the Visi-Goth kings gave still further effect
to the laws by pronouncing corporal punishment, banishment, and confiscation of property, against all Jews who
refused to embrace the Christian faith.   Former laws had
imposed the penalty of death, and this very severity had
frustrated their aims ; the new enactment mitigated the
penalty to a hundred lashes on the naked body, in addition to banishment and forfeiture of goods.

A succession of such enactments reduced the Hebrews
almost to desperation, and there is probably some truth
in the accusation that they had entered into treasonable
correspondence with the Šaracens, whose army was already
appearing on the opposite coast of Africa.   It was reported
that a widely-spread plot existed throughout the country
to introduce the Moslems and overthrow the Christian
religion.   The rumour easily obtained credence, and a law
was hastily passed exceeding even the previous ones in
severity.   The Hebrews were to be seized, sold into
slavery and distributed throughout the country ; all property owned by Jews was to be confiscated, and all the
children under seven years of age were to be taken from
their parents and brought up as Christians.   This acted
like the proverbial " last feather" on the camel's back, and
the Jews took flight *en masse.*

Wittiza, the next king, attempted to conciliate the
much-wronged Hebrews, and to the astonishment and
annoyance of the Roman clergy, compelled a Council at
Toledo, with an archbishop at its head, to sanction his new
laws, restoring the rights of citizenship to the Jews.   But
the act of policy and humanity came too late.   The
Saracens, at once the protectors and avengers of the children of Israel, were at the door ; how it fared with the
latter under the Mohammedan dominion in Spain we shall
narrate in a subsequent chapter.

In France the state of the Jews was little better than in
Spain, and from the very commencement of the kingdom
laws and edicts had been framed against them. In A.D.
540 Childebert prohibited them from appearing in the
streets of Paris during the season of Lent, and the
Council of Orleans about the same time promulgated a

PARIS—THE BOULEVARDS.

similar edict, which obtained throughout the greater part
of the country.

Languedoc was the province in which the Israelites
were most numerous and most prosperous, and Ferreol,
Bishop of Uzés, was deprived of his diocese for attempting to convert them by fair and conciliatory means. On

being restored some years later the bishop determined to avoid such an unpopular course for the future, and drove every Jew out of his diocese.

Avitus, Bishop of Clermont, made great efforts for the conversion of the Jews, and succeeded in obtaining numerous proselytes. One of these being publicly insulted by a member of his own race, the populace were so exasperated that, although the presence of the bishop prevented the offender from being murdered on the spot, yet his authority could not restrain the mob from demolishing the synagogue; so high did popular feeling run on the occasion that the great mass of Jews in the neighbourhood submitted to baptism rather than incur the fate that threatened them.

Chilperic, "the Nero of France," as he is called, was a man of detestable character, and was also a would-be theologian, and the author of several treatises on doctrinal subjects. Having in vain endeavoured to convince a Jew by argument of the error of his ways, his majesty threw his opponent into prison, where he was barbarously murdered.

This was the signal for a fierce persecution, by which means many promising converts were added to the Church.

Dagobert was a monarch of even more atrocious character than his predecessor, and sought to atone for his misdeeds by the same means—persecution of the Jews; then, perhaps, a ready passport to clerical favour and plenary indulgence.

All Jews were commanded to renounce their religion or quit the kingdom, but their frequent appearance in the subsequent history of France shows that the edict was never rigidly enforced.

Wamba, king of the Goths, issued a decree of banishment against all Jews in the province of Languedoc, which he governed. Strange to say, a certain abbot named Raymire joined with the count of Toulouse, and took up arms to oppose this despotic measure. The king sent an army under Count Paul, his favourite, to suppress the rebellion, but the general, having reached the scene of action, joined his forces with those of the insurgents, took Narbonne, and caused himself to be crowned king. Not long afterwards he was defeated and condemned to death, and the king, Wamba, revenged himself for the troubles which the Jews had brought upon him by persecuting them with bitter animosity, and driving them forth from his kingdom. Notwithstanding these calamities the Jewish academy at Lunel continued to flourish during the seventh century, and subsequently acquired great celebrity, many illustrious rabbis having belonged to it.

In the eighth century the Western Empire was the theatre of a civil war, caused by the dissensions of two opposing parties in the Church, the Iconoclasts and the worshippers of images. The Jews were suspected of being the instigators of the quarrel, and Leo the Isaurian, the Greek emperor, punished them by compelling them to subscribe to all the formularies and ceremonies of the Church. When the Iconoclast party ultimately triumphed, the Jews were forced not only to renew their obligations of outward conformity, but to call down upon themselves awful curses if they secretly profaned any of the holy Christian rites.

Leo's successor, Nicephorus, relaxed these severities and refrained from molesting the Jews. Michael, the next emperor, whose creed was of an extremely eclectic, not to say incongruous character, showed himself especially favourable to his Jewish subjects.

In Italy and Spain the Jews fared badly during the eighth and ninth centuries. About 724 their troubles were increased, if not caused, by their own credulity in following one Serenus, who proclaimed himself the Messiah, and led an immense number of his compatriots to Palestine to share with him the kingdom of the Holy Land.

When they returned to Spain from their wild-goose chase, those who did not perish on the journey found that the Christians had taken possession of all the property which they had left behind.

Languedoc as well as part of Spain was in the power of the Visi-Goths; but the greater portion of Spain had been invaded and subjugated by the Saracens. The Arabs now began to make frequent incursions into Languedoc, and on one occasion, traversing Narbonne, they actually penetrated as far as Lyons, devastating the country on their march.

It is said that this invasion was brought about by the Jews, who had invoked the aid of the Mohammedans in order to destroy the Christian power. Whether these accusations were true or not it is difficult to decide; at any rate they served as a pretext for persecution, and Charlemagne's first act, after having reconquered Toulouse and driven the Moslems from French territory, was to inflict grievous punishment upon his Jewish subjects. He at first threatened to exterminate them altogether, but he appears to have been content with executing some of their head men, and making the others submit to a degrading ceremony, namely, a slap on the face three times a-year at the hands of the bishop, and obliging them to pay each three pounds of wax a-year towards lighting the church. Subsequently, Charlemagne seems to have treated the Jews with greater lenity, and we find that even when they openly boasted that they were in the habit of purchasing the sacred ecclesiastical vessels from the bishop and abbots, it was upon the corrupt clergy, and not upon these Jewish dealers, that the king's wrath fell.

Louis Débonnaire openly favoured the Jews, allowed them to build synagogues, and granted them many other privileges. This was, no doubt, due in a great measure to the influence which Zedekiah, a Hebrew physician, had obtained over the sovereign. The favour and privileges which they thus enjoyed aroused the jealousy of the Christians, and Agobard, Bishop of Lyons, endeavoured to counteract

the effect of royal protection by the thunders of ecclesiastical denunciation. The Jews were forbidden not only to
purchase Christian slaves, but also to engage in any traffic
on Sundays and fast-days. The Hebrews complained to the
king, and were immediately reinstated in all their former
rights and privileges. In vain did the bishop protest, and
even appear in person before the monarch to plead his
cause; Louis refused to grant him an interview except
for the purpose of taking leave. To such extraordinary
credit had the Jews risen in the reign of this monarch
that many Christians kept the Jewish Sabbath, and fre-
quented the synagogues, preferring the sermons of the
rabbis to those of their own ignorant monks; it is even
asserted that a certain deacon, named Paudo, left the
Christian Church to officiate in the synagogue.

Under Charles the Bald, the Jewish influence began to
wane, and a certain French bishop, named Remy, ordered
the clergy of his diocese to preach every Saturday in the
Jewish synagogues. An appeal to the king had no other
effect than that of provoking an edict to extend this practice over the whole of the kingdom, and the conversion of
many Hebrew children was the result. Not long after this
the king died. Zedekiah, the physician who had enjoyed
so much power during the preceding reign, was accused of
having poisoned him; the other members of his race were
suspected of complicity in the plot, and a pretext was thus
afforded for new persecutions. No public misfortune or
reverse could ever happen without the Jews being, of
course, at the bottom of it,—it was convenient to have a
scape-goat, something on which to vent the national ill-
humour; accordingly, when the Normans began to make
incursions into the French territory, and Bordeaux and
other places fell into their hands, the Jews were accused of
having betrayed the towns into the hands of the enemy,
and Charlemagne's edict was once more put in force. The
syndic or chief magistrate, however, received the blow in

the name of all his compatriots. In the provinces they were subjected to still greater indignities by the fanatical populace, and at Beziers, in Languedoc, it was a common amusement to stone the Jews by way of celebrating the Easter festivities. They were ultimately freed from these outrages on payment of a tax to the bishop.

CHAPTER XIII.

THE MIDDLE AGES.

Flourishing condition of Jewish learning in the East—David, Prince of the
Captivity, attempts to bring about the independence of the Jews—Rabbi
Sherira—El Hakem bi amr Illah and Sultan Jelal ed Dáuleh persecute the
Jews—Great prosperity under the Spanish Caliphs—Arabic translation of the
Talmud—Troubles in Granada—Ferdinand—Alfonso—Pedro I.—The Crusades
—The Jews in Hungary and Germany—Atrocities of the Crusaders—The
second Crusade—Travels of Benjamin of Tudela; his account of the Jews in
the East and elsewhere—Alfonso VIII. of Spain—Moses Maimonides—Ap-
pearance of false Messiahs—The Jews in Great Britain—William the Con-
queror—William Rufus—Henry II.—Accession of Richard I.—Massacre of
the Jews—The English Crusaders—Frightful slaughter of the Jews at York
—King John endeavours to protect them—Henry III.—" Sir Hugh of Lincoln "
—Henry sells the Jews to his brother Richard for 5,000 marks of silver—
Edward I.—Recurrence of the crusading fever—The Jews banished from
England.

WHILE the Western world was involved in the darkness of
ignorance and superstition, literature, learning, and philosophy were, as we have seen, cultivated in the East, and
munificently patronised by the Mohammedan caliphs.
That the Jewish schools were in the foremost rank, and were
especially successful in their cultivation of the sciences, is
proved by the many valuable Hebrew treatises which have
come down to us. Intellectual supremacy naturally provoked impatience of political servitude ; but in their efforts
at emancipation they were less successful. One of the
Princes of the Captivity named David, contrived, the
Jewish historians tell us, to free his countrymen from the
tribute which they paid to the caliphs. But his motives
were too soon apparent ; he desired himself to exercise
that despotic authority over his countrymen by releasing
them from which he had gained so much credit. Con-

stant quarrels between himself and the heads of the schools were the result, and the Jewish community, divided against itself, sustained many and serious evils.

In the year 1037 the celebrated Rab Sherira Gaon died at Pherutz Schibbur. He was the founder of a new school in that town, had been elected Prince of the Captivity, and enjoyed such a reputation for wisdom and learning that Hebrews from all quarters of the world came to consult him, and bestowed upon him the proud title of "the most excellent of all excellent ones."

At the commencement of the eleventh century, the Fatemite Caliph El Hakem bi amr Illah came to the throne of Egypt. This prince, who at the time of his accession was a mere child, reigned for twenty-five years, during which time he succeeded in perpetrating more follies, atrocities, and blasphemies than any one man in the history of the world. He was the founder of the Syrian sect of the Druses, who still worship him as a god! The Jews were especial objects of his mad and vindictive caprice: "He ordered that they should wear blue robes, and Christians black, and in order to mark them yet more distinctively, that both should wear black turbans. Christians, moreover, were at first ordered to wear wooden stirrups, with crosses round their necks, while the Jews were compelled to carry round pieces of wood, to signify the head of the golden calf which they had worshipped in the desert." *

The accession of the Sultan Jelal ed Dáuleh to the caliphate, under the name of El Káim bi amr Illah, was a black day to the Jews. Other caliphs of the house of 'Abbas had favoured the Hebrew race ; this prince resolved upon exterminating them altogether. With this design he shut up the schools, banished the professors, and put to death the Prince of the Captivity. Many historians date from this time the extinction of that office ; but Benjamin

* Besant and Palmer's "Jerusalem," p. 129.

of Tudela, a Jewish pilgrim of the twelfth century, found
in Persia one of these chiefs, who boasted his descent
from the prophet Samuel.   This proves the fallacy of the
Jewish assertion that all the Princes of the Captivity were
of the lineage of David.   As we do not meet with the
Princes of the Captivity in history after the eleventh century
we may conclude that their authority had become extinct,
and that the empty title alone remained.

STREET IN CAIRO.

The Jews who were thus expelled from the East passed
through Africa to Spain, where the Mohammedan caliphs
who owed their conquest of the Spanish peninsula to
Jewish influence gave them a cordial reception ; hatred of
the Christian formed also a common bond of unity between the two peoples, and the period of the Mohammedan

dominion in Spain forms the brightest epoch in later Jewish history.

As many of their learned men attained to great favour at the court of the Saracen monarchs, the Jewish literature of these times presents a more flourishing aspect than it had

THE ALHAMBRA.

ever before worn. It was now, indeed, breaking through the trammels of tradition and venturing into the wide fields of general literature. For the first time, too, in their history, the Jews began to employ a language other than Hebrew in their writings, and Arabic became the medium

R

in which they expressed their ideas. But although they made this great progress in general literature, the Talmud, the basis of their law and religious observance, and even the rule and guide of their daily lives, was practically so little known that the Spanish schools were compelled to send to the Babylonian academies to decide difficult points of controversy. To remedy this defect, and possibly to gratify his own curiosity as well, El Hakem, one of the Mohammedan sultans of Cordova, caused a translation to be made into Arabic of the entire Talmud. When the Spanish kingdom was torn by wars and revolutions, the Jews knew how to profit even by such events. Rabbi Samuel Levi, secretary and prime minister of the king of Granada, became prince of his nation, and by his influence and talents raised it to an almost unexampled pitch of prosperity. At his death he was succeeded by his son, who was unfortunately as proud and overbearing as his father had been humble and unassuming ; these qualities brought upon him the detestation of all his compatriots.

The prosperity of the Hebrews in Spain received about the middle of the eleventh century a rude shock. One of their most learned Rabbis conceived the mad scheme of converting all the Mohammedans to Judaism, by means of the Arabic version of the Talmud. The fierce but slumbering fanaticism of the Moslem monarch was aroused ; Rabbi Joseph Hallevi, the well-meaning but misguided rabbi, was seized and put to death, and a violent persecution of the whole community followed, to which 100,000 families are said to have fallen victims. Happily El Hakem's successors upon the throne of Granada did not follow his bloody example.

Under Ferdinand, the Jews had an escape even narrower than that experienced at Granada. This prince was preparing to make war upon the Saracens, and conceiving that heaven might be propitiated by a persecution of the Israelites, would have driven them out of his own dominions, but that the Pope, Alexander II., interposed his authority and dissuaded the king from carrying out his unjust measure. Alfonso, Ferdinand's successor, alarmed at the increasing power of the Saracens, endeavoured to gain the Jews over to his side, experience having shown him that from their pecuniary resources they were valuable allies, and that against a Moslem foe they could be formidable enemies. The Pope, Gregory, remonstrated with the king for his indulgence to the enemies of Christ, but, for once in a way, a Spanish king laughed at the thunders of the Church.

Pedro I., grandson of Alfonso, although constantly instigated against the Jews by Nicholas of Valentia, refused to appease ecclesiastical rancour with the blood of peaceful citizens. The crusades, however, made Pedro's clemency of little avail, and thousands of Jews were massacred in every part of Spain by the furious soldiers of the Cross.

But in spite of all these troubles and persecutions the schools of Spain produced many learned men during the 11th century, eminent alike for literature and science.

About the end of the 11th century, St. Ladislas, king of Hungary, prohibited the Jews from marrying Christian women or purchasing Christian slaves ; Coloman, his successor, renewed this edict, but still permitted them the privilege of purchasing and cultivating the land under the jurisdiction of a bishop.

In Germany they had risen to a most flourishing condition, and had synagogues in all the principal towns, especially in Treves, Cologne, Mayence, and Frankfort. In Bohemia, too, they were well received by the people. In the provinces they did not fare so well, and a certain priest named Godeschal, or Gotschalk, inspired by the success of Peter the Hermit, preached a crusade on his own account against the Jews at home. Many of the princes connived at the doings of the impostor and of

R 2

the 15,000 ruffians who followed him. King Coloman of
Hungary, whose dominions they had invaded, discovering
that their pillaging and other atrocities was not confined
to the Jews alone, but extended to the devoutest Christian
who happened to possess any trifling property, very justly
attacked them. Meeting with a rebuff, the Hungarian
king had recourse to guile, and having induced them to
lay down their arms, he slaughtered them.

I have purposely refrained from detailing the enormities
which this band of ruffians committed in their march,
especially upon the persons of the Jews in the towns
through which they passed. Unfortunately, Jewish history is too full, as it is, of such horrors, without going
out of one's way to describe the doings of an erratic
mob.

The crusading army was little superior to the followers
of Gotschalk, either in discipline or humanity, and on
their way through Europe they ruthlessly slaughtered all
the " enemies of Christ " whom they encountered. It is
estimated that no less than 12,000 Jews perished in
Holland alone. To the credit of human nature it must
be confessed that the wretched children of Israel found
some to help them in this time of need, and the venerable
prelates of Mayence and Spires did not shrink from
raising their voices against the excesses that were being
committed in the name of Christ, and even afforded the
sufferers an asylum in their own episcopal palaces.

After a siege of five weeks the Crusaders took Jerusalem by assault, and at once commenced an indiscriminate slaughter of the inhabitants. "As for the Jews
within the city, they had fled to their synagogue, which
the Christians set on fire and so burned them all."[*]

The second crusade under the Emperor Conrad and
Louis VII., king of France, seemed likely to lead to results similar to those of the first expedition, as far as

* Besant and Palmer's "Jerusalem," p. 187.

the Jews were concerned, for the hermit Rodolph was traversing the Rhenish provinces and urging the German princes to exterminate all who did not profess the Christian faith. As other preachers took up the same cry, the Jews in terror fled to Nuremberg and other towns, where the emperor accorded them a favourable reception. The excellent St. Bernard and other prelates warmly denounced the intolerance of the hermit, and used strenuous and successful efforts to save the Jews from the imminent danger which threatened them.

But the fury which the crusades had inspired was not confined to the line of the Crusaders' march; everywhere throughout Europe the people raged and clamoured for the blood of the "deicides," and swore that the name of Israel should be wiped out of the book of human remembrance.

Benjamin of Tudela, a learned Jew who visited various countries in the 12th century, with a view of ascertaining the condition of his compatriots throughout the world, gives us some very interesting details of their condition in the East, although we must, of course, make some allowance for exaggeration in the author's avowed object of glorifying the Hebrew nation. Throughout the East he found his brethren flourishing and happy, exercising their religion without let or hindrance, and possessing many beautiful synagogues. At Bassora alone, one of the islands on the Tigris, there were 4,000 Hebrew inhabitants; and at Mosul, on the site of the ancient Nineveh, there were 7,000. In the latter town resided Zaccheus, who enjoyed the title of Prince of the Captivity, and a Jewish astronomer named Beren Al Pheres, who, Benjamin tells us, was chaplain to the Mussulman king, Zein ed Din. The famous schools of Pumbeditha, Sora, and Nahardea, were still in existence, although they had lost much of their ancient splendour and importance. Pumbeditha contained only a few learned rabbis, with some

2,000 students devoted, for the most part, to the study of the law. Sora had dwindled down to the condition of a small academy, and Nahardea was remarkable only for a synagogue built of stones brought from Jerusalem.

The Mohammedan court of Spain had attracted so many of the learned Jews to the West, that the Babylonian academies naturally began to decline. But, although the rabbis were so few in Asia, the Jewish community itself was large. At Baghdad our traveller found about a thousand Jews and twenty-eight synagogues; their affairs being directed by ten tribunals, each under the presidency of a Jewish noble. These chiefs, however, all obeyed the Prince of the Captivity, about whose pomp and importance Benjamin gives some curious details. Jewish authors have always insisted upon the continuity of this office, and the descent from David of all who held it; but I have before had occasion to remark that these pretensions are, to say the least, doubtful, and Benjamin of Tudela's testimony upon this point must be received with considerable caution.

In the neighbourhood of the ancient Babylon the Jews were very numerous, and a little further eastward still, on the banks of the river Chobar, he found no less than sixty synagogues; here, too, he saw the tomb of the prophet Ezekiel, which both Jews and Persians alike regarded with veneration.

In Egypt the Jews were very numerous, and Benjamin counted 30,000 in one town on the Ethiopian frontier. The chiefs of all the Egyptian synagogues resided at Cairo, where they watched over the interests of their nation.

In the Holy Land itself they were not in so flourishing a state. At Tyre, about 400 Jews resided, who were nearly all employed in glass works, and in Jerusalem itself there were not more than 200. In the other towns of Palestine they were equally poorly represented; but in

Upper Galilee he found a larger number. It will be remembered that after the destruction of Jerusalem many
sought refuge in that province, where they founded the
famous school of Tiberias. The Samaritans at the time of
Benjamin's visit had abandoned their ancient capital; about
200 had retired to Cæsarea, and 100 were residing at
Sichem (Nablous). Here they scrupulously observed all

A GROUP OF SAMARITANS.

their feasts and offered sacrifice upon Mount Gerizim.
Nablous has ever since remained the seat of the Samaritan religion, and a small community of that people
remains there to the present day. The sacrifices upon
Gerizim had fallen into abeyance for some centuries, but
they were resumed a few years ago as a commercial speculation to attract tourists.

In Greece they were neither numerous nor wealthy, but lived in comparative tranquillity. At Constantinople, the Emperor Theodosius had granted them the suburbs of Galata and Pera, where some 2,000 resided. There were also 500 Caraites in the imperial city, but their quarter was divided by a wall from that of the other Jews.

Benjamin next passed through Italy. In the republics of Genoa and Pisa, he tells us, the Jews were oppressed and kept in subjection; but in the other parts of the country, and even in fanatical Rome itself, they were prosperous and wealthy.

In Germany, with the exception of the Rhenish provinces, they had little to complain of; and in France, though not numerous, they were wealthy and possessed several important academies.

The clemency and humanity of St. Bernard operated very beneficially for the Jewish nation, and, owing chiefly to his influence, the Pope, Innocent II., treated them with great toleration. His successor, Alexander III., extended to them the same favour and countenance.

In Spain, during the 12th century, the Jews enjoyed considerable privileges. One of them, named Joseph, was Prime Minister to Alphonso VIII.; he rose to great influence at the court of the Spanish monarch, and surrounded himself with all the pomp and equipage of a grandee. He fell a victim to the treachery of one of his own creatures, named Gonzala, who, having incurred the just displeasure of his master, thought to escape the consequences of his misdeeds by the ruin of his benefactor. This traitor succeeded in arousing the cupidity of the king, and under pretence of filling the coffers of the state, induced him to hand over to him six of the principal Jews; these the ruffian at once put to death and confiscated their property. Not long afterwards Gonzala offered a much larger sum for twenty others; but the king himself confiscated their property, though he was merciful enough to spare their lives. At length Gonzala was thrown into prison, and the persecution ceased. Alphonso had another motive for his clemency. He was violently in love with a young and beautiful Jewess named Rachel, and her people profited by the influence which she had obtained over the king's mind. Their pride and insolence, however, so exasperated the clergy and the court, that Rachel was assassinated; notwithstanding the loss of their patroness, the Jews still contrived to maintain a considerable portion of their power.

The 12th century produced many eminent Jewish writers and commentators upon the Holy Scriptures; but none attained to such an eminence as the celebrated Moses Maimonides. He was born at Cordova in the year 1131, of an illustrious Jewish family claiming descent from King David. His brilliant talents and, perhaps, more than all, his intimate and friendly relations with his master the celebrated Arab philosopher, Ibn Rúh (Averroes), had aroused the jealousy of his co-religionists, and his writings, especially the *Moreh Nevochim* (the guide to those in doubt), raised up for him a crowd of antagonists. This work has for its object the explanation of difficult passages of Scripture, and professes to distinguish between those which are to be taken in a literal sense, and those which are to be understood as allegorical. Maimonides also contended that the law of Moses, though Divine in origin, was founded on the universal principles of reason and justice, and this doctrine was distasteful to the rabbis. But his crowning heresy was that he failed to display the usual superstitious respect for the Talmud, and the Jewish doctors, with Rabbi Solomon of Montpellier at their head, undertook to defend that recondite and incongruous volume against the daring theologian. The most obvious weapon to employ was that which fanatical priestly factions have generally made use of against reformers, viz., personal abuse. This the rabbis employed as freely against

Maimonides as the Roman Catholics did against Luther, acting up to the true spirit of the Arabic proverb, "Dirt thrown at a wall, if it does not stick, will leave its mark." All their abuse, however, could not prevent the name of Maimonides from being handed down to posterity as one of the brightest ornaments of Jewish literature.

The rabbis of Narbonne, led by the famous David Kimchi, warmly defended Maimonides, who had been compelled to leave Spain and seek refuge in Egypt, where he enjoyed the favour of the sultan and established a school.

In spite of the number of learned men which Judaism in the 12th century produced, their common folk were still so ignorant as to be continually led away by impostors and enthusiasts; and pseudo-messiahs appeared from time to time in various countries and brought many evils, not only on their credulous followers, but upon the Hebrew nation at large. One of these, an Arab Jew, in 1167, boldly went before the sovereign and declared that he was a prophet sent by God. The king asked him to prove his mission by a sign; to this he at once consented, and requested that his head might be cut off, assuring his majesty that he would immediately come to life again. The king took him at his word, but it is needless to add that the poor madman never fulfilled his part of the contract.

We pass now to the consideration of the state of the Jews in England. It is difficult to ascertain the exact period at which they were established in this kingdom; but it would seem that they were already numerous at the time of the Norman Conquest.

A colony of Hebrews from Rouen purchased from William the Conqueror the right to settle in Great Britain. In the feudal ages the Jews were the most wealthy and the best educated of all the secular classes. The financial operations of the country also were entirely in their hands, and so completely had they the control of commerce, that the very vessels and ornaments of the Christian churches were purchased from Jewish manufactories.

William Rufus showed himself very favourable to the Jews, and being himself a godless man, he encouraged them to dispute with the clergy, declaring that he would embrace the religion of whichever side should have the best of the argument. During this reign the Jews were a very powerful and even aggressive section of the community.

Henry II. also favoured and protected them, and some idea of their wealth and influence may be formed from the fact, that in the year 1188 the parliament assembled at Northampton taxed the Jews at £60,000 to provide for the expenses of the war, while the Christians of the kingdom were altogether only required to contribute £70,000. It is true that this taxation may as likely indicate the tyranny of the parliament as the number or opulence of the Jews.

On the accession of Richard I., the Jews, anxious to obtain the favour of the new king, came in crowds from all parts of the kingdom to assist at his coronation, bringing rich presents with them. The clergy and the court gave out that the Jews had formed a conspiracy to be-witch the king, and they were consequently excluded from Westminster Abbey at the time of the coronation. Some few, actuated by curiosity to view the pageant, contrived to slip into the abbey with the crowd, but being detected they took to flight, and were pursued by the infuriated people and some of them slain. Immediately the report spread that the king, in honour of his accession, had given orders for a massacre of all the Jews. Mad with excite-ment, fanaticism, and love of plunder, the mob pursued the wretched Jews from house to house, and gave them-selves up to murder, pillage, and the most frightful atrocities. Authority was powerless to quell the disturb-

RICHARD CŒUR DE LION.

ances, and the example of the metropolis was soon followed in the counties. A royal edict for the re-establishment of good order was published the morning after the king's coronation, but the persecution of the Jews continued for the greater part of the year.

The crusades, in which Richard participated more from love of adventure than from devotion, revived all the old hatred against the Jews, and kindled it into a fiercer flame. Popular prejudice confounded all banking transactions under the hateful name of usury, and as this branch of commerce was exercised entirely by Jews, the bad odour in which they were held by the rest of the people was greatly increased. Being a thrifty and industrious race, in strong contrast to the lazy and luxurious Englishmen of the day, they were soon the creditors of half the nation. The estimation in which they were held by their Christian fellow-subjects was not such as to engender any strong feelings of affection for the latter, and we need not wonder that they occasionally proved exacting creditors, or drove hard bargains. Such being the state of feeling between the two parties, we can imagine what the result would be when bands of men, fired with fanatic enthusiasm, were preparing to set out for a distant land to punish the " enemies of Christ." Was it reasonable that they who had sold their all to provide them with means for the journey should leave their families to starve, and allow these other enemies of Christ to remain at home in comfort and opulence. It needed not the specious reasoning of the priests or the sterner eloquence of the needy barons, themselves the Jews' debtors be it remembered, to enforce these arguments.

At York, where a large number of the Jewish bankers, or usurers, resided, the populace began to repeat the scenes of violence and bloodshed which had just disgraced the metropolis. The Jews, in order to escape the fury of the mob, sought and obtained an asylum in the castle ; but suspecting the good faith of the governor, they took the opportunity of his temporary absence in the town to lock the gates against him and defended the castle themselves. The governor, hereupon, made common cause with the popular party and induced the sheriff to give orders for an attack. The sheriff, seeing the frightful consequences which would be likely to ensue, wished the governor to revoke his decision, but it was too late; the enraged people carried the castle by assault, and the Jews, being unable to obtain terms from the conquerors, chose to fall by their own hands rather than encounter the brutal fury of the mob. The tragedy of Masada was enacted over again, and the wretched band, having slain their wives and children, fell upon each other's swords. More than 500 are said to have perished on the occasion, and a few wretched survivors, who had surrendered at discretion, were massacred without mercy. The assault was led by a canon of York cathedral, who, dressed in full canonicals, continued to incite the mob to the work of destruction, shouting out, "Kill the enemies of Jesus Christ." After this frightful catastrophe, the ring-leaders, who were nearly all debtors of the Jews, proceeded to the cathedral, where the records of all financial transactions were laid up, and forcing the custodian to give up the documents to them, solemnly burnt in the church all the bills, acceptances, and other memoranda of their pecuniary obligations. It is probable that the government would have overlooked the slaughter of a few Jewish subjects, and the levying of a small fine might have repaired the damage done to the castle; but the last act of the mob was enough to rouse the virtuous indignation of the king and his ministers, for the law provided that all debts owing to a deceased Jew should revert to the crown. Rydal, Bishop of Ely, and then Lord Chancellor of the realm, was accordingly charged with the exemplary punishment of the ill-doers; but the prelate contented himself with depriving the sheriff and governor,

RICHARD CŒUR DE LION AND HIS KNIGHTS.

and fining some of the richer inhabitants. The principal authors of the outrage had escaped over the Scottish borders ; and Granville, who was instructed to make inquiries as to the guilty parties, found so many implicated that he thought it prudent to desist from the pursuit.

These and similar persecutions at length drove many of the principal Jews to seek refuge in other more hospitable countries. Such a diminution in the revenue was the result that King John, on his accession to the throne, did his utmost to induce them to return, and granted them a charter restoring to them all their ancient privileges with many fresh ones, on condition of their paying a somewhat exorbitant tax. But even the royal protection was not sufficient to shield them from the fanatical hatred of the people, and those who did return were subjected to greater indignities and oppression than before. They were not, however, altogether without revenge, for they found that, provided they paid a sufficient sum to the government, they might extort whatever interest they chose for the monies which they advanced, and we can scarcely blame them if they made use of usury as a weapon of retaliation for the many and grievous wrongs which they suffered.

King John himself, notwithstanding the charter which he had given the Jews, subjected them to torture and imprisonment until he had exacted from them a sum of 60,000 marks of silver. He demanded 10,000 for the ransom of a single Jew of Bristol, and when the victim refused to furnish the money he adopted the cruel expedient of drawing one of the unfortunate man's teeth every day until the sum was paid.

Henry III. was a monarch of more enlightened views ; he protected his Jewish subjects from the fury of the crusading bands, and set at liberty such as had been incarcerated during the previous reign. In 1233, he founded a college for converted Jews, where they might reside without being obliged either to work or practise usury; and the advantages thus held out induced many to embrace Christianity. The mass of the people, however, continued to treat the unfortunate race with as great contumely and tyranny as ever.

In 1235 the old charge was brought against the Jews of having kidnapped children in order to circumcise or crucify them. This was made a pretext for fresh extortions and fresh persecutions. The supposed crime was alleged to have taken place at Lincoln, the body being afterwards discovered at the bottom of a well, and the story is perpetuated in Chaucer's *Prioress's Tale.*

The war with Spain in 1254 caused the king to make fresh demands upon them. The children of Israel would fain have quitted so inhospitable a country, but they were refused permission to depart, and compelled to remain and pay the impost. In the following year he again required 5,000 marks of silver, and, as the Jews declared themselves absolutely unable to satisfy the extortion, Henry sold them to his brother Richard for that sum. The latter was allowed to reimburse himself as best he might; but, more merciful than his royal brother, he forbore to oppress them further.

In the third year of Edward I. a law was passed which somewhat alleviated the condition of the Jews; and, although still subject to humiliating indignities, and prohibited from free intercourse with Christians, they were allowed to purchase houses and landed estates, and were released from a part of their unjust imposts.

Presently the crusading fever seized Edward, with the usual results as far as the Jews were concerned; they were treated with the utmost cruelty, and not only their public but their private liberty interfered with to such an extent that they became at length quite reckless, and were suspected, perhaps not without reason, of having tampered with the coinage, and perpetrated other commercial frauds.

S

Public indignation was not hard to excite when a general loot of Jewish houses was in prospective; and a popular rising took place, in which the whole of the devoted community throughout England were deprived of liberty in a single day, and 280 were put to death in London alone.

Ultimately a royal decree was passed, banishing them entirely from the kingdom, and forbidding them to return under pain of death. The wretched exiles were deprived of all that they possessed, with the exception of a trifling sum, barely sufficient for their journey. A large number were robbed of even this small sum by the sailors of the Cinque Ports, who threw the owners themselves into the sea to hide their crime.

It is but fair to add that those who were found guilty of this dastardly act were tried and executed. It is computed that 16,511 persons left the country in this exodus; and the Jews did not appear again as a people in Great Britain for 350 years.

CHAPTER XIV.

THE MIDDLE AGES—(continued).

THE state of the Jews in France was little better than that of their co-religionists in England. About 1182 Philip Augustus banished them from his dominions, and confiscated all their estates. When, some time afterwards, the king repealed this measure, he excused himself for so doing by declaring that his object in bringing them back was to procure from them the money necessary for carrying on the Crusades.

But they had not long been re-established in the country before their industry and skill in financial and commercial transactions enabled them to amass enormous wealth, which they invested largely in landed property.

For some time the king was willing, for a sufficient consideration, to countenance this proceeding; but the popular
discontent at length compelled him to pass new laws to
prohibit Jews from holding land.

Louis IX. inaugurated his reign by the convocation of
the Council of Melun, at which it was enacted that no
Christians should for the future be allowed to borrow
money of the Jews. At this period the Jews were, in
accordance with the old feudal system, held in absolute
slavery to the barons on whose lands they dwelt, and
could be bought and sold.

The year 1238 A.D. witnessed a horrible persecution;
it commenced in Paris and quickly extended to the provinces, and nearly 2,500 Jews lost their lives. The
pretext for these atrocities was the same as that which
had given rise to the disturbances at Lincoln, namely, the
alleged crucifixion of children. Pope Gregory IX. at
length interfered, and procured for them the royal protection.

When St. Louis was taken prisoner in the Holy Land
some fanatical peasants, pretending to miraculous powers,
preached a crusade for his deliverance. A disorderly
rabble was soon collected, but, instead of marching for
Palestine, they contented themselves with plundering and
murdering the Jews at home. The authorities at last
interfered, and the fanatics were dispersed; but it is
needless to add that the plunder which was taken from
them never found its way back to its original owners or
their families.

The king during his captivity desired that all Jews
should be banished from France, and the Queen Blanche,
who acted as regent, scrupulously fulfilled his decree.

In 1240 the celebrated Council of Lyons enjoined all
Christian princes and sovereigns, under pain of excom-
munication, to compel all Jews in their dominions to give
up whatever monies they might have acquired by usury,

and apply the sums so obtained to the purpose of carrying on the Crusades.

Notwithstanding all these severities, the Hebrew race was still vigorous and flourishing, as is proved by the fact that special laws had to be passed in France, and especially in Languedoc, to prevent them from oppressing their Christian debtors, and that nearly all Jews at that time possessed Christian slaves.

The expulsion of the Jews from France had so ruined commerce, that Philip the Hardy, successor of St. Louis, was obliged to recall them in order to restore the financial prosperity of the country.

Fifteen years later, Edward, king of England, expelled them from Gascony, and Philip the Fair once more drove them out of France, and appropriated their property. Many of the poor exiles perished of want by the way, but some succeeded in reaching the German frontier, and even to the present day the Jews of Germany are considered to be of French origin. Some escaped banishment by submitting to baptism, but all (with very few exceptions) returned at the first opportunity to their ancient faith.

In 1321 a still more dreadful calamity overtook the fated race. I have already mentioned that many of the lower classes during the captivity of St. Louis had banded together and originated a crusade of their own. Now the same madness took possession of the peasantry, and almost the whole of the agricultural population, with a priest and a monk at their head, forsook the fields, and marched vaguely against the Saracens. In every district through which they passed they were joined by their fellows, until the presence of such a vast number of undisciplined fanatics thoroughly alarmed the government. Of course they soon began to suffer from want, and every town and village through which they passed was laid under contribution by them, each member of the band taking just whatever he came across or happened to require. Royal authority and Papal anathema were alike powerless to hold them in check, and they marched wherever the two impostors who led them chose to go. At length the usual catastrophe came : the fanaticism of some, the rapacity of others, the hate and fury of all, were turned upon the defenceless Jews, who were massacred with the most frightful cruelties. In 1348 a second pestilence broke out, and precisely the same results followed.

Ten years afterwards a pestilence broke out in France, and the fierce unreasoning people accused the unfortunate Jews of being the authors of it, by conspiring with the lepers to poison the wells and rivers of the country. There does not appear to have been the least shadow of a foundation for this absurd charge, but direct or circumstantial evidence was not needed to prove an accusation in those times. The investigation was conducted in a speedy and satisfactory manner ; a few lepers were arrested and *put to the torture*, and as soon as the inquisitors had succeeded in wresting the answer they required from some shrieking victim on the rack, the case was considered proved. The entire Jewish community was condemned on this conclusive evidence, and the massacres began, followed, of course, by the confiscation of the victims' property. At Paris fewer were put to death, but the richest Hebrews were thrown into prison until they had given up their treasures to the king, who gained 150,000 livres by the transaction.

It is a curious fact that we owe one of the most important instruments of modern commerce to these constant persecutions and expulsions of the Jews. These latter soon found that the main motive of the Christian princes in banishing or otherwise persecuting them, was to obtain possession of their wealth, and they accordingly began to devise means for making this as difficult as possible for others to lay hands on. When Philip the Tall, following up the excesses of the Shepherds, drove the Jews from France, a great number of them entrusted their effects to various persons and escaped to Lombardy. Here they continued to raise money, principally amongst their co-religionists, upon the property which they had left behind, giving orders upon their trustees as security. Thus arose the system of letters of credit, the very essence of modern banking, and to the present day the name of Lombard Street in the City of London, the well-known bankers' quarter, still bears testimony to the origin of the custom.

This ingenious device proved of eminent service to the inventors, for in 1360, when France had been reduced, by the mismanagement of its own governors and the conquests of the English, to a hopeless state of bankruptcy, and the king, John, was in captivity, the Jews were able to dictate terms to the regent, and purchase the right to return to the country and exercise comparative liberty of conscience.

Charles VI. at first treated them with greater humanity and consideration, but the wretched monarch was a prey to a disordered mind, and was a mere tool in the hands of his confessor, who induced him to consent to an edict banishing them from the kingdom. This time, however, they were allowed some little time to collect their debts and wind up their affairs, and although some of the old charges were brought against them, and the populace were in consequence animated with fury against them, yet their lives and property were comparatively unassailed. They left the French frontier in the month of November, not to return again for many years. A few years before 1380 a serious calamity had overtaken them in Lombardy, their great banking centre. The populace rose against them, and burnt the houses of the principal merchants, thus destroying not only the securities for their own property, but also the pledges which had been entrusted to them by those Christians to whom they had lent money. Here the government, though too feeble to punish the offenders, stepped in, and so far protected them that they were released from all obligations to those who had pawned property with them upon their making oath that the goods had been destroyed in the popular tumults.

The Jews in Spain during the Middle Ages were, if possible, worse treated than in the other countries of Europe.

TOLEDO.

At the beginning of the thirteenth century the Bishop of Toledo incited the populace to plunder the houses and synagogues of the Jews, and himself in person directed the lawless operations of the crowd.

In 1212 the Crusaders passed by Toledo and perpetrated their usual atrocities. The Spanish nobility interfered to put a stop to the carnage, but without avail.

Under James I. they had a respite from these cruelties. Raymond of Pennaforte, General of the Dominicans, confessor and minister of the King and the Pope, used his utmost endeavours to bring about their conversion, but with a liberality, rare in a priest of the time, he adopted toleration and education as the best means to effect his purpose.

Alphonso of Castille protected the Jews, and being himself a great lover of science, encouraged the learned rabbis to translate for him the works of the Arabic astronomers and philosophers, paying them handsomely for their services. The populace, intolerant of this favour shown to the detested race, rose up, and on a perfectly unfounded accusation of murder brought against one of the number, commenced a general massacre of the Jews throughout Spain.

James I., king of Arragon, also afforded his countenance and protection to the learned rabbis; and the favour which they thus enjoyed with the nobles of the realm compensated them to some extent for the indignity and scorn heaped upon them by the common people.

In 1320 a portion of that band of Shepherds who had committed such ravages in France found their way to Spain, where their course was signalised by the same cruelties. By a strange perverseness of judgment the Spaniards accused the Jews of having, by means of sorcery, brought this plague upon the country; and the wretched Israelites, who suffered most severely from the fanatical rabble, were punished by law for introducing them. Fifteen thousand, who refused to submit to baptism, were put to a cruel death.

Alphonso XI. of Castille fully recognised the worth and usefulness of his Jewish subjects, and commenced his reign by showing them so much favour, that a Jew named Joseph became his treasurer and financial secretary. But he, too, was obliged to yield to the inveterate prejudices of his subjects; and on a report that a Jewish child had insulted the Holy Sacrament at a certain place, a solemn council was held, at which the question was gravely discussed, whether a sentence of death or banishment should be pronounced against the entire Jewish race.

In 1396, during the reign of Henry III., Martin, bishop of Astigy, by his denunciations of the Jews in the streets of Cordova and Seville, aroused such a spirit of fanaticism, that the populace of those two cities rose up and massacred the Jews without mercy; and the same bloodthirsty fever extended itself to Toledo, Valencia, and Barcelona. John, the successor of Henry III., encouraged a continuance of this violence.

In the beginning of the fifteenth century the Anti-Pope Benedict XIII., then residing at Arragon, evinced great zeal for the conversion of the Jews. In order to carry out his design he proposed a conference between the most learned rabbis of Spain and the Christian doctors. The Rabbi Vidal was chosen advocate of the Jews on the occasion, and one Jerome of Santa Fé, a converted Jew, defended the Christian cause.

The Christian records of this controversy say that Jerome triumphed signally over his antagonist; the Jewish annals say that their rabbis departed "not without glory" from the encounter. All that we know for certain about the transaction is, that a number of the Jews embraced Christianity, and that Benedict ordered all the extant copies of the Talmud to be collected and burnt. This decree, as well as another against Jewish usury, was annulled when the exiled anti-pope's authority came to an end little more than a year afterwards.

About this period a certain Vincent Ferrer made himself conspicuous by his zeal for the conversion of the Jews, which, according to his "Legend," he effected by the exercise of miraculous powers. As many as 25,000 are said to have yielded to his persuasive eloquence and that of the Christian crowds which it stirred up.

The kingdoms of Arragon and Castille were at last blended together by the union of Ferdinand and Isabella, and the whole of Spain became one united monarchy. It was these sovereigns who introduced the Inquisition into the country ; it was established with the avowed object of preventing such Jews and Moors as had been converted to Christianity from relapsing into their old religion. The queen's confessor, a Dominican friar, persuaded her that this falling off of converts was a great injury to the cause of religion, and Isabella induced her husband to sanction the dreadful tribunal. The whole history of the world scarcely presents so horrible a picture as this so-called Christian court. The Pope issued a bull, giving it the sanction of the Church, and at once all law, authority, humanity, and justice were subjugated to the will of a few raving, arrogant monks. All persons suspected of heresy, Judaism, or even lukewarm Christianity, were either burnt alive, or condemned to perpetual imprisonment in loathsome dungeons ; while the most excruciating tortures were employed to exact confession from the accused. The spies of the Inquisition lurked everywhere, listening even to the most careless conversation, and a chance word, which could by any pretence be wrested into an heretical expression, was punished with death. People were encouraged, nay, forced, to betray their dearest friends ; for not to denounce a suspected heretic was to expose one's self to the self-same punishment.

The prime mover in these atrocities and the head of the so-called Holy Office for many years was Thomas de Torquemada, a Dominican, and it is computed that this ruffian caused 8,800 people to be put to death and 90,000 to perpetual imprisonment during his term of office.

One strange feature in these dreadful persecutions is, that a large number of Jews, nominally converted, but really at heart and in secret true Hebrews, held high office both in the Church and State, and were even found amongst the judges of the Holy Office itself. We can well imagine what use they would make of their power to revenge the wrongs of their nation; and there is no doubt but that the number of Christians who thus perished on the charge of heresy, to satisfy Jewish hatred, was quite as large as that of the real Jews whom the Holy Office condemned to suffer for their religion.

For some time the horrors of the Inquisition affected only the professed Christians; in 1492, after the conquest of the Moors and their expulsion from their last stronghold, Granada, came the turn of the Jews themselves.

An edict was issued commanding them all to embrace Christianity, or leave the kingdom within four months. The Jews endeavoured to induce the king, by a bribe of 30,000 ducats, to alter his decision, and rapacity might have effected what humanity was powerless to perform. But while Ferdinand hesitated to decide, the queen, whose better nature was utterly enthralled and degraded by the influence of her confessor, made a sneering speech against them, while Torquemada boldly advanced and, with crucifix raised in the air, shouted out, "Behold Him Whom Judas sold for thirty pieces of silver. Sell ye Him now for a higher price and render an account of your bargain before God." The superstitious sovereign, instead of ordering the arrogant monk under arrest for blasphemy and insolence, bowed to the will of the Church, and condemned hundreds of thousands of human beings to ruin, disgrace, and death, and that in the name of Christ—the God of love and of humanity!

This forced exodus of the Jews, which was upon an enormous scale, was attended with the usual cruelties and hardships. No less than a million souls were thus, without warning or preparation, deprived of homes and property, and thrown destitute upon the world—a world where every people hated and despised them.

As an instance of what they had to suffer, I may mention the story of a Spanish pilot who, having got a great number of them on board his ship, determined to murder them all "to revenge the death of Jesus Christ."

He was dissuaded from this abominable project by the ready argument of the intended victims, who represented that "Jesus Christ wished the salvation and not the death of sinners;" and as an act of great mercy and forbearance the zealous mariner turned them out on the nearest shore, where most of them perished of hunger, a few who survived being rescued by the humanity of the captain of a passing ship.

Many of the poor exiles perished by shipwreck, others died of the plague which broke out amongst them. Some reached Fez in Africa, but the inhabitants refusing to admit them they were starved to death outside the town. Some, again, reached Genoa; this town was at the time suffering from a scarcity of provisions, and when the famished Jews sought for shelter and food the Genoese refused both, except on the condition of their immediately embracing the Christian faith. The poor wretches who had given home and all that they held dear in order to preserve their ancient religion, thus found their sacrifice at last of no avail, and yielding to the pangs of hunger consented to be baptized.

One thing must strike the reader of this list of atrocities, and that is, how divine, how invincible must be that Christianity which could survive such horrors as were perpetrated in its name!

As for King Ferdinand he did not reap so much benefit as he had looked for by his tyrannical measure, for the facilities, of which we have before spoken, which the Jews possessed of removing their wealth to other countries by the system of letters of credit and other means thwarted him of the greater portion of his expected booty. His shortsighted policy was strongly reprobated by many of the other European powers, and the Pope himself, Alexander VI., offered an asylum to many of the exiles.

Portugal was naturally a tempting region for those whom Spain had thus thrust forth, especially as the king, John II., had already shown some signs of toleration and enlightenment by employing Jews on important geographical missions, and his navigators had been materially assisted by them in their voyages of discovery to the East Indies.

He was not, however, proof against cupidity, and only allowed the fugitives to enter his dominions on condition of their paying an exorbitant poll-tax and undertaking to quit the country after a certain time. He engaged, when the time for their departure came, to furnish them with vessels for their safe-conduct; but, although the king may have acted in good faith, his subjects disregarded his commands, and many of those Jews who embarked on board Portuguese vessels threw themselves into the sea rather than remain to suffer the horrible indignities and persecutions to which the sailors subjected them. Their compatriots, taking warning at their fate, preferred staying in the country, although they knew that they must be sold into slavery, to exposing themselves to such risks and perils.

Emmanuel II., his successor, gave them their liberty, and at first treated them with humanity and consideration. Unfortunately for them he desired to espouse the daughter of Ferdinand and Isabella, and the bigoted queen would not hear of a son-in-law who suffered the "Enemies of God" to remain in his kingdom.

A day was therefore appointed for their departure; but before it arrived the king secretly ordered all the Jewish children under fourteen years of age to be torn from their parents, dispersed through the country and brought up as Christians. The secret transpired before the day named, and was hurriedly put into execution lest the parents should conceal their children and so evade the edict. A most harrowing scene then took place, and mothers threw their children into the wells and rivers rather than see them torn from their arms to be brought up in a strange faith, and amidst a strange people.

Even this was not the end of their troubles, for Emmanuel suddenly refused to allow them to embark at two of the ports named, and the consequence was that a great number were thrown back on Lisbon, and thus made, against their will, to break their contract and thus become amenable to the law. Of these, some were shipped off as slaves, while others consented to be baptized, on condition that the government should restore their children and let them remain in peace for twenty years. But before half that time had elapsed, the populace had seized upon some trifling pretext to rise and murder most of the converts. It is true that the ringleaders were punished for this outrage when the affair came to the king's ears.

The same accusations were laid against the Jews in Germany as in other countries, and led to the same persecutions. They were suspected of encouraging the incursions of the hordes of Mongolian savages, who overran Europe about this period, and at Frankfort, Haguenau in Lower Alsace, and at Munich, Wurtzburg, and Berne, many were massacred by the populace on the old charge of crucifying Christian children.

In Lithuania they lived in comparative security, under the mild and equitable reign of Boleslas, but in 1267 the Council of Vienna imposed a heavy tax upon them, and ordered the demolition of a fine new synagogue which they had built. As the civil authorities did not carry out the arbitrary ecclesiastical acts, and the German princes even openly offered an asylum to fugitive Jews, the clergy at last threatened to excommunicate all who should show such toleration for the future.

While the two rival emperors, Adolphus of Nassau and Albert of Austria, were struggling for the pre-eminence, a fanatical peasant, named Rindfleisch, gave out that he had been sent by Heaven to exterminate the Jews, and continued to instigate the people of Nuremburg, Rothenburg, and other towns to massacre the Hebrew inhabitants. The Emperor Albert could not at first interfere to put a stop to these enormities, fearing lest the populace should side with his rivals ; but as soon as he was firmly established upon the throne, he compelled the inhabitants of Nuremberg to pay a heavy fine for the damage done to the town by fire during the disturbances.

The Council of Vienna, convoked by the authority of Pope Clement V. against the Templars, issued some severe decrees against the Jewish usurers, and declared any one a heretic who should favour or countenance them. These denunciations did not prevent Ménicho, bishop of Spires, from declaring that no one should persecute them in his diocese.

The appearance of the Flagellants in the 14th century was a frightful calamity to the Jews. The black plague had ravaged Germany, and, as usual, the Jews were accused of being the authors of the mischief. In the midst of the general excitement and misery, bands of monks and peasants, raving mad, passed through Germany, with a crucifix at their head, and scourging their naked bodies as they went along till the blood streamed forth. This discipline, they averred, was to express their contrition for the sins of the Christians of the age, the worst of which was harbouring the Jews. This lunatic enthusiasm, the revival of the old charges of crucifying children, poisoning wells, and outraging the Host, and, still more, the rapacity of the mob which followed in the Flagellants' wake, ended, as might be supposed, in the murder and pillage of the unfortunate Hebrews at Spires, Strasbourg, Thuringia, Frankfort, and other places.

In Bohemia affairs were little better, and Venceslas the emperor, who had made himself odious by his vices, hoped to conciliate the people by persecution of the Jews.

He issued a proclamation releasing his Christian subjects from all debts which they had contracted to Jews, and this license led to excesses more horrible still.

About the year 1434 the Council of Basle ordered all bishops to appoint special preachers for the instruction of the Jews in their dioceses, and to compel the unfortunates by severe penalties to listen to the sermons. They were also prohibited from residing in the neighbourhood of the churches, were obliged to wear a distinctive dress, and were cut off from all social intercourse with Christians.

Louis X. Duke of Bavaria banished all Jews from his dominions, confiscated their property, and erected public buildings with the proceeds.

In the year 1499 they were finally expelled from Nuremburg, ostensibly, of course, on the old accusations, but really because of their wealth and the hereditary hatred which the Christians, thanks to the clergy, fostered against them.

The children of Israel were not themselves without credulity and fanaticism, and in 1500 a certain David Leimlein, calling himself chief of the armies of Israel, predicted the speedy coming of the Messiah, and established himself at Lisbon, where he and a young convert to Judaism soon became famous, the former for his fasting and other discipline, the latter for his learning and eloquence. So thoroughly did these two impostors deceive their co-religionists, that, in anticipation of presently eating unleavened bread in Palestine, the Jews of Italy and Spain destroyed their ovens and gave themselves up to the most absurd excesses. At last the government interfered, and both David and his disciple were thrown into prison, where the latter was put to death.

While the wretched children of Israel suffered so many woes and persecutions both from the clergy and the laity, it is gratifying to observe that the popes themselves for the most part discountenanced such injustice, and set

T

examples of toleration. Gregory the Great is, as we have seen, a notable instance. In the 11th century Alexander II. opposed the bigotry of Ferdinand, and endeavoured to moderate the mad fury of the Crusaders; later on Gregory IX., though himself a firm supporter of the Crusades, used the most stringent measures to repress the license of the " Soldiers of the Cross," and to protect the Jews from their violence. In his letters on the subject to Louis IX. of France, and other potentates, he denounced this so-called religious fanaticism as a mere pretext for lawlessness and robbery.

In 1247 Innocent IV. also raised his voice to protest against the persecution of the Hebrews, pointed out the improbability of the charges brought against them, and declared that they were in worse bondage under the Christian princes than ever their ancestors had been beneath the yoke of Pharaoh.

The Jews of Trani, capital of the kingdom of Naples, had become rich and powerful, and the king, to recompense them for some important services, treated them with great consideration, and at his death specially recommended them to the favour of the state. Instead, however, of allowing them the free exercise of their religion, the government began to use every effort to procure their conversion. In order, by seeming compliance, to avoid a persecution, the Jews professed themselves willing to embrace Christianity, provided they were allowed to contract marriages with the highest families in the kingdom. To their astonishment this offer was accepted, and they were obliged to hold to their bargain; and many, having succeeded in contracting advantageous alliances, were baptized, while those who failed to make such matches quietly subsided back again into Judaism. This roused the anger of the clergy, and a certain monk of Trani succeeded, by reiterating the old charges against them, in raising the passions of the populace, and bringing about a general massacre of the Jews. A similar attempt was made at Naples; but the nobles of that city interfered, and offered an asylum to those Hebrews whose wealth or position exposed them more particularly to the fury of the mob. The Pope, Alexander IV., also interposed his authority on their behalf.

In the 14th century Clement V., who had established the seat of the Papacy at Avignon, protected the Jews, as

NAPLES.

far as lay in his power, from the fury of the fanatical "Shepherds;" he also laboured strenuously to convert the Jews by the legitimate means of example and instruction, and established professors of Hebrew in the various universities. John XXII., his successor, was less tolerant, but his zeal was directed rather against the literature than the persons of the Hebrews, and he destroyed all the copies of the Talmud upon which he could lay his hands.

Presently he banished the Jews altogether from the states of the Church ; but the exiles having sought refuge at the court of the King of Naples, contrived to purchase the revocation of the edict. Clement VI. also treated the Jews with great humanity, and did them especial service by shielding them from the violence of the Holy Office.

In 1394 the Jews of Italy had attained such influence and prosperity that they were enabled to build a magnificent new synagogue at Bologna, the Pope, Boniface IX., himself lending his countenance to the undertaking.

Towards the commencement of the fifteenth century Pope John XXIII. departed from the policy of his predecessors, and commenced an active persecution of the Jews, inciting other governments to follow the same course. Under his successor, Nicholas V., their lot was slightly ameliorated, but in 1472 Sextus IV. having canonised a certain Simon, said to have been massacred by the Jews of Trente 200 years before, the popular hatred again burst forth, and a massacre of the Israelites in Trente and Venice was the result.

Those Jews whom the persecution of the time had driven from Spain and Portugal found a ready asylum in Italy. The Christians of that country were indeed kinder to them than their own co-religionists, for the Jewish authors themselves confessed that the Hebrew Consistory of Rome offered a thousand ducats to the Pope (Alexander VI.) to refuse their brethren permission to settle within his territory. The pontiff indignantly rejected this selfish proposal, and even published an edict compelling the petitioners to make way for the new-comers by quitting the states themselves. The Consistory were compelled to pay a heavy sum in order to purchase the revocation of this decree. Many of the refugees from Spain and Portugal fled to Naples, where they were exposed to the terrible cruelty of the Inquisition to such an extent that they at last ventured to revolt. The viceroy banished them from the kingdom, and shortly after declared the Holy Office to be no longer necessary. Charles V. in 1584 approved of his viceroy's act, and refused to tolerate the presence of Jews in the kingdoms of Naples and Sicily.

VENICE.

In 1539 the favour which the Jews enjoyed with the Pope, Paul III., so excited the jealousy of the Cardinal Sadolet that he ventured upon a public remonstrance to the Pope, declaring that the entire patronage of all civil and ecclesiastical offices was in the hands of the infidels; his protest, however, had but little effect.

It is a curious fact that while elsewhere the unrelenting hatred of the clergy pursued the Jews, in Rome, the head-quarters of the Church, they were comparatively free from persecution.

In the thirteenth century the position of the Jews in the East was changed considerably for the worse. En Násir li-dín illah, caliph of Bagdad, issued a peremptory order that all Jews should embrace Mohammedanism or quit the Babylonian territory. Many preferred exile to

ISPAHAN

apostacy, but a few submitted to make a verbal profession of the Mohammedan creed. In Palestine, although the wars between the Saracens and Crusaders had left the country in a very unquiet state, the Jews had contrived to maintain a foothold, and possessed synagogues and schools, which produced many learned rabbis.

The Eastern Jews, and particularly those of Babylon, suffered severely by the Tartar invasion, but they enjoyed an interval of repose under Argoun Khan, who appointed a Jewish physician named Saad-ed-Daulch as his prime minister; but on the death of the prince, the Moslems, jealous of the vizier's influence and partiality for his countrymen, accused him of having poisoned his master; on this charge he was put to death, and a general massacre of the Israelites followed.

SHAH ABBAS.

The irresistible march of Tamerlane through Asia swept away the prosperity of the Jews of Media and Persia, and when, a little later on, they began to recover themselves a little from these disasters the appearance of Ismail Sufi, founder of the Sufiite dynasty of Persia, involved them in

fresh evils. The astounding rapidity of this prince's conquests induced the ever-credulous Hebrews to regard him
as the true Messiah, particularly as he himself declared
that he was a prophet sent to reform the Moslem faith ;
they accordingly hastened to offer him their homage, but
the monarch, who had conceived a violent aversion to the
children of Israel, rejected their advances and treated
them with exceptional rigour.

Shah Abbas, on his accession to the throne of Persia,
found the country well-nigh depopulated, and in order to
restore, if possible, the prosperity of his kingdom, he
accorded unusual privileges to all strangers who chose to
settle there. The Jews were among the first to avail
themselves of this offer ; but their skill in commerce, and
the consequent rapid increase of their wealth, excited the
jealousy of the other inhabitants, who laid a complaint
before the Shah. The monarch was at first unwilling to
exercise a severity which might prove fatal to his policy of
encouraging emigrants ; but he was at length induced to
yield to the demands of fanaticism, and offer the Hebrews
a choice between Islamism and death. The edict was
never carried into effect, but the principal Jewish doctors
were cited before the Sufi tribunal, and ordered to give an
account of the reasons for their belief. The controversy
which followed is exceedingly curious and interesting.
The Shah first demanded of them why they had relin-
quished their sacrifices and the other ceremonies of their
religion since the coming of Jesus Christ. The rabbis
replied by an evasive answer, declaring that they expected
a Messiah, but could not accept as such Him Whom their
ancestors had crucified. The Shah, irritated at their
reply, demanded why they spoke thus disrespectfully of
Jesus Christ, in Whose prophetic office at least he himself
found no difficulty in believing. At length he asked them,
curtly, what was their opinion of Mohammed ? Afraid to
acknowledge their real sentiments, they replied that since

Mohammed was descended from Abraham through Ishmael they did not entirely reject his authority, but that Moses was, they were taught to believe, their chief prophet and only lawgiver. Sensible of the danger which they were running, by engaging in such a delicate contro-

JEWISH PHYSICIAN.

versy, they endeavoured to turn the conversation, and made a humble appeal to the clemency of the Shah, declaring that they had no other object in settling in Persia than to serve him with zeal and fidelity. Their

expectation of a Messiah was particularly distasteful to a
Moslem, who held that Mohammed was " the seal of the
prophets"; "but nevertheless," said he, " in order to
remove this vain pretext, fix now a time for the appearance of your Messiah, and I will tolerate you until the fulfilment of such term; but if your long-expected Messiah
again fail you, you must either embrace the religion of
Mohammed, or lose your goods, your children, and your
lives." The poor rabbis, grateful at the chance thus
afforded them of temporising, fixed the period at seventy
years, trusting that by that time the Shah would be dead,
and that they might be able to make better terms with his
successor. Abbas exacted an exorbitant price for these
years of respite, and a treaty was drawn up, and signed
and registered by either party, in which the Jews of
Persia were bound either to embrace Islamism or suffer
death at the end of seventy years, unless the veritable and
undoubted Messiah should have appeared, in which case
all Persia should become converted to Judaism.

In the continual wars between the Persians and the
Turks this strange convention was forgotten, but on the
accession of Shah Abbas II. the old treaty was discovered,
and the Shah, animated by mingled fanaticism and cupidity, instantly proceeded to put it into force. In the
dreadful persecution which followed some sought refuge
among the Turks or in India, while others purchased
safety by an outward conformity to the Mohammedan religion. It was shortly, however, discovered that the proselytes continued to practice their own religion in secret,
and the Shah was ultimately induced to restore to them
their ancient privileges.

The Jews of Palestine during all the revolutions which
distracted that country enjoyed a comparative immunity,
and the school of Safed, in Galilee, continued to flourish
and produce many learned men. A curious story is
related of a certain Jew of Jerusalem, who had from

interested motives become a convert to Christianity, and had evinced so much zeal for his new religion that he ultimately rose to the dignity of patriarch of the Holy City. About the year 1665 he repaired to Constantinople, in order to intrigue for the bishopric, but being there attacked by a serious illness, he assembled all the dignitaries of the Church around his bed, and solemnly declared that he had never for a moment ceased to be a Jew at heart, and that he died in the profession of his ancient faith.

CHAPTER XV.

THE JEWS IN RECENT TIMES.

The Jews of the Levant—Sabbathai Levi the *sot disant* Messiah; his strange career—Franck—Another Messianic impostor—State of the Jews in Egypt, Morocco, and Germany—The Reformation—Luther's sentiments towards the Jews—Their condition in Poland and Austria—The Jews of Italy; their treatment by the successive Popes—Jewish printing-presses established in Venetian territory—Tolerant edict of Charles, king of Naples—Cardinal Ximenes opposes the recall of the Jews to Spain—The Jews of Portugal join the Archbishop of Braga in a conspiracy against the throne—The Jews in Holland—Spinoza; his life and philosophy—The Jews acquire civil rights in Amsterdam—The Jews in England—Those of Holland send an embassy to Cromwell—Their condition under Charles II. and James II.—Bill of naturalisation passed and repealed by William III.—Removal of Jewish disabilities in England—The Jews in Germany—Jewish soldiers at Prague—Barbarous edict of Frederick the Great of Prussia; it is revoked by Frederick William II.—Mendelssohn; influence of his writings—Jewish communities in Frankfort and Metz—State of the Jews in France—They recover civil rights during the revolution—Napoleon I. convenes the Sanhedrim at Paris—Isolated Jewish communities—The Beni Kheibar in Arabia—Caraite colony in the Crimea—The Chinese Jews—Jews in the new world—Conclusion.

In the Ottoman empire, and especially at Constantinople, the Jews were very numerous, and although they were regarded by the Turks with scorn and hatred they contrived, as usual, to acquire much wealth and influence by their industry and business capacity. It was among the Jews of the Levant, in the middle of the seventeenth century, that one of the most surprising movements on record took place.

A certain young man, named Sabbathai Zevi, the son of a poulterer at Smyrna, had displayed so much aptitude for learning that at the age of eighteen he was already ordained a rabbi. These early honours appear to have inflamed his ambition, and he conceived a project for passing as the Messiah; to this end he began to practise long and rigid fasts, and spent the greater portion of his time in bathing in the sea; these mortifications, his remarkable beauty, and his unusual eloquence gained for him a number of followers, and he was at length bold enough to appear in the synagogue and openly announce himself as the son of David, even daring, in token of his divine mission, to pronounce the ineffable name of Jehovah. The rabbis denounced him as a seditious blasphemer, and he was

SMYRNA.

compelled to seek safety in flight to Salonica. This place soon became unsafe for him, and he fled, successively, to Egypt and Jerusalem, making on his way a convert of a certain Nathan Levi of Gaza, as clever and designing an impostor as himself, who henceforth played the part of his precursor. After a long residence in Jerusalem, he again urged his pretensions, was once more driven out by the rabbis, and this time returned to his native city of Smyrna.

Here the rabbis, as usual, denounced him; but the populace were more easily duped, and warmly espoused his cause. One Anakia, who was particularly active in opposing him, happened that night to be overtaken by a sudden death, and the superstitious crowd at once attributed his fate to his rejection of the Messiah; this, for him, lucky accident gave greater and more speedy currency

CONSTANTINOPLE.

to his pretensions than he himself could have hoped for, and in a short time he found himself strong enough to assume royal pomp, while the fame of his reputed miracles and prophecies went forth throughout the whole world.

At length nothing would please his deluded partizans, but that he should repair to Constantinople and confront the sultan in order by his presence to strike awe into the heart of that potentate. When he did arrive in the capital the sultan was absent, but sent instructions to the Grand Vizier to detain the impostor; Sabbathai was in consequence kept in a kind of honourable captivity in the castle of Sestos, from which place he continued to issue manifestos, and sustain his rather difficult part. All went well with him, until one day he was imprudent enough to attempt to punish a respectable but incredulous rabbi of Constantinople with death, for having remained unconvinced of his divine character. The unbeliever sought the protection of the Moslems in the neighbourhood, who barely saved him from the fury of Sabbathai's followers. The sultan feeling, perhaps, that the affair had gone quite far enough, peremptorily summoned Sabbathai into his presence. The Grand Seigneur expressed his determination of testing his prisoner's miraculous powers by shooting three poisoned arrows at him, promising that if he proved invulnerable he would himself acknowledge his title ; if he refused to submit to this ordeal there was still left him the alternative of death or Islamism. The wretched creature utterly lost his presence of mind, and without hesitation embraced the Mohammedan faith. The sultan bestowed upon him a dress of honour, the title of Capidji Basha, and dismissed him. Strange to say, even this defection did not put an end to the delusion, and he had still impudence and address enough to devise an excuse for his conduct, and so well did he succeed that even after his death, which took place of a colic in the year 1676, his sect numbered a large amount of followers.

Various impostors have from time to time attempted to revive the delusion, but none with so much success as one Franck, who, in the middle of the last century, appeared in Germany, where the credulity of his brethren in all parts of the world supplied him with the means of living in Oriental pomp and magnificence.

Egypt has ever been a favourite residence with the

Jews, but in 1524 the Hebrew community in that country experienced a rude interruption to the prosperity which they had long enjoyed. The governor of Egypt, having revolted against the Sultan Suleiman II., imposed a heavy tax upon the Jews, which they declared themselves unable to pay, as his soldiers had already pillaged their houses and property. The governor in a rage ordered the instant seizure of all the Jews in the kingdom, but a conspiracy which opportunely broke out against his life at this period saved them from further evils. Since that time they have been very numerous in the country, especially in Cairo, where a large portion of the commerce, and especially the banking, is in their hands.

In Morocco, Tunis, and Algeria, they have also been always numerous, for, being well received by the Moham-medan governments of Africa, those countries became a natural refuge when the constantly recurring persecutions drove them out of Spain and Portugal.

At the commencement of the 16th century the Bishop of Cologne banished the Jews from his diocese, being instigated to, or at least supported in this arbitrary measure by a convert from Judaism, named Victor à Carbé. Not long after another convert named Pfepfercorn, coun-selled the Emperor Maxmilian to destroy all the Jewish books, and would probably have obtained his desire had the great Reuchlin pointed out that only those works which contained blasphemies against Jesus Christ could be deemed worthy of destruction, and that it was a manifest absurdity to destroy in the emperor's dominions works which were distributed over the whole world, and could be easily reprinted. The matter was ultimately referred to the Pope ; and Hochstrat, a creature of the Inquisition, re-paired to Rome, where he attempted by bribes and threats of schism to influence the decision of the pontiff. Reuch-lin was, however, successful, and when taunted and threatened by the monks for his share in the transaction, he answered, "that Martin Luther, whose party was already making headway in Germany would soon give them too much trouble to leave them time to occupy themselves with the Jews."

The Reformation gave a curious impulse to Jewish learning throughout Germany, for as the Protestant theologians were well versed in the learned languages, and constantly quoted rabbinical and other authorities, the Catholic priests and monks were obliged to study the same subjects in order to refute them, and the Jews themselves, seeing the request into which their sacred language was coming, began to publish grammars and dictionaries, and to take up the cudgels on behalf of their own religion. The Reformation, indeed, wrought wonders for the Jews, inasmuch as the people, when once freed from the trammels of bigotry and superstition which the Romish clergy had imposed upon them, ceased to lend credence to the false charges which had been so often brought against the devoted race with such fatal effect; but against Luther himself the Jews entertained a strong aversion, to a certain extent well grounded, as he appears to have prevented certain Christian princes from receiving them into their territories.

In Poland, as early as the beginning of the fourteenth century, the Jews enjoyed perfect liberty of conscience, their prosperous condition being due in the first instance to the influence of a beautiful Jewess named Esther, who lived as mistress with Casimir the Great. Even when fanaticism had risen to such a pitch as to banish the Reformers from Poland the Jews were unmolested in the enjoyment of their wealth, and in the possession of their magnificent synagogues and schools. Johannes Sobieski extended unwonted favour towards them, but his successor was induced by the clergy to put in force an old law of Sigismund I., debarring them from many of their privileges. But the other Slavonic Jews were not exempt entirely

U

from persecution ; those of Cracow and Posen were from time to time exposed to the violence of the populace on the old charges, and such outbreaks have occurred at intervals even as late as 1811.

About the year 1660 the Jews obtained permission to build a magnificent synagogue and to found an academy in Vienna ; but when they were on the point of opening them, the empress, who attributed her sterility to the toleration displayed towards the Jews, induced her husband to break faith with them, and banish them from the country. At her death, in 1673, they were recalled, and speedily attained, as was their wont, to wealth and distinction ; but their good fortune so excited the jealousy of the populace that they became the victims of much violence and injustice. During the war with the Turks, the Jews aided the latter in maintaining the siege of Buda, and this did not tend to increase the good-will of the emperor towards them.

The Jews of Italy in the Middle Ages, as we have seen, enjoyed much greater tranquillity and prosperity than their compatriots elsewhere, thanks to the toleration of the Roman pontiffs. In later times the same good fortune attended them, though chequered by occasional bigotry and persecution. In 1554 Julius III. conceived a violent antipathy to their favourite Talmudic work, the Gemara, and seized and burnt every copy of it which he could obtain. Paul IV., in the following year, not only waged war against the books of the Jews, but issued an edict forcing them to sell their landed property, to wear a distinctive and humiliating costume, and to renounce all intercourse with Christians, limiting the number of their synagogues, and imposing other grievous conditions upon them. There seemed every prospect of a violent persecution breaking out, as the popular mind was already inflamed by the accusations of a number of female converts from Judaism, who pretended to be possessed by devils through the sorceries of the Jews. The Pope himself lent credence to this absurd story, and confessed that he was on the point of sanctioning a general massacre, had it not been for the good sense of one of his cardinals, who exposed the imposture. The women were punished with death ; and the Pope, ashamed of his credulity, declared that he would never molest the Jews again so long as he lived.

Pius V., in 1569, treated them with great harshness, banishing them from every city in the Papal States except Rome and Ancona, where he only tolerated them for the sake of maintaining their commerce with the East.

Gregory XIII. added certain other vexatious laws to those already in force against them ; but Sextus V. revoked all these unjust decrees of his predecessors, and accorded the Jews perfect liberty of conscience and civil freedom. He made no secret of the fact that it was their money and their commerce which made him regard them as such valuable citizens.

In 1593 Clement VIII. partly put in force the Bull of Pius V., expelling them from the Papal States, but he allowed them to dwell at Avignon, wishing, he said, to effect their conversion.

In the Venetian territory the Jews were also suffered to remain without molestation, and this indulgence they owed to their signal services in the wars against the Turks, especially at the siege of Candia. A great many learned rabbis issued from the Venetian schools, and from the Hebrew press at Venice proceeded some of the earliest printed works in that language. At Padua, also, they possessed an important academy.

Towards the latter end of the 17th century, the affairs of the Italian Jews began to assume a more favourable aspect even than heretofore, and when the Venetian general, Morisini, returned victorious from the Morea, with many Jewish captives, the Pope, Innocent XI., used his influence to procure their liberation.

In 1740, Charles, king of Naples, published an edict permitting Jews to enter his dominions, and promising them that they should remain in the undisturbed exercise of their religion for fifty years. Those who professed medicine were also honoured with the degree of doctor of that faculty. The clergy were, as might have been expected, furious at these concessions; but the king insisted upon carrying out his tolerant project. Unfortunately, however, their own misconduct, or perhaps, more probably, the intolerance of the priests, brought about a revocation of the law not long afterwards.

I have already related how the Jews of Spain were, after a long series of terrible persecutions, ultimately banished from that country. On the accession of Charles V., they earnestly petitioned to be allowed to return; but Cardinal Ximenes employed all his eloquence and influence to prevent the king from acceding to their request, and Charles V. preferred the advice of the cardinal to that of his ministers and the still more substantial argument of 800,000 golden crowns, with which the Jews offered to back up their application.

In Portugal, about this period, the Jews mixed themselves up in the intrigues which the Archbishop of Braga had set on foot in order to recover that country for the throne of Spain, from which it had successfully revolted. The archbishop, in the name of the king of Spain, promised them entire liberty of conscience if they would aid in re-establishing him upon the throne. They were to commence by setting fire to houses in various parts of the capital and its suburbs, and while the people were engaged in extinguishing the flames, they were to fly to the palace and assassinate the king. The plot was discovered before it could be put into execution, by the confession of a rich Jewish merchant who was put to the torture; and the principal members of the conspiracy suffered the extreme penalty of the law. Disappointed in their hopes of regaining their liberty, the Jews of Spain and Portugal (for there were still many secretly lurking in the former country) continued to exercise their Jewish religion, although ostensibly professing the Christian faith. It is a strange but undoubted fact that for centuries staunch, exclusive and staunch Jews were to be found amongst the Spanish and Portuguese nobility and clergy, and even beneath the cowl of the monks.

The Spanish Jews claimed descent from the royal tribe of Judah, and so proud are they of this illustrious origin, that they will not countenance any matrimonial alliances between their own people and the Jews of any other part of Europe.

The toleration which the Jews met with in Holland made that country a favourite refuge for those whom persecution had driven from other parts of Europe. But though they were free from active injury, yet they laboured under many disabilities, and were forbidden to practise the useful arts or trades, and were excluded from all honourable and lucrative employments.

In Amsterdam they were placed under the surveillance of syndics, who treated them with great ignominy and rigour. The Revolution at length worked a change in their condition, and in 1796 the National Convention of Batavia accorded the freedom of the city to the Jews. It could not, however, exempt them from the effects of private ill-feeling, and they experienced for a long time considerable difficulty in obtaining the free exercise of their newly-acquired rights.

In Holland the Jews have always enjoyed greater religious toleration than in, perhaps, any other country in the world.

The Jews of Amsterdam allowed themselves to be led astray by the teaching of one Zeighler, a German Jew of considerable reputation for learning, who foretold the speedy advent of the Messiah. They do not appear, however, to have been betrayed into any great excesses by their belief in this impostor, but only to have paid for their folly and credulity by pecuniary loss and ridicule.

Of the many learned Jews which Holland has produced, none, perhaps, has had so much influence upon modern thought as the celebrated Benedict Spinoza. He was born at Amsterdam, his father being a merchant of Portuguese origin. He commenced his studies by learning Latin from a certain physician of a sceptical turn of mind, and the influence of his early teaching was so strong that, after a few years of theological study, he openly renounced his belief in the Jewish religion. He still continued, nevertheless, to frequent the synagogue ; but he refused many tempting offers which his fellow-countrymen made him, in the hope of inducing him to dissimulate his opinions and to continue in the ostensible profession of his ancient faith. At length, an attempt being made upon his life by one of his fanatical compatriots, he is said to have separated himself thenceforth entirely from the Jewish community and professed Christianity; but although he assiduously attended both the Lutheran and Calvinistic churches, his Christianity sat as lightly upon him as his Judaism had done. Finding that all their attempts to reclaim him were in vain, the Jews accused him of apostacy and blasphemy, and drove him forth from Amsterdam. He retired to La Haye, where he died in 1677, having published many works on philosophy and metaphysics. His system is the undoubted parent of modern rationalism.*

The flourishing Jewish community of Holland naturally cast longing eyes upon so tempting a field of commercial enterprise as England; but it was not until the time of the Commonwealth that an opportunity was afforded them of seeking once more an establishment in this country.

A learned physician named Manasseh Ben Israel was deputed to present a petition to the Protector. Cromwell

* Milman, Vol. III., p. 374.

received the embassy with great courtesy, and referred the question to a committee composed of two lawyers, seven citizens of London, and fourteen divines. The lawyers decided upon the legality of re-admitting the Jews; the citizens were divided as to its expediency; but the clergy disputed so long and so warmly, that Cromwell, at length weary of the controversy, adjourned the question *sine die.*

Charles II. saw in the new impulse to the trade of the country, which the re-admission of the Jews would necessarily give, a means of replenishing his attenuated treasury. They were allowed quietly to establish themselves in the kingdom, where they have ever since maintained a hold.

Under James II., an alien duty, which had hitherto fettered them grievously in their commercial transactions, was removed, but it was re-imposed under William III. In 1753, a bill was introduced for the naturalisation of all Jews who had resided for three years in the country, without having been absent for any single period of more than three months, and passed the two houses of parliament, and received the royal assent. But this measure of toleration was somewhat premature: popular hatred, commercial jealousy, and clerical rancour, all combined to attack the bill; and so high did the feeling run that parliament was obliged to repeal the obnoxious Act. It has been reserved for the reign of our Most Gracious Queen to witness the removal of the last of Jewish disabilities.

By the memorable edict of 1782, the Emperor Joseph II. removed all the disabilities under which the Jews of Germany had hitherto laboured, making them liable at the same time to military service. A company of Jewish recruits was especially blessed by the chief rabbi of Prague on being enrolled, and was furnished with certain religious adjuncts to their uniform, in the shape of the silk fringes called *zizith,** and two leathern bands called *tephilim,* having the Decalogue written on parchment

* Cf. Numbers xv. 37—41.

attached. During the war which terminated in the division of Poland, an army encamped near Warsaw in which were five battalions of Jewish soldiers.

Leopold, Joseph's successor, accorded the Jews the right of taking degrees in the various faculties and of entering the legal profession. In 1791, a Jew was received as a doctor in the University of Prague.

Frederick the Great of Prussia, in 1750, published an edict for the regulation of the Jews in that country, which in the severity of its provisions, and the restrictions and disabilities which it imposed upon them, was scarcely less barbarous than the laws of the princes of the Middle Ages. The father of a family was only allowed to find a wife for one, or at most two of his sons, the rest being condemned to celibacy. Every Jew on his marriage was moreover compelled to purchase a large quantity of porcelain at the royal manufactory. In 1809, these unjust regulations were repealed by Frederick William II.

The emancipation of the Jews in Germany was due in no small degree to the influence of some of their own writers, who, by their enlightened views and brilliant talents, commanded the respect of their Christian fellow-countrymen. Of no one is this more true than of the celebrated Moses Mendelssohn, one of the greatest and best philosophers which Judaism has produced. He began life in the humblest circumstances, but his perseverance enabled him to overcome the terrible obstacles of poverty and ill-health, and while still a young man to be recognised as one of the most brilliant literary men of his day. Unlike Spinoza, he had a simple and childlike faith, which kept him safe from the whisperings of unbelief, and, although his philosophical mind could not brook the trammels of rabbinical control, yet he remained faithful to the synagogue, only tempering his creed with a warmer and more Christian-like spirit. His fame, and the high esteem in which he was held by persons of all ranks and persuasions, excited many Hebrews to emulate his example and devote themselves to literary studies.

In Frankfort the Jews had for centuries endured the utmost scorn and oppression at the hands of their fellow-citizens, and although they never ceased to struggle for freedom and civil rights, yet as late as 1826 all the old regulations were in force against them, and they were subjected to the most ignominious restrictions.

The Jews of Metz retained their privileges even after the banishment of the Jews from France by Charles VI., in 1394.* In 1566 they were expelled from the city; but four families obtained permission to return during the following year, and in 1603 we find the number increased to twenty-four, who obtained letters patent from Henry IV., granting them the right of residence.

When again expelled from France in 1615 they were still allowed to settle in Metz and Bordeaux. In 1718 they had so largely increased in numbers and importance in the former city as to excite the jealousy of the Christian merchants, who obtained from the king, Louis XV., a decree limiting the number of resident Jewish families to twenty-four.

On the commencement of the great French Revolution the Jews seized the opportunity of petitioning the assembly to grant them civil rights. A long and lively discussion followed, which ended in their demand being acceded to.

In 1806 Napoleon I. astonished Europe by summoning a grand Sanhedrim of the Jews at Paris, and propounded twelve questions for their consideration, which amounted in brief to a demand whether they were willing, or considered it lawful, to submit without reserve to the laws of the realm. As the assembly responded in a satisfactory manner to all these questions a regular scheme for the organisation of the Jewish community was devised and confirmed both by the Jewish and imperial authorities;

* See page 263.

after this the entire enjoyment of civil rights was conceded to them.

In Russia the Jews, for many centuries, experienced very harsh treatment, at the hands both of the Government and the people. But, curiously enough, in this very country there sprang up a sect of converts to Judaism, who, while they rigorously kept to the Christian ceremonies, yet secretly renounced their Christianity, and declared that Moses alone was the recipient of a Divine mission, and that the Messiah was yet to come. This sect had its origin in the teachings of a Jew named Zacharias, at Novgorod, about the year 1490, and numbered amongst its members many priests and nobles, and the heresy even extended to the royal family itself. It was, however, discovered later on by the Archbishop of Novgorod, and the chief culprits punished. Still the heresy, fostered as it was by the Metropolitan itself, was not for a long time thoroughly suppressed.

As the Russian empire was extended in subsequent centuries, vast numbers of Jewish subjects were added to the Muscovite rule—the partition of Poland alone bringing nearly half a million. As these were some of the wealthiest and most industrious of the population, the Government was wise enough to encourage rather than persecute them. They were, nevertheless, placed under great social disadvantages, until the ukase of 1835, when they were admitted to the privilege of citizens. The number of Jews in the Russian empire is estimated at no less than two millions.

I must not omit to mention, in conclusion, a few Jewish communities existing in remote quarters of the world, and which, from their very isolation, have escaped the vicissitudes to which their compatriots elsewhere were exposed.

In Yemen (Arabia Felix) there is a large number of Jews, as many as 2,000 residing in San'á, the capital. They, as usual, monopolise the greater part of the mercantile transactions of the country. Amidst the mountains of the Hejjàz are several small tribes of Jews, known by the name of the Beni Kheibar. I have already pointed out the fact that the Fellahin of Petra, although nominally Moslems, are undoubtedly of Jewish origin.

In the Crimea a curious little colony of Caraite Jews exists, occupying a picturesque fortress. They number about 1,200.

The Jews began to gain a footing in China during the Han dynasty, which lasted from 600 B.C. to 220 of the Christian era; but the exact time of their settlement is unknown. At first they appear to have become numerous and wealthy, many of them even being created governors of provinces and mandarins. By degrees, however, they dwindled down to a small community, inhabiting Kaisong-Fou, capital of the province of Honam, 150 leagues from Pekin. In 1704, a Jesuit missionary named Gozani visited them and obtained some interesting information upon their condition and belief. They observe the Sabbath very scrupulously, and considering the length of time during which they have been separated from their brethren, they have preserved the rites and ceremonies of their religion with great exactitude. They have, nevertheless, many usages which they have borrowed from the Chinese, such as the worshipping of their ancestors and burning fragrant perfumes. When Gozani spoke to them of Jesus Christ, he found that they had never so much as heard of the Christian religion or its Founder, knowing no other Jesus but the son of Sirach.

In various parts of the Indian peninsula Jews are also numerous; and a colony exists at Malabar. They are divided into two classes, white and negro; the latter claiming to be the most ancient in origin, but occupying an inferior position.

In the New World they have increased incredibly, between 70,000 and 80,000 being found in the United States alone, while there are large numbers in all the British colonies.

INDEX.

PASSAGES OF THE BIBLE QUOTED OR REFERRED TO IN THIS WORK.

UNWIN BROTHERS, LITTLE BRIDGE STREET, 71A, LUDGATE HILL, E.C.

PUBLICATIONS

OF THE

Society for Promoting Christian Knowledge.

Star Atlas.

Gives all the stars from 1 to 6.5 magnitude between the North Pole and 34° South Declination, and all Nebulæ and Star Clusters, which are visible in telescopes of moderate power. Translated and adapted from the German of Dr. KLEIN, by the Rev. E. McCLURE, M.A. Imp. 4to. With 18 Charts and 80 pages illustrative letterpress. Cloth Boards, 7s. 6d.

History of India.

From the Earliest Times to the Present Day. By Captain L. J. TROTTER. With eight page Woodcuts and numerous smaller Woodcuts. A new and revised edition. Post 8vo. Cloth boards, 6s.

Beauty in Common Things.

Illustrated by twelve Drawings from Nature, by Mrs. J. W. WHYMPER. Printed in Colours. Demy 4to. Cloth boards, 10s. 6d.

The Fern Portfolio.

By FRANCIS GEORGE HEATH. With fifteen Plates, elaborately drawn, life size, exquisitely coloured from Nature, and accompanied by descriptive texts: all the species of British Ferns, which comprise a large proportion of the Ferns of America, and many other parts of the World. Elegantly bound in cloth, 8s.

Scenes in the East.

Consisting of twelve Coloured Photographic Views of Places mentioned in the Bible, beautifully executed, with descriptive letterpress. By the Rev. CANON TRISTRAM, Author of " The Land of Israel," &c. 4to. Cloth, bevelled boards, gilt edges, 6s.

Sinai and Jerusalem; or, Scenes from Bible Lands.

Consisting of Coloured Photographic Views of Places mentioned in the Bible, including a Panoramic View of Jerusalem with descriptive letterpress. By the Rev. F. W. HOLLAND, M.A. Demy 4to. Cloth, bevelled boards, gilt edges, 6s.

Bible Places; or, The Topography of the Holy Land.

A succinct account of all the Places, Rivers, and Mountains of the Land of Israel mentioned in the Bible, so far as they have been identified; together with their modern names and historical references. By the Rev. CANON TRISTRAM. With map. Crown 8vo. Cloth boards, 4s.

The Land of Israel.

A Journal of Travel in Palestine, undertaken with special reference to its Physical Character. By the Rev. CANON TRISTRAM. Fourth edition, revised. With Maps and many Illustrations. Large Post 8vo. Cloth boards, 10s. 6d.

Narrative of a Modern Pilgrimage through Palestine on Horseback, and with Tents.

By the Rev. ALFRED CHARLES SMITH, M.A., Author of " The Attractions of the Nile," &c. Numerous Illustrations and four Coloured Plates. Crown 8vo. Cloth boards, 5s.

The Natural History of the Bible.

By the Rev. CANON TRISTRAM, Author of " Bible Places," &c. With numerous Woodcuts. Crown 8vo. Cloth boards, 5s.

A History of the Jewish Nation.

From the Earliest Times to the Present Day. By the late E. H. PALMER, M.A., Author of " The Desert of the Exodus," &c. With Map of Palestine and numerous Illustrations. Crown 8vo. Cloth boards, 4s.

Pictorial Architecture of the British Isles.

By the Rev. H. H. BISHOP. With about 150 Illustrations. Royal 4to. Cloth boards, 4s.

Pictorial Architecture of Greece and Italy.

By the Rev. H. H. BISHOP. With numerous Engravings. Royal 4to. Cloth boards, 5s.

Pictorial Geography of the British Isles.

By MARY E. PALGRAVE. With numerous Engravings. Royal 4to. Cloth boards, 5s.

British Birds in their Haunts.

Being a Popular account of the Birds which have been observed in the British Isles; their Haunts and Habits; their systematic, common, and provincial Names; together with a Synopsis of Genera; and a brief Summary of Specific Characters. By the late Rev. C. A. JOHNS, B.A., F.L.S. Post 8vo. Cloth boards, 6s.

A Chapter of English Church History.

Being the Minutes of the S.P.C.K. for the years 1698-1703. Together with Abstracts of Correspondents' Letters during part of the same period. Edited by the Rev. E. McCLURE, M.A., Editorial Secretary of the S.P.C.K. Demy 8vo. With a Woodcut. Cloth boards, 5s.

Africa, seen through its Explorers.

By CHARLES H. EDEN, Esq. With Map and several Illustrations. Crown 8vo. Cloth boards, 5s.

Australia's Heroes.

Being a slight Sketch of the most prominent amongst the band of gallant men who devoted their lives and energies to the cause of Science, and the development of the Fifth Continent. By C. H. EDEN, Esq. With Map. Crown 8vo. Cloth boards, 5s.

Christians under the Crescent in Asia.

By the Rev. EDWARD L. CUTTS, B.A., Author of "Turning Points of Church History," &c. With numerous Illustrations. Post 8vo. Cloth boards, 5s.

Some Heroes of Travel; or, Chapters from the History of Geographical Discovery and Enterprise.

Compiled and re-written by W. H. DAVENPORT ADAMS, Author of "Great English Churchmen," &c. With Map. Crown 8vo. Cloth boards, 5s.

The Fifth Continent, with the Adjacent Islands.

Being an Account of Australia, Tasmania, and New Guinea, with Statistical Information to the latest date. By C. H. EDEN, Esq. With Map. Crown 8vo. Cloth boards, 5s.

Frozen Asia : A Sketch of Modern Siberia.

By CHARLES H. EDEN, Esq., Author of "Australia's Heroes," &c. With Map. Crown 8vo. Cloth boards, 5s.

Heroes of the Arctic and their Adventures.

By FREDERICK WHYMPER, Esq., Author of "Travels in Alaska." With Map, eight full-page and numerous small Woodcuts. Crown 8vo. Cloth boards, 3s. 6d.

China.

By Professor ROBERT K. DOUGLAS, of the British Museum. With Map, and eight full-page Illustrations and several Vignettes. Post 8vo. Cloth boards, 5s.

Russia : Past and Present.

Adapted from the German of Lankenau and Oelnitz. By Mrs. CHESTER. With Map and three full-page Woodcuts and Vignettes. Post 8vo. Cloth boards, 5s.

LONDON:

NORTHUMBERLAND AVENUE, CHARING CROSS, W.C.;

43, QUEEN VICTORIA STREET, E.C.; 97, WESTBOURNE GROVE, W.

BRIGHTON: 135, NORTH STREET.